Johnson's Sermons

A Study

JAMES GRAY

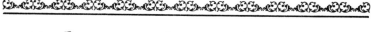

Johnson's Sermons

A Study

OXFORD
AT THE CLARENDON PRESS
1972

Oxford University Press, Ely House, London W. 1

GLASGOW NEW YORK TORONTO MELBOURNE WELLINGTON
CAPE TOWN IBADAN NAIROBI DAR ES SALAAM LUSAKA ADDIS ABABA
DELHI BOMBAY CALCUTTA MADRAS KARACHI LAHORE DACCA
KUALA LUMPUR SINGAPORE HONG KONG TOKYO

PRINTED IN GREAT BRITAIN
AT THE UNIVERSITY PRESS, OXFORD
BY VIVIAN RIDLER
PRINTER TO THE UNIVERSITY

TO MY WIFE

PREFACE

MUCH of the preparatory work on this book was done in the Beinecke Rare Book and Manuscript Library of Yale University, where the manuscript of an unpublished sermon by Samuel Johnson is deposited, and an extensive collection of the books and papers of Johnson and Boswell is housed. To the Librarian, Mr. Herman W. Liebert, and the Research Librarian, Miss Marjorie G. Wynne, my very warm thanks are due. The Future State letter which forms the Appendix is a copy of the one in the Beinecke Library at Yale.

Of the many other debts which might be mentioned, the greatest is to Professor Jean H. Hagstrum of Northwestern University, with whom I have had the honour of collaborating in the compilation of the Yale Edition of the Sermons of Samuel Johnson. Most of my remaining obligations are mentioned in the Introduction and in footnotes, but I would like to record here my special gratitude to the Humanities Research Council of Canada and the administrators of the Pollack Research Fund at Bishop's University, whose financial assistance enabled me to carry out much of my work at Yale, the Morgan Library in New York, the New York Public Library, the British Museum, and elsewhere.

For reading the book at various stages in its development, and for offering helpful advice and valuable criticism, my sincere appreciation is due to Professors Robert Browne, Joyce Hemlow, Hugh Hood, and William Kinsley, and to that indefatigable dean of Johnsonian studies, Dr. L. F. Powell.

JAMES GRAY

CONTENTS

x   CONTENTS

LIST OF PLATES

LIST OF ABBREVIATIONS USED
IN FOOTNOTES

Bibl.   Reference to Bibliography at end of this book.

Diaries   *Samuel Johnson: Diaries, Prayers, and Annals*, Yale
                         Edn. (see below).

Letters   *The Letters of Samuel Johnson*, with Mrs. Thrale's
                         genuine letters to him, collected and ed. R. W.
                         Chapman (3 vols., Oxford: Clarendon Press,
                         1952). The letters are referred to by their num-
                         bers in this edition.

Life   *Boswell's Life of Johnson*, ed. George Birkbeck
                         Hill; revised and enlarged by L. F. Powell
                         (6 vols., Oxford: Clarendon Press, 1934–50).

Nichols, *Anecdotes*   *Literary Anecdotes of the Eighteenth Century*, by John
                         Nichols (9 vols., London: Nichols, Son, &
                         Bentley, 1812–15).

Works   *The Works of Samuel Johnson, LL.D.*, ed. F. P.
                         Walesby (9 vols., Oxford: Talboys & Wheeler;
                         and London: W. Pickering, 1825).

Yale Edn.   Yale Edition of the *Works of Samuel Johnson*:

                         Vol. i: *Diaries, Prayers, and Annals*, ed. E. L.
                             McAdam, Jr., with Donald and Mary Hyde
                             (New Haven: Yale University Press, 1960).

                         Vol. ii: '*The Idler*' and '*The Adventurer*', eds. W. J.
                             Bate, John M. Bullitt, and L. F. Powell (1963).

                         Vols. iii–v: '*The Rambler*', eds. W. J. Bate and
                             Albrecht B. Strauss (1969).

                         Vol. vi: *Poems*, ed. E. L. McAdam, Jr., with George
                             Milne (1965).

                         Vols. vii and viii: *Johnson on Shakespeare*, ed. A.
                             Sherbo (1968).

                         Sermons forthcoming.

Mr. Beauclerk's great library was this season sold in London by auction. Mr. Wilkes said, he wondered to find in it such a numerous collection of sermons; seeming to think it strange that a gentleman of Mr. Beauclerk's character in the gay world should have chosen to have many compositions of that kind. JOHNSON. 'Why, Sir, you are to consider, that sermons make a considerable branch of English literature. . . .'

(*Life*, iv. 105)

INTRODUCTION

WHILE the study of the religious views and moral philosophy of Samuel Johnson has been a subject of widespread interest for more than two hundred years, few scholars have turned their attention to his sermons.[1] The reasons for this apparent lacuna in Johnsonian scholarship are referred to or implied in the present work: among them, the doubt, going back to their first publication, about the authorship of the sermons in the Taylor collection; their consequent omission from most of the early editions of the Works of Samuel Johnson; and an understandable, if regrettable, inclination on the part of some scholars to pass over them lightly as homiletic, and therefore inferior, versions of the *Rambler* essays.

Since nearly all of Johnson's interests clearly share the one common denominator, religion, it would seem logical and desirable to consider in some detail the single context, apart from his *Prayers and Meditations*, which contains his religious views in their most concentrated form. This the present study sets out to do. Moreover, as Johnson himself regarded sermons as an important branch of literature, and applied to their composition the same care for form and method, the same attention to the rules governing the chosen art, that he devoted to other rhetorical genres (in spite of what he says about spinning them off to meet a deadline or to catch the evening post), the Johnsonian sermon as a species of literary composition is one of the major concerns of this book.

In Johnson's lifetime, sermon literature enjoyed a popularity that may now appear incredible, unless we recall that it was the source of much more than spiritual instruction and solemn exhortation: within its compass, political controversies were aired, contemporary events discussed, social problems defined, and theories of

---

[1] See Bibl. 39, pp. 121–4, and Bibl. 40, pp. 337–8. Between the publication of Robert Armitage's somewhat diffuse and desultory study, *Dr. Johnson: his Religious Life and his Death* (Bibl. 15), and Maurice J. Quinlan's *Samuel Johnson: a Layman's Religion* (Bibl. 47), no published work of any substance was devoted exclusively to Johnson's religious views. Professor Quinlan, recognizing that the sermons 'provide the fullest insight into [Johnson's] theological views', devotes a useful chapter to them (pp. xiii and 85–100).

education propounded. For eighteenth-century readers it had
something of the interest of present-day manuals of popular
psychology, as well as the status of a model of English prose.
The work of a Tillotson or an Atterbury was held up as a literary
example, while an address by a Wesley or a Whitefield was often
welcomed as a directive for a way of life.[1] Booksellers' catalogues
were sometimes devoted exclusively to collections of sermons and
devotional treatises, which competed with the novel and the political pamphlet as the best-sellers of the day, and leading critics gave
what would now be regarded as disproportionate space to them in
the columns of the literary magazines.

As a young assistant in his father's bookstall Johnson reaped
the benefits of this homiletic harvest. Throughout his later career
he kept so well abreast of current sermon literature that he was
able to pass judgement on most of the important preachers of his
time. For reasons that will be discussed in this book, he found a
few of the earlier divines more congenial to him than most of the
modern interpreters of God's word, but he was conversant with
both the old and the new.

His own sermons, however, are far from being exercises in
eclecticism. As might be expected, they have their own unmistakably Johnsonian stamp and personality. To compare them with
those of, say, Swift or Sterne, would be to do them an injustice.
As he wrote them for other people, and hence at one remove
from the pulpit, it was no part of his design to attack or amuse
his congregation, or to hypnotize it with polemical brilliance or
theatrical ingenuity. His intention was not to vilify, but to instruct;
not to entertain, but to convince. His effects are produced, not by
Sternian aposiopesis, Swiftian denunciation, or Wesleyan dynamism,
but rather by that characteristic blend of eloquence, dignity, and
masterful emphasis which issues sometimes in *ex cathedra* thunder,
but more often in the quietly reasoned assertion of unassailable
truths.

This is not to say that Johnson was unmoved by the work of
the great theologians. On the contrary, he assimilated so much of
their writing that the task of tracing their effect upon him becomes

[1] See *The Eighteenth-Century Pulpit* (Bibl. 89), p. 10.

at once important and formidable. In preparation for this task, many of the sermons of those whom he held in special veneration, such as Clarke, Baxter, Tillotson, South, and Jortin, have been examined, with a view to finding out why he was impressed by them, and how, if at all, they affected his own homiletic work. In this book only such findings as seemed to make a reasonable case for demonstrable influences have been reported; but when one is dealing with a mind as richly stocked as that of Samuel Johnson, all conclusions must be tempered with due caution, together with a painful awareness that much has been missed.

Johnson's sermons contain a wide variety of subject-matter and treatment. Some were composed for delivery in a small country parish, others for presentation to an audience of parliamentarians in Westminster. One was written to be preached by a famous prisoner at Newgate on the eve of his execution. Whether advising parishioners how to choose a partner in marriage, instructing those in authority how to govern wisely, or showing condemned captives how to meet their fate with resolution, Johnson the preacher is always in his element, dealing confidently with the humble domestic virtues as well as the great issues of state; with the familiar themes of repentance, fear, charity, misery, self-deceit, vanity, love, godliness, and death, as well as the legal niceties of fraud, calumny, and civil disobedience.

Previous studies of Johnson, such as those of Professors Joseph Wood Krutch, Walter Jackson Bate, and James L. Clifford, have focused attention on the deep spiritual foundations of Johnson's social, moral, and literary beliefs and principles, while the work of Professor Donald J. Greene has done much to reveal the interdependence of his political and religious philosophies. In particular, Professor Greene observes that, in the sermon he wrote for the Revd. Hervey Aston, Johnson 'works out a rationale of public charity that inevitably impinges on political theory', and he shows Sermons XXIII and XXIV to be significant statements of Johnson's theory of government.[1]

Professor Robert Voitle treats the sermons in relation to the main purpose of his book, *Samuel Johnson the Moralist*, which is to

---

[1] *The Politics of Samuel Johnson* (Bibl. 41), pp. 148, 223–30.

provide 'a comprehensive view of Samuel Johnson's moral notions' by considering them 'in the terms of his own century', and comparing his moral ideas with those of 'more systematic' thinkers such as Bishop Richard Cumberland and John Locke, both of whom 'strongly influenced Johnson's moral thinking'.[1]

In his references to the sermons Professor Voitle alludes particularly to the themes of charity, self-love and social responsibility, authority, power and wealth, and duty, and demonstrates Johnson's 'dogged and practical empiricism' in his approach to all those subjects. Discussing Johnson's theory of society 'as a purely political structure', Professor Voitle finds in his 'altruistic utilitarianism' the closest parallels between his views and those expressed in Cumberland's *De Legibus Naturae*. Like Professor Greene, moreover, he finds that Johnson says more in his sermons, especially Sermon XXIV, than anywhere else on the subject of the origin and purposes of government.[2]

Sharing Professor Voitle's view that Johnson's ethical theory strongly resembles the utilitarianism of Richard Cumberland, Professor Chester Chapin notes that Johnson 'finds no incompatibility between the New Testament ethic and the ethic of social utility'. Thus, in Sermon V, he argues that God originally created man for happiness in this world. The Fall changed that, but men may still do much to promote happiness in this life by practising the Christian virtues.[3]

Professor Chapin's book, one of the most valuable of recent studies, is substantially an intellectual history of Johnson, with careful biographical and philosophical documentation. After discussing the significance of the childhood instruction in religion Johnson received from his mother, Professor Chapin points out that the spiritual awakening which followed a period of rebelliousness against authority was closely related to his reading, not only of Law's *Serious Call*, but of the Portuguese Jesuit Jeronymo Lobo's account of his voyage to Abyssinia, translated by Joachim Le Grand, and published in 1728 as *Voyage historique d'Abissinie du R. P. Jerome Lobo*. Johnson's curiosity about 'a third branch of

---

[1] Bibl. 49, pp. vii–ix.   [2] Ibid., pp. 134, 60, 63–4.
[3] *The Religious Thought of Samuel Johnson* (Bibl. 38), pp. 92–4.

Christianity, unfamiliar to most Europeans but possibly quite as authentic a branch of the historic faith as the European varieties', led him to translate the work into English. Professor Chapin, like Joel J. Gold before him, observes that Johnson 'slanted' his translation in such a way as to show Lobo and the Jesuit Portuguese missionary enterprise in an unfavourable light.[1]

Turning to Johnson's attitude to the Evangelical movement, Professor Chapin discusses the correspondence over two-and-a-half years with Miss Hill Boothby, who, he told Mrs. Thrale, 'pushed her piety to bigotry, her devotion to enthusiasm'. Johnson could not believe, argues Professor Chapin, that '"divine evidence for divine truths" was *ordinarily* granted to even the most devout Christians'.[2] Then, dealing with Johnson's views on eschatology, evil, free will and necessity, the relationship between Church and State, and his attitude to the non-Christian world, Professor Chapin concludes that orthodoxy is 'right' for Johnson, who 'finds Christian doctrine and teaching so exactly consonant to the human condition that it is difficult to assume impulses in him constantly at war with his faith'. While Johnson is 'sceptical about a number of matters of considerable importance to orthodox Christianity', his doubts led him to the conclusion, not that religion is 'unreasonable', but that human reason is limited.[3]

The present study accepts in part the findings of these scholars, to whose useful insights it is greatly indebted. It also derives some valuable suggestions from the work of Miss Katherine C. Balderston, particularly in the section on William Law; and for the establishment of the canon of Johnson's sermons it stands on the shoulders of the previous work of Professor Jean Hagstrum, Dr. R. W. Chapman, and others. It breaks fresh ground, however, in a number of ways, including its examination of the nature of the collaboration between Johnson and John Taylor of Ashbourne, its study of the influence of Richard Baxter, its emphasis on happiness as the dominant theme of the sermons, and its particular attention to matters

[1] Ibid., pp. 41–50.
[2] Ibid., pp. 53–70. In a letter dated 13 Oct. 1787 the Revd. Dr. John Taylor expresses the view that Johnson's exchanges with Miss Hill Boothby ought not to have been revealed (Rylands Eng. MS. 892 (R74733)).
[3] Ibid., pp. 156–8.

of form and style. In the last respect, it attempts to complement the work of Professor W. K. Wimsatt, Jr., whose two studies of Johnson's prose style make little or no mention of the sermons.

No single study can be exhaustive. The present work formulates more problems, no doubt, than it solves. It certainly indicates that few answers are final. In a very real sense, work on Samuel Johnson must always be work in progress.

I

The Composition of the Sermons

JOHNSON AS HOMILIST: THE CANON OF HIS SERMONS

ALTHOUGH the cast of his mind was both pedagogical and homiletic, Samuel Johnson never, in the formal sense of the word, delivered a sermon. He did, however, write and dictate sermons, some forty of them, and the world is the richer for the fact that twenty-eight of these have survived. Of the twenty-eight, only two were published in Johnson's lifetime, twenty-five appeared posthumously, and one will appear in print for the first time in the Yale Edition of the *Works of Samuel Johnson.*

The two sermons published in Johnson's lifetime were written in 1745 and 1777, the first for the Revd. Henry Hervey Aston, a close friend, who delivered it before the Sons of the Clergy, and the second for the Revd. William Dodd, an imprisoned clergyman awaiting the death sentence to be carried out against him for forgery, who preached it before his fellow prisoners at Newgate. The Aston sermon was published as an octavo pamphlet of twenty-eight pages,[1] and the Dodd sermon as an octavo pamphlet of twenty-four pages.[2] The attribution of the Aston sermon to Johnson was established by Dr. L. F. Powell,[3] and we have Johnson's own acknowledgement of the authorship of the Dodd sermon.[4]

The main corpus of sermons by Samuel Johnson is known as the Taylor collection. The Revd. John Taylor, an intimate and lifelong friend of Johnson's, died in 1788, four years after Johnson's own death, leaving among his effects a number of sermons. One of these, a sermon Johnson had written for the funeral of his own wife, was published, in the year of Taylor's death, as an octavo pamphlet of eighteen pages, by the Revd. Samuel Hayes.[5] It was prefaced by the following note, dated 18 March 1788:

[1] Bibl. 6.   [2] Bibl. 8.   [3] Bibl. 135.   [4] *Life*, iii. 141–2.
[5] Bibl. 9. Hayes (1749–95) had been a close friend of Taylor, who had talked of

The following Sermon (the Authenticity of which cannot be doubted) came, with many others, into the Hands of the Editor by the Death of Dr. Taylor, late of Westminster, &c.

It is now published for two Reasons: First, as it is a Composition that will reflect no Disgrace on the Author; and, Secondly, as it is upon a Subject of the highest Importance to Mankind.[1]

Towards the end of May of the same year thirteen of the sermons from John Taylor's collection were published in an octavo volume of 285 pages, with the interesting, if ambiguous, title, *Sermons on Different Subjects, left for Publication by John Taylor, LL.D.*[2] In July of the following year, 1789, a second octavo volume, of 239 pages and containing twelve more sermons, including the one written by Johnson for the funeral of his wife, was published by the same Samuel Hayes.[3] In addition to these published sermons, there is extant, in the Beinecke Rare Book Library at Yale, a sermon in manuscript, with corrections in Johnson's handwriting.[4] That the composition of this sermon was by Johnson himself was first suspected by Dr. R. W. Chapman,[5] and later established by Professor Jean Hagstrum.[6]

Johnson evidently found the task of writing sermons agreeable, easy, and moderately profitable. 'I myself have composed about forty sermons', he said in 1773. 'I have begun a sermon after dinner, and sent it off by post that night.'[7] In a letter he wrote to a young clergyman, the Revd. Charles Lawrence, on 30 August 1780, he testified: 'The composition of sermons is not very difficult: the divisions not only help the memory of the hearer, but direct the

---

bequeathing his fortune to him. See Nichols, *Anecdotes*, ix. 59, and the *Gentleman's Magazine*, LVII, Part I (Mar. 1788), 274.

[1] Bibl. 9, unnumbered page following title-page.   [2] Bibl. 3.

[3] Bibl. 4. Between the publication of the first volume and that of the second, Hayes had resigned his post at Westminster because of the School's failure to promote him to the position of under-master. See Southey, Bibl. 146, i. 135–6.

[4] See below, pp. 42–6.   [5] Bibl. 78.   [6] Bibl. 44.

[7] *Life*, v. 67. See also M. Waingrow (ed.), *The Correspondence and Other Papers of James Boswell Relating to the Making of the Life of Johnson* (London: Heinemann, 1969), pp. 250–1, for the testimony of William Bowles (1755–1826): 'Of Sermons at the sollication of friends he had written several (about 40). The first he ever wrote was on the subject of Pride begun after dinner and sent away by one of the night coaches to the preacher for whose use it was intended . . .' (possibly Sermon VI in the Taylor collection).

judgement of the writer; they supply sources of invention, and keep every part in its proper place.'[1] The 'divisions' to which he referred were the rhetorical partitions, usually numbered, into which a sermon was traditionally broken up—a practice to which Johnson adhered consistently, despite the fact that it was now frowned upon by some authorities.[2]

Some of his diary entries indicate the speed with which he accomplished his composition. On 7 September 1777 he had completed 'part of a sermon' ('*Partem concionis*');[3] on 21 September 1777 he noted that he had completed one for Taylor ('*Concio pro Tayloro*');[4] on 13 October 1777 he mentioned that he was composing sermons while proceeding rapidly with his *Lives of the Poets*: '2 sermons. 2 more sermons 4 in all.'[5] A later entry, dated 20 April 1778, reads: 'I have made sermons perhaps as readily as formerly.'[6] Sir John Hawkins tells us that, before 1760, Johnson composed 'pulpit discourses' at the request of 'sundrey beneficed clergymen', usually at a fee of two guineas.[7] Hawkins goes on, '. . . and such was his notion of justice, that having been paid, he considered them so absolutely the property of the purchaser, as to renounce all claim to them. He reckoned that he had written about forty sermons; but, except as to some, knew not in what hands they were—"I have," said he, "been paid for them, and have no right to enquire about them." '[8] No doubt in keeping with his general view that 'no man but a blockhead ever wrote, except for money',[9] Johnson insisted on remuneration for his sermons. Again, according to Hawkins, 'He was never greedy of money, but without money he could not be stimulated to write. I have been told by a clergyman of some

---

[1] *Letters*, 704.

[2] See, e.g., Samuel D'Oyley, Bibl. 90, pp. 100–21. (A translation of Blaise Gisbert, *L'Eloquence Chrétienne dans l'idée et dans la pratique*.) See also pp. 193 f. below.

[3] *Diaries*, p. 276.   [4] Ibid., p. 277.   [5] Ibid., p. 279.

[6] Ibid., p. 292.

[7] *The Life of Samuel Johnson, LL.D.* (Bibl. 19), pp. 391–2. In the first edition 'one guinea' is given as the fee, but this is corrected in subsequent editions to 'two guineas'. See also *Life*, iii. 507, where Hawkins's account is confirmed by the Revd. John Hussey, whom Johnson informed that the sermons 'were generally copied in his own study by those that employed him, and when finished he always destroyed the original in their presence'. Hussey's remarks are written in his copy of the *Life*, later owned by Professor D. Nichol Smith, and now in the D. Nichol Smith Collection in the National Library of Australia, Canberra.

[8] Hawkins, pp. 391–2.   [9] *Life*, iii. 19.

eminence with whom he had been long acquainted, that, being to preach on a particular occasion, he applied, as others under a like necessity had frequently done, to Johnson for help. "I will write a sermon for thee," said Johnson, "but thou must pay me for it."[1]

Hawkins is more precise than Boswell in describing occasions on which he heard Taylor deliver sermons of Johnson's composition:

Myself have heard, in the church of St. Margaret Westminster, sundry sermons, which I and many others judged, by the sentiments, style, and method, to be of his composition; one in particular, Johnson being present. The next visit I made him, I told him that I had seen him at St. Margaret's on the preceding Sunday, and that it was he who then preached. He heard me, and did not deny either assertion, which, if either had not been true, he certainly would have done.[2]

Hawkins's daughter, Laetitia, provides testimony to the same effect:

Of his detached and miscellaneous biographical pieces, or such as are the result of thought, the merit is as various as the subjects; and in reading many of them, it may occur to those familiar with his style, that it is often kept down—and sometimes with difficulty. This is, perhaps, no where more evident than in those sermons, which are published under the name of Dr. Taylor of Westminster; and the restraint seems to have been intolerable, for the secret betrays itself perpetually. At the time these were preached, we lived in Westminster, and our parish-church being that of Dr. Taylor's preferment, we heard them, as did Johnson himself, when he spent his Sunday with the preacher. My father made no scruple of attacking him on the subject—he preserved a profound silence.[3]

Boswell is a little less explicit on this point. While he recalls finding on Johnson's table part of a sermon he was composing for John Taylor,[4] and while he adds the sermons for Taylor to his list of the prose works of Johnson,[5] he is careful to acknowledge that the evidence for Johnson's authorship is mainly internal, and he observes, perhaps diplomatically:

---

[1] Hawkins, pp. 84–5.   [2] Ibid., p. 392 n.
[3] *Memoirs, Anecdotes, Facts, and Opinions* (Bibl. 20), i. 163.
[4] *Life*, iii. 181. The date, 21 Sept. 1777, is the same as that of Dr. Johnson's diary entry, 'Concio pro Tayloro'.
[5] *Life*, i. 24.

I, however, would not have it thought, that Dr. Taylor, though he could not write like Johnson, (as, indeed, who could?) did not sometimes compose sermons as good as those which we generally have from very respectable divines. He shewed me one with notes on the margin in Johnson's handwriting; and I was present when he read another to Johnson, that he might have his opinion of it, and Johnson said it was 'very well.' These, we may be sure, were not Johnson's; for he was above little arts, or tricks of deception.[1]

As will be shown later, evidences of collaboration between Taylor and Johnson in the composition of a letter on the subject of a future state point at least to the possibility of similar collaboration in the composition of sermons;[2] but there can be little doubt that Johnson's mind provided most of the substance in the Taylor collection.

Support for the view that Johnson was the author of most, if not all, of the sermons left for publication by John Taylor comes from a variety of authorities, including the editor of the 1825 edition of the *Works* of Johnson, Francis Pearson Walesby, who incorporates them unhesitatingly in the Johnson canon;[3] Robert Anderson, who describes them as 'unquestionably Johnson's';[4] and Arthur Murphy, who refers to them as 'the fund, which Dr. Taylor, from time to time, carried with him to his pulpit'.[5]

Even before the publication by Hayes, in 1788 and 1789, of the two volumes of sermons which constitute the Taylor collection, public interest in the whereabouts of Johnson's homiletic works was very much alive. In the *General Evening Post* for 20–2 April 1786 the writer of a news column entitled 'London' noted that a number of pieces which Dr. Johnson had given away 'conferred fame, and probably fortune, on several persons', and went on to observe, 'to the disgrace of some of his *clerical friends*, forty sermons which he himself tells us he wrote, have not yet been *déterré*'.[6] The *Gentleman's Magazine*, on the occasion of the appearance in print of the sermon for Mrs. Johnson's funeral, commented that 'the public

[1] *Life*, iii. 182.   [2] See pp. 29 f. below.
[3] *Works*, ix. 193 n.
[4] *The Life of Samuel Johnson, LL.D.* (Bibl. 14), p. 182.
[5] Essay prefixed to *Works* (1825), i, p. lxxix. First published in 1792.
[6] p. 3, col. 2.

curiosity has long been awakened on the subject of Johnson's Sermons'.[1] The *Critical Review*, in May of 1788, the month in which the first volume of the Taylor collection was published under the editorship of Samuel Hayes, urged further publication: 'It has been said, that Mr. Hayes, to whom this Sermon devolved on the death of Dr. Taylor, has some more discourses by the same author. He cannot bestow a more acceptable present on the world, than to publish them.'[2] The *Monthly Review*, referring to the first volume published by Hayes, noted what it described as 'the general opinion' about the sermons:

Although these discourses came into the world under 'a questionable shape,' the general opinion concerning them is, that they are, in reality, the productions of the late Dr. Samuel Johnson. It is well known that he frequently employed his talents in this way, and the discourses in the present volume bear the strong and characteristic features of his original genius. We may, therefore, with no small degree of confidence, point out this volume to the attention of our Readers, as a curious specimen of what might have been expected from the author of the Rambler, had that manly sense, deep penetration, and ardent love of virtue, which rendered him so useful a public monitor in the capacity of an Essayist, been professionally employed in the service of religion.[3]

It may seem strange that Boswell, who was well aware that Johnson had composed sermons for his friends, was unsuccessful in locating them. Several of his acquaintances had indeed urged the biographer to try to find them and to arrange for their publication. In a letter dated 20 September 1786 the Revd. George Vanbrugh made such a request in these terms:

I have been informed, by persons who had the honour of being known to him, that he had written many sermons. Since his death, I find this confirmed by his own words to Dr. Watson of St. Andrew's, in your highly entertaining Journal of a tour to the Hebrides; and that he had, when you were together in Scotland, composed about forty. In all probability . . . he has since increased that number. I have never seen but one sermon by him, that which he wrote for the late unhappy Dr. Dodd.

[1] LVIII, Part I (1788), 234.   [2] LXV (1788), 397.
[3] LXXIX (Dec. 1788), 528–9. This review was written by William Enfield.

If all the sermons Dr. Johnson had written could be collected, they would make a most valuable publication: one of the first, I have no doubt, with respect to utility, in the English language. Wonderful must be the effect of his clear and nervous style, illustrating the principles of the Christian Religion! The full persuasion in the propitiatory sacrifice of Jesus Christ must afford the greatest satisfaction to every serious reader. Indeed in the present age we stand in need of such an eminent writer (and this writer being a layman his support of our Religion will be attended with a yet higher degree of efficacy) capable of defending the doctrines of Christianity against the cavils and objections of modern deists, infidels, and free-thinkers.

Perhaps some difficulty may arise in collecting the sermons, as the persons to whom Dr. Johnson gave them may be unwilling to acknowledge having been obliged to any other's labours. But I should hope no one would hesitate a moment to relinquish them, with the reflection that by this means they could do real good to mankind. If only a few could be procured, the publication even of these would be of great advantage to the world. . . .[1]

On page 7 of this letter, Boswell scribbled, in his usual way, the draft of a reply, in which he said he was 'much afraid' that he would never find out who the owners of the sermons were; 'at least all the inquiry which I have hitherto made has proved ineffectual'.[1] This draft reply is dated 23 October 1786.

Even from the other side of the Atlantic Boswell received an inquiry regarding the sermons. Writing on 2 January 1792, James Abercrombie of Philadelphia mentioned that he had in his possession 'two thin Octavo Volumes' of Johnson's sermons, bound together (presumably the Hayes edition of the Taylor collection), and added: 'Can you inform me Sir, whether any more of the Forty he is said to have written have yet been discovered, or whether any other of his writings yet remain to be published. . . .'[2]

Some months later, in a letter dated 11 June 1792, Boswell told Abercrombie: 'I have not yet been able to discover any more of his [Johnson's] Sermons besides those *left for Publication by Dr. Taylor.* I am informed by the Lord Bishop of Salisbury that he gave an excellent one to a clergyman who preached and published it in his

[1] MS. Yale (unnumbered).   [2] MS. Yale C1.

own name on some publick occasion. But the Bishop has not as yet told me the name and seems unwilling to do it yet I flatter myself I shall get at it. . . .'[1] In a later note to Abercrombie, dated 28 July 1793, Boswell recorded at least partial failure in his quest: 'I have not yet obtained from the Bishop of Salisbury the name of the Clergyman to whom Johnson gave a Sermon which was preached on the fifth of November; for that I find was the public occasion. I will endeavour if possible to find it out.'[2]

Meanwhile, a young clergyman from Ashbourne in Derbyshire, where John Taylor lived, had written to Boswell to say that he had in his possession two fragments of sermons 'that carry with them evident testimony of the rich mine from whence they sprung'.[3] These fragments, which the clergyman, the Revd. Daniel Astle, obligingly copied out for Boswell in a small quarto notebook, together with a number of rather trivial reminiscences of his acquaintance with Dr. Johnson, are in fact portions of Sermons V and XXIV (or, more precisely, Sermon V of vol. i and Sermon XI of vol. ii, in the Hayes edition) as they later appeared. Astle's notebook is dated December 1786, and thus pre-dates the Hayes edition by two years.[4] It appears that Boswell was a little doubtful about the authenticity of the fragments, as he wrote to Astle on 28 December 1786, in these terms:

> As to the Fragments,—I am sure you will not take it amiss that as I pledge myself to the Publick for a most scrupulous attention to authenticity, I request of you to inform me where the originals are, and if you are possessed of them or can procure them, to favour me with a sight of them. . . .[5]

Replying from Ashbourne on 23 January 1787, Astle observes:

> Being an inhabitant of Ashbourne, you will, perhaps, suspect that I have more of the Doctor's productions to present you with, since

---

[1] MS. Yale L1.

[2] MS. Yale L2. See Waingrow (cited p. 8, n. 7 above), p. 548.

[3] MS. Yale C43 (Fettercairn 1591).

[4] The notebook, which is now in the Beinecke Rare Book Library at Yale, is discussed by Marshall Waingrow in an unpublished Yale doctoral dissertation (Bibl. 33), pp. 98 ff. and Appendix D. I am grateful to Dr. Waingrow for bringing this notebook to my attention. See Waingrow, *The Correspondence*, etc., pp. 611 ff., where the fragments are printed as an Appendix.   [5] MS. Yale L19.

an anonymous correspondent in one of the public papers has lately
pointed out a person in this place as the fortunate possessor of many
of the Doctor's valuable originals: but my residence here has been
of short continuance, and I have not the smallest acquaintance with
the person before hinted at; so that nothing is likely to be derived
through the channel of my interest even from this very copious
source.

The papers which I have already communicated to you, were long
ago intrusted to me under a strict injunction of secrecy; so that you
may safely rely upon their being authentic. The Originals from
whence these were taken, are now in London, where it is not in my
power to obtain access to them. . . .[1]

Writing to Astle on 14 February 1787, Boswell contented himself
with saying, 'I *guess* at the way in which the *Fragments* are known
to be authentic, but shall not express it, in my Compilation. . . .'[2]

It is not difficult to reconstruct Boswell's guess: the originals
from which Astle's fragments were transcribed probably came
from the Ashbourne mansion of the Revd. John Taylor, who had
taken them to his house in London. The important fact is that we
have, in the Astle fragments, unmistakable evidence of the existence of portions of Johnson's sermons in Ashbourne in 1786, and
we know that the same sermons found their way into the Taylor
collection published by Hayes two to three years later.

At this point it may be well to bring together the various
strands of testimony which support the view that Johnson was
indeed the author of most of the sermons in the Taylor collection.
First, we have Johnson's own statement that he had composed
about forty sermons;[3] second, Boswell's listing of the Taylor
collection as part of the Johnsonian canon; third, Johnson's diary
note, '*Concio pro Tayloro*'; fourth, the personal accounts of friends
who were close to both Johnson and Taylor, particularly that of
Boswell; fifth, the crucial documentary evidence in Daniel Astle's
notebook; and last, and most conclusive, the internal evidence
from the substance and style of the sermons themselves.

---

[1] MS. Yale C44.
[2] MS. Yale L20: draft by Boswell, written on verso of Astle's letter of 23 Jan. 1787.
The letter itself is now in the Hyde collection. See Waingrow, *The Correspondence*, etc.,
p. 202.   [3] *Life*, v. 67.

In view of the weightiness of this testimony, it seems odd that it was not until 1823 that two of the sermons were published as part of the collected works of Dr. Johnson, and not until 1825, when the nine-volume edition of the works appeared, that all the sermons in the Taylor collection were included. Yet the 1819–21 series entitled *British Prose Writers* had devoted two duodecimo volumes to the sermons, describing them as 'indisputably' Johnson's, and ranking them with 'the original writings of Bacon and Boyle, of Clarendon and Locke'.[1] Perhaps there was a lurking suspicion on the part of the earlier editors of Johnson's works that some of the sermons were the products of collaboration between Taylor and Johnson: a suspicion which, as will be shown later, was not entirely without foundation.

Another possible deterrent to the publication of the sermons as part of the Johnsonian canon was the unusual circumstance that their ownership and their authorship were not one and the same. The clerical custom of preaching borrowed sermons was no new phenomenon, but the publication of other men's flowers under the name of the borrower or purchaser no doubt seemed a little irregular, even to a generation of hardened plagiarists.

As venerable an authority as St. Augustine of Hippo could be cited in justification of judicious sermon-borrowing: 'There are, indeed, some men who have a good delivery, but cannot compose anything to deliver. Now, if such men take what has been written with wisdom and eloquence by others, and commit it to memory, and deliver it to the people, they cannot be blamed, supposing them to do it without deception.'[2] In the eighteenth and nineteenth centuries sermons were frequently borrowed and purchased. Whether their authorship was acknowledged from the pulpit we cannot be sure. It will be remembered that Sir Roger de Coverley presented to his parish priest 'all the good Sermons . . . in English',[3] and the parson who succeeded Jonathan Swift as incumbent at Kilroot painstakingly transcribed the sermons Swift had left behind him, thus evoking Swift's comment that he would be utterly

[1] Bibl. 5.
[2] *On Christian Doctrine*, IV. xxix. 63. The translation is from the Philip Schaff edn., Bibl. 142, ii. 596.
[3] *Spectator* 106.

disgraced by their content.[1] Johnson himself advised the young clergyman mentioned earlier (p. 8) to 'attempt, from time to time, an original sermon', but he evidently assumed that most of his pulpit addresses would be at least partly derivative: 'Take care to register, somewhere or other, the authors from whom your several discourses are borrowed; and do not imagine that you shall always remember, even what perhaps you now think it impossible to forget.'[2]

Boswell's closest English clerical friend, William Johnson Temple, frequently admits that he borrows sermons: 'I have great compunction for not composing more sermons', he writes on 10 June 1788, but adds that he does not 'look upon borrowing a good sermon sometimes of Barrow or Jeremy Taylor as a theft. One may be prevented and may not be in health and spirits to draw from ones own fund, and it is better to give the good sense of another than ones own insipidity. Mr. Mason borrowed largely from the French divines. . . .'[3] In a published *Essay on the Clergy* Temple even suggested emulating the styles of a variety of eminent divines according to the levels of the congregation:

Hence, perhaps, one might infer, that the calm and ingenious reasoning of Clarke or Sherlock is the proper style of discourse to a polite audience; the primitive and ingenious piety of Tillotson to one of the middle rank of people; the figurative and declamatory manner of Barrow to a popular and mixt assembly: such seems to be the character of the style and manner of these great Moralists and Divines, though not strictly applicable to several of their discourses. . . .[4]

Sometimes, too, clergymen would write 'request' sermons for one another. Joseph Cradock tells us that he wrote a 'Visitation Sermon' for a young man just ordained,[5] and the Revd. Charles Jenner notes that his curate would not divulge the authorship of some 'incomparably good' sermons he had delivered.[6]

[1] Louis A. Landa, Bibl. 115, p. 97.
[2] *Letters*, 704. A reviewer of the 1789 volume of the Taylor collection recommended it 'to those young divines who are unable or unwilling to compose their own sermons'. See p. 200 below.
[3] MS. Yale (unnumbered).   [4] Bibl. 152, p. 75.   [5] Bibl. 18, i. 185.
[6] Ibid., iv. 220–1. Jenner later discovered that the sermons were those of Edward Young.

C

Such practices were criticized, both in prose and in verse:

> But some with lazy Pride disgrace the Gown,
> And never preach one Sermon of their own;
> 'Tis easier to transcribe than to compose,
> So all the Week, they eat, and drink, and doze.[1]

Hawkins is more soberly censorious:

The practice of preaching sermons composed by others is now become so common, that many of the clergy scruple not to avow it, and think themselves justified by the authority of Mr. Addison, who in one of his Spectators has very incautiously given countenance thereto; . . . as it is an assumption of the merit of another, the practice is unjust, and, as it leads to a belief of that which is not true, in a high degree immoral.[2]

It is clear that Dr. Johnson did not share this scandalized point of view. He had composed for others, not only pulpit discourses, but prologues, prefaces, dedications, political speeches, and lectures. Once they had left his pen, he was quite content to consider them the property of their recipients, or part of the common storehouse. The wide generosity of his mind triumphed over the narrow morality of lesser men. Perhaps such magnanimity is characteristic of the truly great original creative spirit.

THE JOHNSON–TAYLOR FRIENDSHIP

The man for whom Johnson composed so many sermons, the Revd. John Taylor, has been poorly served by his biographers. The only detailed study of his life, by Thomas Taylor, is largely taken up with genealogical details and offers a rather sketchy

---

[1] Robert Dodsley, *Art of Preaching* (Bibl. 88), p. 17. A more ingenious method of multiple borrowing is described in a poem with the same title by 'the late Reverend Christopher Pitt' and published in *The Oxford Sausage*: being Select Poetical Pieces: By the most celebrated wits in that university. A new edn. Cambridge: Printed by Weston Hatfield, 1822, pp. 53–4:

> Such is a sermon, where confus'dly dark,
> Join Hoadly, Sharp, South, Sherlock, Wake, and Clarke,
> So eggs of different parishes will run
> To batter, when you beat six yolks to one.

[2] Hawkins, pp. 391–2 n.

portrait of the man.[1] This sketchiness is not entirely the fault of the biographer, as materials for a satisfactory life of John Taylor are singularly lacking. Apart from a moderately useful entry in the *Dictionary of National Biography*, a number of fairly detailed references to Taylor in Boswell's *Life of Johnson*, the letters exchanged between Johnson and Taylor, and sporadic comments in *Thraliana*, Mrs. Piozzi's *Letters to and from the Late Samuel Johnson*, and her *Anecdotes of the Late Samuel Johnson*, the record is tantalizingly bare. Even that great rag-bag of Johnsoniana, A. L. Reade's *Johnsonian Gleanings*, yields but a few usable scraps of biographical material.

Yet the man for and with whom Johnson composed the bulk of the pulpit addresses under review here is a fascinating figure—fascinating because of his closeness to Dr. Johnson, who described him as being 'better acquainted with my heart than any man or woman now alive',[2] and because of the paradox that he appeared to embody many of the characteristics Johnson openly detested: among them, a blatant disregard for his sacred calling, a consuming greed which placed him in constant pursuit of wealthy and influential patrons, and an overriding vanity that expressed itself in ostentatious display and sumptuous living.

John Taylor (1711–88) was the son of Thomas Taylor, an attorney of Ashbourne. He was taught at Lichfield Grammar School, along with Johnson, by the Revd. John Hunter, whom he described as 'an excellent master',[3] although Johnson had found him to be 'wrong-headedly severe'.[4] It was at Lichfield that the strong friendship between Taylor and Johnson began to develop. In 1728 Taylor went up to Oxford, where, at his friend's persuasion, he entered Christ Church rather than Pembroke, because Johnson had been dissatisfied with the teaching there.[5] At Christ Church Taylor had the benefit of Edmund Bateman's instruction. Boswell tells us that Bateman's lectures were so informative that Johnson 'used to come and get them at second hand from Taylor'.[5] When Johnson went down from Oxford, Taylor accompanied him as far as Banbury. Although Taylor himself left the University somewhat

---

[1] *A Life of John Taylor, LL.D.* (Bibl. 30).
[2] H. L. Piozzi, *Anecdotes* (Bibl. 27), p. 31. See also *Life*, i. 26 n.
[3] *Life*, i. 44. (Transcribed from a revised draft, MS. Yale LR 12², p. 11.)
[4] *Life*, i. 44.   [5] *Life*, i. 76.

prematurely, he became a Master of Arts in 1742 and a Doctor of Laws in 1752.

His original intention was to become an attorney like his father, and he may have practised law for some time after leaving Oxford. When his father died in 1731, Taylor came into a considerable fortune. The following year he married Elizabeth Webb. There were no children by this marriage, but by all accounts it was a happy one, unlike his second, contracted between 1746 and 1751 to Mary Tuckfield, which ended in separation.

Sometime between 1736 and 1740 Taylor was admitted to Holy Orders, and in the latter year he was presented to the rectory of Market Bosworth in Leicestershire. According to his biographer, this preferment was obtained by purchase, a practice that was neither illegal nor unusual in the eighteenth century. Indeed it was all too easy at that time for a parson to become spiritual head of several parishes without being resident in any one of them. Taylor

is not known to have resided for any considerable length of time in any parish of which he was incumbent, and at the time of his death he held at least three if not more benefices, besides a prebend in the collegiate church of Westminster, and a chaplaincy to the Duke of Devonshire. In addition to the rectory of Market Bosworth he acquired a prebend of Westminster in 1746, the preachership of the chapel in the Broadway, Westminster, in 1748, the rectory of Lawford in Essex in 1751, the perpetual curacy of St. Botolph's, Aldersgate, in 1769, resigning the same in 1776, and the rectory of St. Margaret's, Westminster, in 1784. His desire for preferments was insatiable. A letter in 1742 from Johnson to him shows that he was expecting to obtain something considerable—a bishopric or a deanery—through the offices of his patron, the Duke of Devonshire, who was at that time Lord Lieutenant of Ireland; in 1776 a letter from Johnson to Mrs. Thrale states that livings and preferments were running in his head as if he were in want with twenty children; in 1779 he was hoping for the deanery of Rochester; and in 1781 for that of Lincoln.[1]

In this account, Taylor's biographer has given him one rectory too many, that of Lawford in Essex, which was held by another John

[1] Thomas Taylor, op. cit., p. 18. See *Letters*, 17. The biographer is, perhaps, slightly exaggerating Taylor's aspirations in 1742.

Taylor. It should also be pointed out that most of Taylor's preferments were tenable with his prebendal stall at Westminster,
which he had probably obtained through the influence of the Duke
of Devonshire. The prebend itself carried a stipend of £300, but
the duties of the office were nominal, and the obligation to preach
twice each year in Westminster could be discharged *aut per se aut per
alium*.[1]

Taylor's secular honours and activities were almost equally
numerous and impressive. He owned extensive estates in both
Ballidon and Ashbourne, and in 1767 he became a magistrate for
the county of Derby. By this time, too, Taylor appears to have
been in the commission of the peace for the county of Leicester.
He was appointed to the position of Assistant Governor of the
'Free Grammar School of Elizabeth Late Queen of England in the
Town of Ashbourne' in 1768, and Governor in 1773. He evidently
had a variety of business interests as well, for his friends included
two retired innkeepers, a cheese factor, and two tanners.

But Taylor's most engrossing activity was farming. In Johnson's
letters from Ashbourne, where he frequently stayed in Taylor's
impressive mansion, he makes repeated remarks about his host's
enthusiasm for cattle and sheep breeding. 'He is, in his usual way,
very busy, getting a bull to his cows and a dog to his bitches. . . .
Taylor is now going to have a ram; and then, after Aries and Taurus,
we shall have Gemini.'[2] Johnson does not mention the fact that
Taylor was an acknowledged expert in deer as well as cattle raising.
He jests about his host's pride in his champion bull. 'The great
bull has no disease but age. I hope in time to be like the great
bull.'[3]

Elsewhere, I have tried to piece together the various descriptions
of Taylor's opulent ménage, including those of Boswell and Mrs.

---

[1] A. S. Turberville (ed.), *Johnson's England* (Bibl. 157), i. 20–1. A racy account of
'The Church Militant' is also given in T. H. White, *The Age of Scandal* (Bibl. 158),
pp. 184 ff., with statistical details of plural livings in eighteenth-century England.
White quotes (p. 192) a letter from Thomas Gray on the subject of Dr. Plumptre,
a typical pluralist, who, when sitting for his portrait, prescribed the motto, *Non
magna loquimur, sed vivimus*. Gray's translation was: 'We don't say much, but we hold
good livings.'

[2] *Letters*, 553. See also *Letters*, 237 281, 282, etc.

[3] *Letters*, 254.

Thrale, who fondly described Taylor's mansion as 'home'.[1] They add up to a very palatial mansion and entourage, ruled over by a prosperous and self-indulgent squire-cum-parson who liked to entertain lavishly and whose regal disposition well entitled him to the sobriquet, 'King of Ashbourne'. Two extant portraits of Taylor, by Opie and by Wright of Derby, lend support to Boswell's pen picture of 'a hearty English 'Squire, with the parson super-induced'.[2] Both indicate rubicund features, a double chin, and a total impression of monarchical well-being.

Johnson once confided to Boswell: 'I do not suppose he is very fond of my company. His habits are by no means sufficiently clerical: this he knows that I see; and no man likes to live under the eye of perpetual disapprobation.'[3] So often do Johnson's letters from Ashbourne refer to his host's neglect that we may suppose his fears to have been well grounded. There is even a pathetic note in some of his direct appeals to his friend. In a letter dated 12 April 1784 he asks Taylor why he has not heard from him: 'Do not omit giving me the comfort of knowing, that after all my losses I have yet a friend left.'[4]

Taylor's attitude to Johnson was usually cordial, yet, because of the enormous differences between them, it sometimes appeared unsympathetic. When Johnson was staying at Ashbourne, Taylor would often leave him on his own from breakfast to dinner. 'I have no company', Johnson complains in a letter to Boswell. 'The Doctor is busy in his fields, and goes to bed at nine, and his whole system is so different from mine, that we seem formed for different elements.'[5] On many other occasions Johnson confesses boredom with the uniformity of the Ashbourne regimen: 'I have here little company and little amusement, and thus abandoned to the contemplation of my own miseries, I am sometimes gloomy and depressed. . . .'[6] This to Dr. Brocklesby in August 1784. 'I have no company here, and shall naturally come home hungry for conversation.'[7] This in September of the same year. 'Everything is very liberally

[1] Bibl. 96, pp. 242–52.
[2] Life, ii. 473–4. See also iii. 157, 190, and 498–9; and iv. 378 and 548–9.
[3] Life, iii. 181.   [4] Letters, 951. Life, iv. 270.
[5] Letters, 981. Life, iii. 504.   [6] Letters, 1000. Life, iv. 356.
[7] Letters, 1010.

1. Opie's portrait of the Revd. Dr. John Taylor

provided for me but conversation.'[1] The complaint is the more poignant when we remember that this was the last year of Johnson's life.

When Johnson was dying, Taylor exhibited a degree of callousness that is almost incredible. Instead of offering comfort or assistance, he merely sent a note to Johnson advising him to abstain from full meals.[2] In reply, in the last letter Johnson ever addressed to him, the ailing man wrote: 'Coming down from a very restless night I found your letter which made me a little angry. You tell me that recovery is in my power. This indeed I should be glad to hear, if I could once believe it. But you mean to charge me with neglecting or opposing my own health. Tell me therefore what I do that hurts me, and what I neglect that would help me. Tell it as soon as you can.... Answer the first part of this letter immediately.'[3] In reply, Taylor quoted the words of advice Johnson himself had given to Henry Thrale when he was dying: 'After the denunciation of your physicians this morning, such eating is little better than Suicide.'[4] The tactlessness of this warning to Johnson is underlined by Boswell's observation that, in his final days, he could hardly be persuaded to eat anything at all.[5]

At Johnson's funeral Taylor read the burial service. In an editorial note to the *Life* we are told that there was much criticism of the conduct of the funeral, and Dr. Charles Burney, in a letter written the following day, described Taylor's reading of the service as 'so-so'.[6] Taylor also conducted the subsequent negotiations for the erection of a memorial to his illustrious friend.[7]

In the light of all that has been said and written about the incompatibility of the interests and intellects of the two men, and of the apparent indifference that Taylor displayed towards Johnson, it is not easy to find motives for the continuance of their long association. Perhaps the simplest explanation is that they were, from time to time and in different ways, useful to each other. Not

---

[1] *Letters*, 994. [2] *Life*, iv. 444. [3] *Letters*, 1028.
[4] *Thraliana* (Bibl. 16), i. 488. See also ibid., ii. 629, for a discussion of the controversy surrounding Johnson's warning to Thrale.
[5] *Life*, iv. 415, 419. But see Taylor's version in Waingrow, op. cit., pp. 100–1.
[6] *Life*, iv. 420 n. See also J. Johnstone, Bibl. 110, i. 535.
[7] *Life*, iv. 464 (Appendix I).

only did Johnson write, dictate, and annotate sermons for Taylor; he assisted and advised him in a number of lawsuits in which Taylor was involved, including that which arose from his disastrous second marriage (*Taylor* v. *Tuckfield* in the Chancery Records for 1769–70).[1] In return, Taylor offered Johnson the hospitality of his mansion, and at least the assurance of his friendship. On one difficult occasion, it was Taylor who helped to heal the breach between Johnson and Garrick, during the planning of the production of *Irene*.[2]

Johnson undoubtedly admired his friend's physical energy. He praised the acuteness of his mind and the strength of his understanding.[3] He told Boswell that Taylor 'had great activity in some respects, and yet such a sort of indolence, that if you should put a pebble upon his chimney-piece, you would find it there, in the same state, a year afterwards'.[4] In his turn, Taylor told Boswell that he admired Johnson for his very clear head, his great power of words, and his very gay imagination. 'But', he added, 'there is no disputing with him. He will not hear you, and having a louder voice than you, must roar you down.'[5]

The two temperaments clashed now and then, but Johnson did not do all the roaring. It will be remembered, *pace* Professor Donald Greene,[6] that Johnson entertained very positive views about Whigs, and Taylor was a Whig. Once Johnson had remarked: 'I do not like much to see a Whig in any dress. But I hate to see a Whig in a parson's gown.'[7] In a heated argument with Taylor on the subject of the popular attitude in England to the royal family of Stuart, which Boswell reports for us, he went so far as to say that ' "if England were fairly polled, the present King would be sent away to-night, and his adherents hanged to-morrow." Taylor, who was as violent a Whig as Johnson was a Tory, was roused by this to a pitch of bellowing. He denied, loudly, what Johnson said; and

---

[1] Thomas Taylor, op. cit., p. 24. See also *Life*, i. 472–3, and *Letters*, 155 to 159; 161; and 165.

[2] *Life*, i. 196. See also Waingrow, *The Correspondence*, etc., p. 106.

[3] *Life*, iii. 139.   [4] *Life*, iii. 138.   [5] *Life*, iii. 150.

[6] *The Politics of Samuel Johnson* (Bibl. 41), pp. 203–4 and 223.

[7] *Life*, v. 255 (*Journal of a Tour to the Hebrides*). The immediate reference is to the Revd. James Granger (1723–76), the author of *A Biographical Dictionary of England* (1769).

maintained, that there was an abhorrence against the Stuart family, though he admitted that the people were not so much attached to the present King.'[1] Johnson went on to argue that popular loyalty to the king had diminished to the point of indifference. People, he said, would not *pay* to restore the exiled house of Stuart. But if it were a mere matter of a vote, twenty to one would be in favour of restoring the Stuarts, largely on the grounds of their hereditary rights. The argument then subsided.

In the light of this heated exchange, Sermon XXIII makes particularly interesting reading, as it was written for Taylor to preach on 30 January, in commemoration of the martyrdom of Charles I. Johnson takes a strongly conservative view of public disorder:

Of the strife, which this day brings back to our remembrance, we may observe, that it had all the tokens of *strife* proceeding from *envy*. The rage of the faction, which invaded the rights of the Church and the Monarchy, was disproportionate to the provocation received. . . .

As the end was unjust, the means likewise were illegal. The power of the faction, commenced by clamour, was promoted by rebellion, and established by murder. . . .

This war . . . was a war of the rabble against their superiors; a war, in which the lowest and basest of the people were encouraged by men a little higher than themselves, to lift their hands against their ecclesiastical and civil Governors, and by which those who were grown impatient of obedience, endeavoured to obtain the power of commanding.

This *strife*, as we all know, ended in *confusion*. Our laws were overruled, our rights were abolished. The soldier seized upon the property, the fanatick rushed into the church. The Usurpers gave way to other Usurpers; the Schismaticks were thrust out by other Schismaticks; the people felt nothing from their masters but alternatives of oppression, and heard nothing from their teachers but varieties of errour.

Such was the *strife*, and such was the *confusion*. Such are the evils which God sometimes permits to fall upon nations, when they stand secure in their own greatness, and forget their dependence on universal sovereignty, depart from the laws of their Maker, corrupt the

[1] *Life*, iii. 156. For a discussion of the apparent inconsistency of Johnson's opinions on the Stuarts in particular, and of royalty in general, see Greene, op. cit., pp. 180–2 and 240–1.

purity of his worship, or swerve from the truth of his revelation. Such evils surely we have too much reason to fear again, for we have no right to charge our Ancestors with having provoked them by crimes greater than our own.[1]

It will be noted here that Johnson tactfully steers away from any comments on the popularity, or otherwise, of the Stuart dynasty, and concentrates his attack, instead, on the evils arising from sedition and rebellion. In this way, he managed to express his own views honestly and forthrightly, without in any respect displeasing his friend.

Another sermon which must have called for nice judgement on Johnson's part was the first one in the Taylor collection, on marriage. Unfortunately, we cannot date this, or any other sermon in the collection, with any precision;[2] but if it was written after Taylor's second marriage, it must have had for him a special poignancy, not to say irony, since his wife deserted him in 1763, on the grounds of cruelty. Interestingly enough, Johnson's personal advice to Taylor on that occasion, in a letter written on 13 August 1763, and in later letters, bears a distinct resemblance to the subject-matter of *Rambler* 64 and of the sermon mentioned. The sermon reads, in part:

That Marriage itself, an Institution designed only for the promotion of happiness, and for the relief of the disappointments, anxieties, and distresses to which we are subject in our present state, does not always produce the effects, for which it was appointed; that it sometimes condenses the gloom, which it was intended to dispel, and increases the weight, which was expected to be made lighter by it, must, however unwillingly, be yet acknowledged.[3]

Even more significant is the paragraph preceding this:

. . . Offences against Society in its greater extent are cognizable by human laws. No Man can invade the property, or disturb the quiet

---

[1] *Works*, ix. 504–6. For the convenience of the reader, references are given to this, the most accessible edition of the Sermons; but where there are special points of emphasis, the earliest text (see p. 8, nn. 2 and 3 above) is used.

[2] See Maurice J. Quinlan, Bibl. 47, pp. 209–12 (Appendix: 'The Dating of Johnson's Sermons'). Professor Quinlan's attempt to establish dates by the method of word counts is, in my view, of doubtful value. See below, p. 91, n. 1.

[3] *Works*, ix. 292.

of his Neighbour, without subjecting himself to penalties, and suffer-
ing in proportion to the injuries he has offered. But cruelty and pride,
oppression and partiality, may tyrannize in private families without
controul; meekness may be trampled upon, and Piety insulted, without any appeal, but to conscience and to Heaven. A thousand methods
of torture may be invented, a thousand acts of unkindness, or disregard, may be committed, a thousand innocent gratifications may be
denied, and a thousand hardships imposed, without any violations
of national laws. Life may be embittered with hourly vexation; and
weeks, months, and years be lingered out in misery, without any
legal cause of separation, or possibility of judicial redress. . . .[1]

Both the author and the preacher could speak with authority on
this subject; Johnson's own marriage to 'Tetty' could scarcely be
described as paradisal, and Taylor's second marriage ended, as
has been mentioned, with a deed of separation. Incidentally, by
one of the provisions of this deed, Taylor allowed his wife £160 a
year, contrary to Johnson's strong advice to avoid 'paying for her
disobedience and elopement'.[2]

   There are other ironies implicit in the sermons composed for
Taylor. That a man whose financial and property concerns were so
much at the forefront of his life should preach against the evils of
business and interest; that a prosperous farmer who maintained a
regal board and substantial ménage should recommend the austere
and arduous life to others; that a man of litigious disposition,
'brisk and vigorous, fierce and fell',[3] as Johnson describes him, in
the continual prosecution of lawsuits, should plead in the pulpit
for toleration of opinions and modesty in manners; and that a man
of whom Johnson said, in a moment of exasperation, 'Nothing in
all life can be more *profligater* than what he is',[3] should advise his
parishioners to cultivate a life of watchful abstinence and prayerful
self-discipline: all of these are ironies indeed. One wonders whether
Johnson, in composing such homilies, hoped for some amendment
in the preacher himself.

   Johnson once said to his college friend, Edwards: 'The life of a
parson, of a conscientious clergyman, is not easy. . . . No, Sir, I do

   [1] Ibid., pp. 291–2.
   [2] Thomas Taylor, op. cit., p. 24. See also *Life*, i. 472–3, and *Letters*, 156 to 159;
161; and 165.   [3] *Letters*, 672.

not envy a clergyman's life as an easy life, nor do I envy the clergy-man who makes it an easy life.'[1] Here, unmistakably, is an implicit criticism of John Taylor. Yet, as we have seen, Johnson aided and abetted his friend in making his life an easy one; and we have no record of his having taken Taylor to task for his inordinate pre-occupation with his farming and business interests. Although he remonstrated with Taylor in a half-hearted way on the subject of his epicurean way of life, and looked upon his secular habits with 'the eye of perpetual disapprobation', he went again and again to Ashbourne, often at his own bidding, and gladly accepted the bounty of his friend's table and the hospitality of his mansion.

Out of this strange and incongruous association, or perhaps in some ways in spite of it, arose some of the most eloquent and impressive productions of Johnson's homiletic genius. In the pages that follow, some attempt will be made to evaluate these sermons, and others that Johnson composed, and to show how their creator brought to bear upon them his reading, his talents, and his experience. Before leaving the subject of John Taylor as catalyst, however, I would like to express an opinion, perhaps an unpopular one, about the part he played in the association.

For better or worse, Taylor was Johnson's closest friend. It was invariably to Taylor that he appealed for spiritual aid in times of extremity, illness, and misfortune. It was to Taylor, moreover, that he turned when his fears and anxieties about death and the hereafter were at their height. I believe that Taylor, for all his shortcomings, managed to impart to Johnson something of his own serene attitude to that greatest 'enemy to human quiet',[2] death itself. Thus the English squire-cum-parson, with his broad worldliness and his staunch Whig partisanship, offered to Johnson, through his faith in God's purposes and in the reality of the here-after, the solution to the most deeply perplexing problem of his life. In the words of the Rambler himself, 'A long life may be passed without finding a friend in whose understanding and virtue we can equally confide, and whose opinion we can value at once for its justness and sincerity.'[3] Of all the circle of Johnson's friends,

---

[1] *Life*, iii. 304.   [2] *Works*, ix. 518 (Sermon XXV).
[3] *Rambler* 28, *Works*, ii. 139; Yale Edn. iii. 155.

Taylor, with all his faults and weaknesses, came nearest to this ideal.

COLLABORATION WITH JOHN TAYLOR

A close study of all the sermons in the Taylor collection reveals that there are, here and there, marked variations in the prose style, and occasional local references to Ashbourne which could only have been made by Taylor himself. Although most of the sermons are quite obviously of Johnson's composition, then, there is reason to believe that at least one of them was mainly, if not entirely, of Taylor's creation, and that some parts of the others were interpolations or interpositions of Taylor's too. That the two men were capable of such collaboration will now be demonstrated, first by reference to a published letter which was, apparently, their joint composition, and secondly by evidence from the sermons themselves.

According to Boswell's account, Johnson had remarked that he would prefer a state of torment after death to one of annihilation.[1] When this remark was relayed to Taylor, the latter was greatly disturbed by it, for, as he noted, 'coming from a person of Johnson's weight and character, it might be productive of evil consequences'.[2] Johnson then asked Taylor to arrange his thoughts on the subject. The result was Taylor's *Letter to Samuel Johnson on the Subject of a Future State* (reprinted in the Appendix below, pp. 233 ff.), which received both applause and condemnation from the literary periodicals of the day.

A remarkable feature of this *Letter*, which is a very scarce document today, is that it has the earmarks of Johnson's own style, and it bears evidence of Johnson's hand in several places.[3] It would appear, then, that Johnson deliberately helped Taylor, in this instance, to argue against him. Whether he realized that Taylor would, after Johnson's death, take the liberty of publishing the

---

[1] *Life*, iii. 295–6. See pp. 32–3 below. It would appear that the editors of the *Life* have not taken into account Taylor's own report of the conversation which evoked Johnson's remark.

[2] *A Letter to Samuel Johnson, LL.D. on the Subject of a Future State* (Bibl. 13), Advertisement (page unnumbered). See also *Life*, iii. 296 n.

[3] See R. W. Chapman, Bibl. 79, pp. 338–9, and J. H. Hagstrum, Bibl. 44, pp. 258–9.

letter, as he did, is another matter. At any rate, Taylor was sufficiently circumspect to conclude the piece by saying, 'I hope you will
approve the part which I have done; and I have no doubt but that
I shall be perfectly satisfied with your superstructure upon this
foundation.'[1] While this does not prove that Johnson had a hand in
the final draft of the *Letter*, it indicates that he was, at least,
invited to make revisions. Taylor claims in his preamble that the
arguments in the *Letter* were enlarged *after* Johnson's death,[2]
and we must take his word for this.

What motives could Taylor have had for publishing the *Letter*
after Johnson's death? For one thing, we know that Taylor was
not a conspicuously modest man. As has been pointed out, he
enjoyed the last word in an argument almost as much as his celebrated friend did, and here was a unique opportunity to prove
himself in the right and Johnson in the wrong. The prestige value
of beating the Rambler at his own game, even using his own
stylistic weapons for the purpose, would appeal strongly to a
man whose intellectual capacities were much less noteworthy than
his abilities as a stock-breeder. Again, his detractors might say,
Taylor may have been planning at this very time (1787) to publish
the sermons that Johnson had written for him, or helped him to
compose, and the *Letter* would serve as a foretaste of the homiletic
material that Taylor more or less claimed to be his own.

Taking a more charitable view, one might argue, with equal
plausibility, that Taylor was genuinely concerned over the possible
consequences of Johnson's reported utterances on the subject of
annihilation, and he may well have believed that his rejoinder
would provide the desired corrective. Taylor had no illusions
about his limited prowess as an author, and it is unlikely that he
expected fame or fortune from the publication of one isolated letter.

As it happened, the *Letter* met with a mixed reception. 'Candidus'
in the *Gentleman's Magazine* welcomed it as an important contribution to 'natural Theology',[3] while Erasmus Darwin complimented
Taylor on an argument which he considered 'coincident with an

---

[1] John Taylor, op. cit., p. 18.
[2] Ibid., Advertisement (page unnumbered).
[3] *Gentleman's Magazine*, LVII (Oct. 1787), 873-4.

observation of the great Malbranche who in some parts of his metaphysical researches was a more accurate observer of the powers of the human mind than Mr. Locke'.[1] At the opposite extreme, the *Monthly Review* found the *Letter* factually vague and theologically incomplete.[2] The *Gentleman's Magazine* expressed an editorial opinion that Johnson himself would have treated the subject with greater propriety.[3] The conflict of opinions became quite heated. Whether Taylor was gratified with the publicity or not we do not know. The fact that he ordered his executors to publish the Sermons after his death, which occurred a year later, in 1788, suggests that he felt some foundation had been laid for his literary reputation.

Turning to the *Letter* itself, we find that it was inscribed to the fifth Duke of Devonshire, to whose family Taylor was a chaplain, and prefaced by a complimentary sonnet from the pen of Brooke Boothby, Jr., the eldest son of Sir Brooke Boothby, fifth baronet of Ashbourne Hall. This sonnet praises Taylor in fulsome terms, declaring that his 'clearer reason' had chased away the clouds from Johnson's mind, so that his faith was re-established and he died in 'full reliance on his God'. Let the whole world have the benefit of this 'bright conviction', continues Boothby, and

> Teach weaker minds the mighty truths to scan,
> Not more the friend of Johnson, than of man.[4]

After this grand outburst of eulogium one might expect to find in the *Letter* something more than a sketchy reaffirmation of Christian hope, but one is disappointed. It begins by reminding us, in phrases almost identical with those used by Johnson in Sermon XXV,[5] that 'death is the great disturber of human quiet'. Religion, it goes on, offers an explanation of death which should

---

[1] Ibid.

[2] *Monthly Review* or *Literary Journal*, LXXVIII (1788), 83–4.

[3] *Gentleman's Magazine*, LVII (June 1787), 521–2. See also LVIII (Jan. 1788), 39–40, and the *Critical Review*, LXIV (July 1787), 75–6, for other opinions of the *Letter*.

[4] John Taylor, op. cit., unnumbered page following Advertisement. See Joseph Tilley, *The Old Halls, Manors, and Families of Derbyshire* (Bibl. 153), ii. 202 ff., for a discussion of Boothby's merits as a poet and of his attachment to the literary circle at Lichfield.

[5] John Taylor, op. cit., p. 2. Cf. *Works*, ix. 518 (Sermon XXV).

calm the troubled mind. Death, in fact, is simply a change in the manner of life, a change from relative darkness to the light of God's revelation. Arguing from the mortality of matter to the immortality of the soul, the *Letter* then shows how Christ's example proves the reality of resurrection. The present life, it continues, is a state of probation, in which the only restraint is the hope of rewards or the fear of punishments. If the nature of the future state were known to man here and now, many would be tempted to commit suicide.[1] Such knowledge, indeed, would invalidate the necessity of faith. A righteous life will lead naturally to the transition from the earthly to the heavenly state. The day of judgement will thus become, for the righteous, a day of rejoicing.

In this *Letter*, which is little more than a summary of arguments in favour of the soul's immortality and of a future state, we have an example of an unusual and interesting partnership at work. Johnson's fears and anxieties about death and the hereafter are well known, both through his own more intimate writings, such as the *Prayers and Meditations*, and through his recorded conversations. Taylor, on the other hand, appears to have had a serene attitude to death. Moreover, shallow and worldly though he may have been, he possessed an invincible faith in God's purposes and in the reality of the life to come. Using Johnson's help, and even some of his own phraseology, Taylor articulated this faith in the crude, unpolished fashion of the *Letter*.

Although we do not know precisely how the two men collaborated in the composition of this curious work, we can piece together the various fragments of evidence provided by Taylor, first in the Advertisement to the *Letter*, and secondly in the interpolated paragraphs in which he makes direct reference to Johnson. In the Advertisement Taylor refers readers to a sentence in Johnson's *Prayers and Meditations*: 'At Ashbourne, I hope to talk seriously with Taylor.'[2] This was written on 14 October 1781. Taylor implies that this serious talk resulted from the concern which he had expressed when it was reported to him, by Richard Paul Jodrell, that Johnson had said, in conversation with Dr. Richard

---

[1] John Taylor, op. cit., pp. 7–8. Cf. *Life*, iv. 225.
[2] *Diaries*, p. 310.

Brocklesby, 'he would prefer a state of torment to that of annihilation'.[1] It appears likely that the 'talk' took place during Johnson's next visit to Ashbourne, between 9 and 30 November 1781. While no reference is made to it in Johnson's letters from Ashbourne during that visit, one that he wrote to Mrs. Thrale on 28 November contains what may be a significant sentence. After discussing Taylor's disappointments in horse-breeding and in seeking the deanery of Lincoln, Johnson observes that the parson-farmer is, none the less, 'happier than if he had no desire': 'To be without hope or fear, if it were possible would not be happiness; it is better that life should struggle with obstructions, than stagnate and putrefy.'[2] Now a part of Taylor's *Letter* is taken up with the question of worldly disappointments. The philosophers who had come to the conclusion that the soul of man is 'a substance distinct from matter' had reasoned that God would not have created 'a being to desire so much, and to obtain so little', unless there were some compensatory future state.[3]

Putting Johnson's serious talk with Taylor into perspective, then, we can see that, while Johnson tried to persuade his friend that worldly disappointments were, as he said in a letter written just before the particular visit mentioned, 'the common incidents of life',[4] Taylor took the more optimistic view that they were unmerited calamities which would be made good in the life to come. Out of such optimism arose his unshakable belief in the immortality of the soul, which, in turn, proved 'the absurdity and folly of annihilation':

When I told you that I had heard from Mr. Jodrell, of your conversation with Dr. Brocklesby about annihilation; you said, 'that nothing could be more weak than any such notion; that life was indeed a great thing; and that you meant nothing more by your preference of a state of torment to a state of annihilation, than to express at what an immense value you rated vital existence'. Upon this part of the subject it is very necessary that you should be precisely exact, and very forcible.[5]

[1] John Taylor, op. cit., p. 6.   [2] *Letters*, 751.1.
[3] John Taylor, op. cit., pp. 5–6.   [4] *Letters*, 739.1.
[5] John Taylor, op. cit., p. 6.

Now what follows in the *Letter* has the ring of Johnsonian author-ity about it, as if it were a direct answer to Taylor's demand for precision and force:

Our all-merciful Creator has made men free and moral agents; as such he has sent them into this world, into a state of probation; suffers them to be masters of themselves, and restrains them only by coercions applied to their reason; by the hope of rewards, or the fear of punishments. But to prevent the sin of suicide, a sin that most opposes the designs and schemes of his providence, and the most heinous of all sins in his sight, our God omnipotent has applied every exertion of his almighty power; and by his prescient care at our creation in framing, in mixing, and in uniting, in our nature, in our reason, and in our senses, this first principle, this miraculous law of self-preservation, He, the mighty Lord, hath taught us how offensive in his sight is the crime of self-murder; . . .[1]

The first part of this statement is almost a paraphrase of what Johnson had written, many years before, in his Preface to *The Preceptor*, and had repeated several times in conversation as well as in his writings. It is to be remembered, he had written in the Preface, that

the laws of mere morality are of no coercive power; and, however they may, by conviction, of their fitness please the reasoner in the shade, when the passions stagnate without impulse, and the appetites are secluded from their objects, they will be of little force against the ardour of desire, or the vehemence of rage, amidst the pleasures and tumults of the world. To counteract the power of temptations, hope must be excited by the prospect of rewards, and fear by the expecta-tion of punishment; and virtue may owe her panegyricks to morality, but must derive her authority from religion.[2]

On the subject of suicide, however, Johnson was notably silent. Only one reference to it is made in the *Life*,[3] and the one scrap of evidence to indicate that Johnson once talked to Taylor about the possibility of suicide is so unreliable as to be dismissed as third-hand testimony.[4] That he coupled thoughts of suicide with fears

---

[1] John Taylor, op. cit., p. 7.   [2] *Works*, v. 243–4.   [3] *Life*, iv. 225.
[4] A. L. Reade, Bibl. 139. A Mrs. Nicholas is the writer of a letter, dated 1786, in which the reference appears. See James L. Clifford, Bibl. 17, p. 129 and note.

of annihilation is, none the less, a distinct possibility. Boswell's single quotation on the subject is as follows:

JOHNSON. 'Sir, if a man has led a good life for seven years, and then is hurried by passion to do what is wrong, and is suddenly carried off, depend upon it he will have the reward of his seven years' good life; GOD will not take a catch of him. Upon this principle Richard Baxter believes that a Suicide may be saved. "If, (says he,) it should be objected that what I maintain may encourage suicide, I answer, I am not to tell a lie to prevent it." '[1]

It was Baxter who also argued, however, that 'sin doth unquestionably deserve a natural death and annihilation', and that 'Nature teacheth men to choose a great deal of pain and misery, rather than not to be at all: even so much as will not utterly weigh down the love of life, and of vital operations.'[2] This view is expressed by Johnson several times in the *Life*, and it accords with what is said in the second half of the paragraph quoted from the *Letter*: the 'miraculous law of self-preservation' is, in fact, illustrated by man's determination to hold on to life, even in the face of the greatest agony.

From such examples we can see how Johnson and Taylor probably collaborated in the composition of the *Letter*. After the 'precisely exact' and 'very forcible' argument supplied, one conjectures, by Johnson himself, Taylor continues: 'I was once desired by a Friend to give my opinion of the crime of suicide. My answer was the argument above; and the effect of it was most amazing. He immediately turned pale; his lips were convulsed; and it was some time before he could recover himself. You have frequently, and very lately, reminded me of this occurrence.'[3] Is it possible that the 'Friend' was Samuel Johnson? And is it not likely that the

---

[1] *Life*, iv. 225.

[2] *The Reasons of the Christian Religion* (Bibl. 64), p. 165. See p. 105 below.

[3] John Taylor, op. cit., p. 8. See also Waingrow, op. cit., p. 468, where James Hutton (1715–95), founder of the Moravian Church in England, is quoted as writing (29 Jan. 1792): 'I recollect having heard in Derbyshire that Dr. Taylor had boasted at a Table there that Dr. Johnson had consulted Him about the admissibility of Suicide, and that He had set him right by the most paltry common place Stuff that could be. I grew so angry and so disgusted that I despised Taylor as unworthy of Society, if what he uttered was in any Degree True, as a Confessors Breach of Confession Fidelity, and if not True, it certainly was not, how disgraceful. . . .'

argument provided by Taylor, who offered him the reassurance he sought, was cast in the strong and precise terms illustrated above by Johnson himself? Was this the kind of 'superstructure' that Taylor asked Johnson, at the very end of the *Letter*, to add to his 'foundation'?[1]

If such collaboration was possible in the composition of a document of this kind, there is surely no reason to doubt that a similar form of co-authorship was at work in the production of some parts, at least, of the sermons. In most of these, however, the Johnsonian 'superstructure' is much more in evidence than the Taylorian 'foundation'. The mind of the creator of the *Rambler*, the *Idler*, and *Rasselas* is never far from the foreground of the discourses in the Taylor collection; verbal echoes, even repeated phrases, from these works of Johnson are to be found again and again. While such similarities may not constitute conclusive evidence of Johnson's authorship, or part-authorship, since Taylor could have been quoting or paraphrasing his friend's essays, they are strongly suggestive of '*Conciones pro Tayloro*'. The themes and ideas are also familiar: the vanity of human wishes and the shortness of life; typically Johnsonian approaches to the subjects of charity and friendship; reiterations of favourite texts, frequently noted in the *Life* and in the *Prayers and Meditations*; warnings to the unrepentant, counsels to those who seek domestic happiness, and admonitions to those in power to account for their stewardship: these have a truly Johnsonian slant and focus.

A careful study of a sermon and a *Rambler* essay on the same theme reveals much more, of course, than verbal echoes, similarities in approach, and stylistic identity: it shows that, in spite of adaptations to a different audience and a different genre, the same great mind is at work on the same idea. Parallels between the sermons and Johnson's other works will be dealt with later, but one or two striking instances may be mentioned here. Sermon II bears a close resemblance to *Rambler* 110, treating the theme of repentance in similar sequence: (1) the character of God: fear and mercy; (2) the inadequacy of external repentance only; (3) superstition in piety; (4) the definition of repentance as a change of life

---

[1] John Taylor, op. cit., p. 18.

and practice; (5) the consideration of future punishment; (6) repentance as the result of sorrow and fear. This example affords a convincing testimony to Johnson's authorship: the same idea, broken up into similar component parts, and carrying almost identical intellectual and emotional associations. There are important differences in detail, however. The *Rambler* essay quotes Milton, while the sermon adheres to the text of Isaiah; the essay is a much more succinct performance; the tone is altogether less hortatory, less homiletic; and the sermon consolidates and reiterates its main points in ways that would be inappropriate to an essay.

It might be argued that someone else could have sat down and written a sermon such as Sermon II, with *Rambler* 110 lying open on his desk, or that Taylor could have asked Johnson to compose a discourse based upon the *Rambler* essay. I do not believe that either of these explanations is correct. A study of the *Life* and of Johnson's writings reveals, on the whole, a remarkable consistency in his thinking. In his conversations, for instance, similar stimuli appear to produce similar arguments, almost in so many words, time and again. His remarkable memory, together with a propensity for arranging his thoughts in sequential patterns, contributed to this effect. Hence we find similar sequences of ideas between *Ramblers* and *Idlers* dealing with parallel themes, between *Rasselas* and *The Vanity of Human Wishes*, between what he writes about Milton in *Ramblers* 139 and 140 and in the *Life of Milton*, between his published correspondence and what he is reported as having said in his conversations, and so on. There are notable exceptions to this, of course, and it would be manifestly wrong to say that Johnson never changed his mind or his patterns of thinking on any subject; but the fact remains that he rarely altered these patterns when dealing with matters of intense conviction. What he did alter was his phrasing and his emphasis, as in the example just discussed: composing a sermon for someone else would, after all, require something more than a mere repetition or paraphrase of an essay written for popular consumption.

Another instance of close correspondence between the argument of a sermon and views which Johnson expressed elsewhere will be found in Sermon VI, where, dilating on a favourite theme, the folly of pride, he attacks the arrogance of the philosophers and speculatists in much the same way as he does in *Ramblers* 173 and 181, parts of his review of Soame Jenyns's *A Free Inquiry into the Nature and Origin of Evil*, and his *Life of Boerhaave*.

Where such obvious parallels and similarities do not exist, and where the style is clearly un-Johnsonian, we should be right to suspect the hand of Taylor, or of someone else, at work. Close examination of the Taylor collection reveals only one sermon of this kind, Sermon XXI. Professor Jean Hagstrum has advanced strong arguments for dismissing this sermon from the Johnsonian canon.[1] Professor Maurice Quinlan, while accepting the substance of these arguments, points out at least one parallel between a passage in the sermon and a sentence in *Rambler* 149.[2] Before presenting my own view, I would like to quote some of Professor Hagstrum's observations for consideration:

We are justified . . . in believing that a sermon in the collection left for publication that reveals the very faults that seem to have been Taylor's and certainly could not have been Johnson's should be withdrawn from the Johnsonian canon and attributed to Dr. Taylor. The sermon is No. XXI; its theme is the goodness of God as revealed in creation. This theme, based here, as it usually was, on Ps. 145: 9 ('The Lord is good to all, and his tender mercies are over all his works'), was treated more often than perhaps any other in the homiletical literature of the period. Clarke, South, Tillotson, Barrow, Jortin, and others all had sermons on it, some of them singularly parallel in outline and even phraseology to the one in Taylor's collection. The theme, briefly put, is that God's goodness compelled him to create and give life; that all life is good; that the universe is perfect and therefore reveals its creator; that man and his instincts point to God. This is the natural religion and optimism typical of much eighteenth-century theology and bordering closely upon the unorthodox Leibnitzian theory of the 'best of all possible worlds.' The following sentences from the sermon under discussion are typical of the idea:

'He [God] created to communicate. . . . His goodness dictated the bestowing of existence, in all its forms, and with all its properties. . . .

[1] J. H. Hagstrum, loc. cit., pp. 259–61.
[2] Maurice J. Quinlan, op. cit., p. 221 n. 20.

His goodness connects unnumbered worlds together in one spacious, vast, and unbounded universe, and embraces every system.

'In the first place, to illustrate this, we need only to take a transient view of the outworks of the visible creation, a general survey of the nature and correspondence of the various parts of this regular and grand machine, *this finished and stupendous fabrick*, in which everything is contrived and concluded for the best.'

Now it is impossible to believe that such a profession of naturalistic optimism could come from the author of *Rasselas*. The sermon on the goodness of God, moreover, has an idea that comes very close to a belief which Johnson was also at pains to refute—the notion (to Johnson unorthodox) of the Great Chain of Being, which held that man, beast, and all things created were links in a great cosmic chain, that each was in its rightful place, and that it was, therefore, the veriest cosmic impertinence to complain of one's lot. Here are typical paragraphs from Sermon XXI:

'It is evidently the same with respect to all the other creatures we are acquainted with. Their nature and condition, their qualities and circumstances, are so adapted to one another, that, as the intellectual powers of a being of a more exalted nature would not probably suit an inhabitant of the lower world, so neither would the capacities of human nature guide the fowls of the air, or conduct the beasts of the field, to so much happiness, as they find, by following the motions and impulses of sense and instinct. . . .

'But these universal notices, and undeniable testimonies of divine goodness, throughout the animated regions of earth, sea, and air, in the *propriety and suitableness of creatures to their state, and objects to their appetites*, are too evident and obvious to all men to need enlargement.'

Such statements are strikingly similar to those of Soame Jenyns, which Johnson refuted with relentless indignation. Jenyns wrote (I quote from Johnson's citation of his opponent's words):

'It is, moreover, highly probable, that there is such a connexion between all ranks and orders, by subordinate degree that they mutually support each other's existence, and every one, in its place, is absolutely necessary towards sustaining the whole *vast and magnificent fabric*. . . . A man can have no reason to repine, that he is not an angel; nor a horse, that he is not a man; much less, that, in their several stations, they possess not the faculties of another; for this would be an insufferable misfortune.'

Such speculations aroused Johnson's scorn: 'To these meditations humanity is unequal.'[1]

Perhaps there is less scorn than realism in the last remark of Johnson's. Although he disagreed with the optimistic views of Leibnitz, he did not treat them uniformly with contempt. For the present discussion, however, it is not necessary to consider Johnson's philosophy in detail. We can accept Professor Hagstrum's argument that Sermon XXI does not represent Johnson's own views; but does that necessarily imply that Johnson had no part in its composition? After all, as has been shown, Taylor's *Letter on the Subject of a Future State* contained opinions contrary to Johnson's own; yet we have demonstrated that Johnson aided Taylor in its composition.

In fairness to Professor Hagstrum, it should be observed that his reason for rejecting Sermon XXI from the Johnsonian canon is based on the style of the piece at least as much as on the content or argument. He quotes from the text generously and underlines some phrases, grammatical constructions, and 'violations of good sense and idiom' which are 'notorious' examples of un-Johnsonian English.[2] Two of his examples are the following:

In this *devout, masterly, and useful performance*, the author appears deeply sensible of the divine greatness, and peculiarly transported with contemplating God's infinite goodness; even to that degree, that he cheerfully engages in, and absolutely *devotes himself to*, the *very important* service of adoring and obeying this almighty, unbounded, and *most* benevolent Being. . . . [The performance referred to is the text, Ps. 145: 9.]

Our great Lord and Master has taught us, that there is none good but one, that is God. By *which* expression we may understand, that there is none so *perfectly* disinterested, so *diffusively*, and so *astonishingly* good, as God is. *For*, in another place, he instructs us both how to comprehend, and rely on this unchangeable and never-failing attribute of the divine nature; *resembling it to, or representing it by*, a human

[1] J. H. Hagstrum, loc. cit., pp. 259–60.   [2] Ibid., p. 260.

quality of virtue, namely, the affection and tender regard of parents to their children.

Professor Hagstrum concludes:

This sermon, then—a pompous and offensive attempt to be fashionable in theology and Johnsonian in style—proclaims itself the work of the author of the derivative *Letter to Samuel Johnson*. It is not difficult to see how one of Taylor's own sermons might easily have come in among those written for him by Dr. Johnson and 'left for publication'.[1]

With this finding it would be hard to disagree. Sermon XXI is a mediocre discourse, full of the blemishes he mentions. Yet I would favour its qualified retention as part of the Johnsonian canon, on the grounds that, however imperfect it may be, it shows some of the signs of the kind of collaboration which produced the *Letter*. Taylor probably discussed the theme of the sermon with Johnson, jotted down some ideas at the latter's dictation, and in the end botched the job of transcription and revision. Not having the reportorial ability or the retentive memory of a Boswell, who on occasion managed to record, from dictation, scraps of homiletic material thrown to him by his great mentor,[2] Taylor patched together this sermon to the best of his ability.

Another sermon which shows some evident additions of Taylor's own composition is Sermon XVIII. The last six paragraphs of this discourse strongly criticize magistrates who withhold charity funds from those who are in need. The subject is broached in the first person, with a directness and vehemence that strongly suggest a local situation in Ashbourne:

Truth requires, that I warn you against a species of fraud, sometimes found amongst you, and *that* of a *very* shameful and oppressive kind. . . . He declares himself, *perhaps*, unable to work, by *which* nothing more can reasonably be meant, than that he is no longer capable of labour equal to his livelihood. This man is found employing the *remains* of his strength in some little office. For this surely he deserves to be commended. But what has been the consequence? He has been considered as an impostor, who claims the benefit of the fund by counterfeited incapacity; and that feeble diligence, which, among

---

[1] Ibid., p. 261.   [2] See James Gray, Bibl. 97.

reasonable and equitable men, gives him a title to esteem and pity, is *misapplied* and *misrepresented into* a pretence for depriving him of his right, and *this done* by judges, who vainly imagine they shall be benefited themselves by their own wicked determination.[1]

Professor Hagstrum's comment is understandable:

> Although less offensive than the style of the sermon on the goodness of God, this direct and homely exhortation also betrays, it seems to me, the hand of Dr. Taylor. The looseness of the grammatical structure, the vagueness of the pronominal reference, and the carelessness of the vocabulary can point to only one conclusion.[2]

Nevertheless, there is a vestige of Johnsonianism in the phrase 'by counterfeited incapacity', and the spirit of Johnson is not far removed from the sentiments, however awkwardly expressed by John Taylor.

We may conclude, then, that the collaboration between Johnson and Taylor took several forms: sometimes Johnson composed a whole sermon for his friend; sometimes he dictated it, in whole or part; sometimes Taylor supplied the 'foundation' and Johnson the 'superstructure', as in the *Letter on the Subject of a Future State*; and sometimes, as in Sermon XXI and the conclusion of Sermon XVIII, Taylor did most of the composition, using an occasional Johnsonian turn of phrase. A rare example of their collaboration in action will be discussed in the next part of this chapter.

THE YALE MANUSCRIPT SERMON

One sermon not included in the Hayes edition of the Taylor collection of sermons, the only one of the joint productions of Johnson and Taylor to exist in manuscript, provides a unique illustration of one of the methods by which the two friends collaborated. Hitherto unpublished, it is in the possession of the Beinecke Library at Yale University, and will be printed in the Yale Edition of the Sermons of Dr. Johnson. It does not appear to have been in Taylor's keeping at the time of his death, and it may never have been seen by Hayes.

---

[1] *Works*, ix. 457.   [2] J. H. Hagstrum, loc. cit., p. 261.

This sermon was first described by Dr. R. W. Chapman in the London *Times* in 1933,[1] and it was discussed at greater length by Professor Jean Hagstrum in 1943.[2] It consists of an unstitched quire of fourteen leaves, measuring $7\frac{3}{4}$ by $5\frac{1}{2}$ inches. The text, as Hagstrum convincingly demonstrates, is written in the hand of Dr. Taylor, and bears corrections in the hand of Dr. Johnson. The outer wrapper is inscribed, also in manuscript, 'MS Sermon by Dr. Johnson found in the library at Bradley by R. Gifford, and given to him by Hugo Meynell Esq.'

Although Samuel Hayes appears not to have examined this sermon, it was well known to a number of his contemporaries, including Thomas Cadell, for whom the Hayes edition of the *Sermons Left for Publication* was printed. As will be shown, however, Cadell had some doubts about its authorship. It was also known to at least four others: Richard Gifford, Hugo Meynell, John Nichols, and George Strahan.

The early history of this manuscript sermon can be established by reference to correspondence between Gifford and Nichols. In reply to a letter which has not survived, but in which Gifford presumably told Nichols of the discovery of the sermon, Nichols observed that the internal evidence of Johnson's authorship was 'indisputable'.[3] Gifford then wrote the following letter to Nichols:

Duffield, June 3, 1790

Dear Sir,

By the *internal* evidence, which you admit to be indisputable, you undoubtedly mean the language and the turn of the periods. But did you not overlook the corrections, which are certainly in Dr. Johnson's handwriting? Mr. Cadell, who must have seen many autographs of his, must admit this; and I cannot but think it a kind of *external* evidence. I found the MS. in the library of Hugo Meynell, esq. of Bradley in this county. Dr. Johnson was intimately acquainted with Mrs. Fitzherbert, Mr. Meynell's sister, a circumstance mentioned by Mr. Boswell or Mrs. Piozzi, I forget which. Mr. Meynell had never seen

[1] See Bibl. 78.
[2] J. H. Hagstrum, loc. cit., pp. 261–6.
[3] Ibid., p. 262.

the MS. before I shewed it to him; nor could he or any of his friends recollect the hand of the person to whom, it is clear from the corrections, the Doctor dictated it. Mr. Strahan read the MS. when I was in Essex last summer; and was not only convinced that it was of the Doctor's composition, but that he had alluded to this very sermon in a conversation he once had with him. Mr. Cadell will receive perfect satisfaction on this head the first opportunity he has of mentioning the business to Mr. Strahan. Mr. P. Coke had not an opportunity of acquainting you, that Mr. Meynell, when he gave me leave to publish it, desired that what it might be sold for might be given to the Infirmary at Nottingham. It may be decent to say this to others; but I will not suspect you of entertaining the idea that I am capable of profiting in this way by the works of another. If the Doctor knows anything of this business, I have no doubt but he will be well-satisfied with the intended application of the money. . . .

I am

Your faithful, humble Servt.

R^d Gifford.[1]

The 'Doctor' referred to in the last sentence quoted appears to be Dr. Johnson who had, of course, been dead for five years; the implication that he might still be aware of what was going on is presumably a humorous one. The interesting feature of this letter is the fact that Gifford and Strahan were both convinced that Johnson was the author of the sermon. Strahan even recalls an occasion when Johnson made some reference to it. Nichols's reply to Gifford accompanies the sermon in the Beinecke Library at Yale. It shows that, while Nichols was convinced of the sermon's authenticity, Cadell was reluctant to print it.

June 15, 1790.

Dear Sir,

I had not overlooked the *external* Evidence, such as it is, arising from the Doctor's Corrections; about which there can be *no Doubt*: but those Corrections alone do not ascertain the Work to be his. I could produce some Articles that are certainly *not his*, but which have *his Corrections*.—This is not to invalidate the Value of the Sermon; for, I repeat it, I have no Doubt of its being genuine. Yet Mr.

[1] J. H. Hagstrum, loc. cit., p. 263.

Cadell hesitates to publish it as *Johnson's*, unless more positive Proof could be had.—What shall we do? . . .

Your faithful humble Servt
J. Nichols[1]

Gifford, in return, appears willing to drop the matter.

Duffield, June 17, 1790.

Dear Sir,

I will not give you any more trouble about the MS. sermon. It is safe in your hands; and I am not only satisfied with what has been done respecting it, but equally so, that nothing more can be done consistently with common prudence.[2]

Thus the idea of publishing the manuscript was scrapped, and no more was said or heard of it until 1933, when it was brought to the attention of the public by Dr. Chapman.

A careful study of the manuscript leads me to accept the findings of Professor Hagstrum: that the sermon is undoubtedly in the handwriting of John Taylor, as a comparison between it and Taylor's autograph letters clearly shows, and that the corrections are in the handwriting of Dr. Johnson. The reason why Cadell, who must have been familiar with the autographs of both men, and who had published the Taylor collection only a short time previously, still had doubts about the sermon's authorship, can only be surmised. Perhaps there might have been copyright complications, about which the publishers at that time were particularly sensitive.[3]

Any doubts that Cadell might have had about the Johnsonian substance of the manuscript sermon would have been hard to justify. Apart from occasional lapses that could have been the result of inaccuracies of transcription, the sermon seems to be a fine product of the Johnson–Taylor collaboration, the bulk of the composition having been suggested and dictated by Johnson, a

[1] MS. Sermon—by Dr. Johnson (Bibl. 7). Unnumbered page accompanying the sermon. See also J. H. Hagstrum, loc. cit., p. 263.

[2] Ibid., p. 263.

[3] On the problems of shared copyrights see J. A. Cochrane, *Dr. Johnson's Printer* (Bibl. 85), pp. 136 ff.

few interpolations inserted by Taylor, and the whole corrected by Johnson, but prepared for delivery by Taylor.

If the sermon is compared with *Rambler* 114, it will be found to have a similar central idea or theme, and parallel, but not identical, phrasing. At times, indeed, the sentences are too tortuous and careless to be Johnson's, but the core idea in each one is quite plainly his. The strongly moralistic tone towards the end has a shrill quality similar to that of the conclusion of Sermon XVIII, indicating that Taylor's own emphasis has been introduced. The combined efforts of the two friends are, therefore, clearly in evidence in this discourse.

II

Johnson's Homiletic Sources and Models

FOR the task of composing and collaborating in the composition of the sermons discussed in the previous chapter Samuel Johnson was unusually well qualified. His natural propensity to think homiletically, his deep and comprehensive knowledge of the Book of Common Prayer and of the Bible, and his virtually lifelong immersion in sermon literature fitted him splendidly for the production of pulpit discourses. It is with his background in sermon-reading that the present chapter concerns itself, and with some of the most important sources and models from which he derived both inspiration and ideas.

Boswell records one occasion when Johnson's opinion was sought as to 'what were the best English sermons for style':

I took an opportunity to-day of mentioning several to him.—'*Atterbury?*' JOHNSON. 'Yes, Sir, one of the best.' BOSWELL. '*Tillotson?*' JOHNSON. 'Why, not now. I should not advise a preacher at this day to imitate Tillotson's style: though I don't know; I should be cautious of objecting to what has been applauded by so many suffrages.— *South* is one of the best, if you except his peculiarities, and his violence, and sometimes coarseness of language.—*Seed* has a very fine style; but he is not very theological.—*Jortin's* sermons are very elegant.—*Sherlock's* style too is very elegant, though he has not made it his principal study.—And you may add *Smallridge*. All the latter preachers have a good style. Indeed, nobody now talks much of style: every body composes pretty well. There are no such unharmonious periods as there were a hundred years ago. I should recommend Dr. *Clarke's* sermons, were he orthodox. However, it is very well known *where* he was not orthodox, which was upon the doctrine of the Trinity, as to which he is a condemned heretick; so one is aware of it.' BOSWELL. 'I like Ogden's Sermons on Prayer very much, both for neatness of style and subtilty of reasoning.' JOHNSON. 'I should like to read all that Ogden has written.' BOSWELL. 'What I wish to know is, what sermons afford the best specimen of English pulpit eloquence.' JOHNSON. 'We have no sermons addressed to the passions that are good for anything; if you mean that kind of eloquence.' A CLERGYMAN: (whose name I do not recollect.) 'Were not Dodd's sermons addressed to the passions?' JOHNSON. 'They were nothing, Sir, be they addressed to what they may.'[1]

Although this passage is primarily concerned with questions of homiletic style and pulpit eloquence, it gives some idea of the enormous fund of sermon-reading that formed so much of Johnson's intellectual background and contributed so substantially to his habits of thought. His own sermons were, in one sense, uniquely his; in another, the distillation of English pulpit influences from the latter half of the sixteenth century to the middle of the eighteenth, and from the 'highest' Anglican to the 'lowest' Puritan strains. On the whole, these influences were assimilated so completely that it is not easy to identify individual examples of ideas, doctrine, or arguments that spring from any one of them. In short, almost the entire body of Christian writing in English forms their background.

In Johnson's view, a sermon should be a practical discourse, having an immediate and important application to the purposes of life.[2] With the finer points of theology, and with the niceties of doctrinal exposition, he was rarely concerned. As will be demonstrated, there is only a subtle difference between the moral essay and the sermon as he practised the two forms, a difference in the quality and the degree of didacticism. Above all, he regarded the sermon as a genre of English literature, and the writing of sermons as an art no less important, if slightly less exacting, than the art of poetry.[3] This is why he was a little reluctant to recommend to Boswell the work of John Tillotson (1630–92), whose sermons he found deficient in beauty and embellishment, though powerful in impact and worthwhile in substance;[4] and why Richard Hooker (1554?–1600), with his measured sentences and his meticulously selected phrases, appealed to him as a model of sermon prose.[5]

Because he preferred a style of pulpit discourse free from verbal

---

[1] *Life*, iii. 247–8.   [2] *Life*, i. 459.   [3] *Life*, iv. 105 and iii. 437.
[4] *Life*, iii. 247.   [5] *Life*, i. 219.

tricks and metaphysical wit, Johnson avoided the special kinds of eloquence that so enriched the sermons of John Donne, Lancelot Andrewes, and Henry More.[1] The paradox, the neatly turned conceit, the convoluted symbol, the far-fetched analogy—all of these are conspicuously absent from his own homiletic prose, and he did not admire them in others.

As Professor Maurice Quinlan has observed,

Johnson himself was probably more devout and certainly better informed on Christian doctrine than most clergymen of his time. He had a special interest in sermons. He read with discrimination, analyzing the style and comparing the views expressed. He observed who wrote best on evidence, on prayer, on free will and necessity. Furthermore, he could recall what writers on religion, as on other subjects, had said, years after he had read them. When Joshua Reynolds praised the sermons of Zachariah Mudge, he commented, 'Mudge's sermons are good but not practical. He grasps more than he can hold. . . . I love Blair's sermons.' He observed that Jeremy Taylor 'gives a very good advice: "Never lie in your prayers; never confess more than you really believe." ' When asked about Richard Baxter's sermons, he replied, 'Read any of them; they are all good.' On the subject of prayer he favoured Samuel Ogden as a preacher who 'fought infidels with their own weapons'. For style Johnson heartily recommended Atterbury, South, and Seed. . . .

. . . Some indication of how widely he ranged, though by no means a complete record of his reading, is supplied by the list of books he owned at the time of his death. His personal library contained a rich assortment of philosophical, devotional, and theological works. Among them were a few rare items, like a 1491 edition of *De Consolatione Philosophiae* by Boethius. Many of the earlier volumes were printed in Latin, such as the *Opera* of St. Thomas Aquinas, and those of St. Anselm and of Erasmus, as well as the *De Legibus* of Suarez. The first centuries of Christianity were represented by Eusebius' *History of the Christian Church*, and the works of St. Ambrose, St. Athanasius, St. Augustine, and Justin the Martyr. Also on Johnson's bookshelves were volumes of such diverse nature and different dogmas as the *Roman Missal*, Sale's *Koran*, and the writings of Calvin. English authors were represented by works like Goodman's *Penitent Pardoned*, Pearce's

---

[1] *Life*, ii. 162.

Commentary on the Evangelists, and Fuller's *Church History*. There were also dozens of volumes of sermons by seventeenth- and eighteenth-century divines.[1]

For this information on Johnson's collection of religious works Professor Quinlan consulted the *Sale Catalogue of Dr. Johnson's Library* (privately printed by A. Edward Newton, 1925), which is, unfortunately, a rather inadequate listing, originally prepared by an unskilled auctioneer,[2] but it serves as an indication, at least, of the very considerable resources on which Johnson could depend.

Professor Quinlan points out that, of the many authors of religious writings whom Johnson had read, two were singled out by him as having made the greatest contribution to his Christian outlook: William Law (1686–1761) and Samuel Clarke (1675–1729).[3] To these one would be justified in adding a third: Richard Baxter (1615–91).

WILLIAM LAW

William Law, whose influence on the religious thought and practice of the eighteenth century as a whole was enormous, played a particularly important role in Johnson's early spiritual development, about which Boswell has this to say:

> He communicated to me the following particulars upon the subject of his religious progress. 'I fell into an inattention to religion, or an indifference about it, in my ninth year. The church at Lichfield, in which we had a seat, wanted reparation, so I was to go and find a seat in other churches; and having bad eyes, and being awkward about this, I used to go and read in the fields on Sunday. This habit continued till my fourteenth year; and still I find a great reluctance to go to church. I then became a sort of lax *talker* against religion, for I did not much *think* against it; and this lasted till I went to Oxford, where it would not be *suffered*. When at Oxford, I took up Law's

[1] *Samuel Johnson: a Layman's Religion* (Bibl. 47), pp. 3–4.

[2] Arthur Wollaston Hutton, Bibl. 109, pp. 117 ff. A different view is taken by Percy Colson, Bibl. 86, p. 34. Mr. Colson gives credit to James Christie, the auctioneer (then in his fifty-fifth year), for a very successful sale. The sum realized was £247. 9s. 0d.

[3] Quinlan, pp. 3–45. See also *Life*, i. 68, ii. 122, iv. 286, n. 3, 311; and i. 398; iv 416, 524.

Serious Call to a Holy Life, expecting to find it a dull book (as such books generally are), and perhaps to laugh at it. But I found Law quite an overmatch for me; and this was the first occasion of my thinking in earnest of religion, after I became capable of rational inquiry.' From this time forward religion was the predominant subject of his thoughts; though, with the just sentiments of a conscientious Christian, he lamented that his practice of its duties fell far short of what it ought to be.[1]

Mrs. Thrale also testifies to the deep and abiding impression made upon Johnson's mind by Law's *Serious Call*.[2] Recent scholarship strongly supports her testimony. Professor Katherine C. Balderston, Stuart Gerry Brown, and Walter Jackson Bate, in particular, have all drawn attention to the continuing influence of Law's work in Johnson's maturity and throughout his later life.[3]

Miss Balderston begins an important article on this subject by quoting Sir John Hawkins, who, she points out, 'accounted for Johnson's intense religious convictions, and the exemplary piety of his behaviour which made him so conspicuously different from the generality of Christian men in his own society, by his reading in the older Christian literature':

To speak of . . . his religion, it had a tincture of enthusiasm, arising, as is conjectured, from the fervour of his imagination, and the perusal of St. Augustine and other of the fathers, and the writings of Kempis and the ascetics, which prompted him to the employment of composing meditations and devotional exercises. It farther produced in him an habitual reverence for the name of God, which he was never known to utter but on proper occasions and with due respect, and operated on those that were admitted to his conversations as a powerful restraint of all profane discourse, and idle discussion of theological questions; and lastly, it inspired him with that charity, meaning thereby a general concern for the welfare of all mankind, without which we are told that all pretensions to religion are vain.[4]

Miss Balderston believes that all the important aspects of Johnson's religious life which Hawkins ascribes to the influence of the Church

---

[1] *Life*, i. 67–9.   [2] *Thraliana*, i. 421.
[3] Bibl. 57; 73; 34, pp. 134 and 162. See also Quinlan, pp. 3–26, and Chester F. Chapin, Bibl. 38, pp. 36–41.
[4] Balderston, Bibl. 57, p. 382, and Hawkins, pp. 162–3.

Fathers may, in fact, be attributed to the effect of Law's *Serious Call*. Notwithstanding Johnson's own warning, in *Adventurer* 95, against finding 'sources' for moral utterances, and charging moral writers with plagiarism, she attempts to show that

> many of Johnson's moral and religious ideas stem from Law, as well as many of his psychological insights into human motivation. I have tried . . . to ignore views held in common by the two which might be called the basic concepts of Christian belief and Christian morality, or be classed as what Johnson calls 'general truth'. And if I have allowed any such ideas to intrude, it may at least be argued that Johnson met them first in Law. It must be remembered that Johnson read the *Serious Call* when he was only nineteen years old, before he began his omnivorous reading in religious literature. Of the one hundred and fifteen volumes which constituted his library when he left Oxford, only three—*Sherlock on Death*, the Bible, and the Book of Common Prayer—were religious.[1]

The latter fact is not especially significant. More to the point would be some information about the books Johnson borrowed, while at Oxford, to supplement his own library. One of these, indeed, was the *Serious Call* itself. In general, however, Miss Balderston's thesis is a valid one; and an important indication of the sustained impression made by Law's work on Johnson's mind is the fact that, in the revised fourth edition of his *Dictionary*, published in 1773, after Law's death, Johnson quotes the *Serious Call* no fewer than 195 times.[2]

It will be remembered that Johnson had found Law to be an 'overmatch' for him when he read the *Serious Call* during his Oxford days.[3] By this he appears to have meant that Law had somehow persuaded him of the hopeless superficiality of his attitude to religion. Furthermore, his inability to discipline himself to 'the devout and holy life' for which Law so earnestly appeals shamed and perhaps even disheartened him. What Law practised, and demanded of others, was a total dedication of oneself to a blameless and perfect Christian existence: 'If a man should keep this whole law of love, and yet offend in one point, he would be guilty of all.'[4]

---

[1] Balderston, pp. 382-3.   [2] Ibid., p. 383.   [3] *Life*, i. 68.
[4] *Serious Call* (Bibl. 117), p. 279.

To achieve this totality of dedication a man must first be convinced of his responsibility for his own salvation, using his God-given reason to find out the truth, and his free will to respond to that truth. Thus, in his view, the abuse of reason becomes a primary sin, as it makes us 'rebels against God . . . and subject to his wrath'.[1] The Christian religion 'requires a life of the highest reason', since it is 'only the refinement and exaltation of our best faculties'.[2]

As Miss Balderston states,

> Law's conception of the Christian life and the exigency of his standards were something quite apart from the Christian teaching and practice of his day, and only Jeremy Taylor in the seventeenth century could be remotely comparable to him. He was appalled by the laxness and complacency of the religious life of his day, and set out to show the average Christian how far he fell short of what his religion, in Law's view, really demanded of him. His book is addressed, not to atheists or flagrant sinners, but to the practising Christian who thinks that he is 'good enough'. No man is good enough, says Law, who does not dedicate his entire life, his time and his estate, the thoughts, words, and deeds of every hour of his life, in loving obedience, to God. . . . He holds the general Protestant belief in every man's individual responsibility for his own salvation, and the Christian-humanist faith in reason as God's gift to show us the truth, and free-will to obey the truth which reason reveals. . . .[3]

It is not difficult to trace, in Johnson's sermons, evidences of the impact of Law's *Serious Call* upon his mind. In Sermon IX, for instance, we find that the steps advocated by Law for self-examination before Evening Prayer are closely followed by Johnson in his words on preparation for Holy Communion. 'Nothing can be more reasonable before this solemn profession [of repentance]', Johnson insists, 'than that a man examine himself, whether it be true; whether he really and unfeignedly resolves to accept the conditions of salvation offered to him, and to perform his part of the covenant which he comes to ratify. . . .'[4] 'The necessity of this examination', Law explains, 'is founded upon the necessity of repentance. For if it is necessary to repent of all our sins, if the guilt of unrepented

---

[1] Ibid., p. 102.   [2] Ibid., p. 53.   [3] Balderston, p. 384.
[4] *Works*, ix. 376.

sins still continues upon us, then it is necessary, not only that all our sins, but the particular circumstances and aggravations of them, be known and recollected, and brought to repentance. . . .'[1] Johnson, likewise, lays stress, not only on the sins themselves, but 'those occasions which betray us'[2] to them. Both men advocate a methodical approach to self-examination, Johnson suggesting that it be arranged under 'the three chief and general heads' of 'faith, repentance, and subsequent obedience',[3] while Law stipulates a particularization of one's sins, followed by a rational and sustained effort to understand the rightness and wisdom of divine regulation: hence repentance becomes an instrument by which one's faith is reinforced and subsequent obedience is ensured:

> To proceed; in order to make this examination still farther benefi-cial, every man should oblige himself to a certain method in it. As every man has something *particular* in his nature, stronger inclina-tions to *some vices* than others, some infirmities that *stick closer* to him, and are harder to be conquer'd than others; . . . so it is highly neces-sary, that these particularities of our natures and tempers should never escape a severe trial. . . . I say, a *severe trial*, because nothing but a rigorous severity against these natural tempers, is sufficient to conquer them. . . .
>
> For if there is an infinitely wise and good Creator, in whom we live, move, and have our being, whose Providence governs all things in all places, surely it must be the highest act of our *understanding* to con-ceive rightly of him; it must be the noblest instance of our *judgment*, the most exalted temper of our nature, to worship and adore this universal Providence, to conform to its laws, to study its wisdom, and to live and act everywhere, as in the presence of this infinitely good and wise Creator. . . .[4]

In his sermon, Johnson also emphasizes a full understanding of 'the ideas of God and religion' as a means of conquering 'the inordinate passion', for 'by dwelling upon, and indulging any idea, we may

---

[1] Law, p. 325.   [2] *Works.*, ix. 373.   [3] Ibid., p. 376.
[4] Law, pp. 331 and 350–1. The italics are those of the original edition (1729), which are not reproduced in the Everyman edition. As the original edition is some-what rare, the Everyman is quoted for convenience. (The copy in the possession of the Beinecke Library at Yale, consulted for the material of this chapter, was Boswell's copy.)

increase its efficacy and force, make it by degrees predominant in the soul, and raise it to an ascendant over our passions, so that it shall easily overrule those affections or appetites which formerly tyrannized within us'.[1]

Similar examples of this close correspondence between the thought and belief of Law and those of Johnson can be found elsewhere in the sermons. Like Law, Johnson hammers out his arguments with convincing logic and persuasive rhetoric, always appealing to an enlightened self-interest which leads men to wish strongly for the rewards of eternity. Ever conscious of the many ways by which they try to escape from a real and thorough knowledge of their own shortcomings, he invests his arguments with a powerful sense of urgency, demanding an immediate and total commitment to the right way. Johnson adopts a variation of the 'either-or' formula by which Law presents this commitment in the *Serious Call*: 'Either, therefore, you must so far renounce your Christianity, as to say that you need never perform any of these good works; or you must own that you are to perform them all your life in as high a degree as you are able. There is no middle way to be taken.'[2] Johnson expresses it thus:

In condemnation of those who presume to hope, that the performance of one duty will obtain excuse for the violation of others, it is affirmed by St. James, that he who breaks one commandment is guilty of all; and he defends his position by observing, that they are all delivered by the same authority.

His meaning is not, that all crimes are equal, or that in any one crime all others are involved, but that the law of God is to be obeyed with compleat and unreserved submission; and that he who violates any of its ordinances, will not be justified by his observation of all the rest, since as the whole is of divine authority, every breach, wilful and unrepented, is an act of rebellion against Omnipotence. . . .

The power of godliness is contained in the love of God and of our neighbour; in that sum of religion, in which, as we are told by the Saviour of the world, the law and the prophets are comprized. The love of God will engage us to trust in his protection, to acquiesce in

---

[1] *Works*, ix. 373.
[2] Law, p. 64. Arthur W. Hopkinson, Bibl. 106, pp. 4–6, has likened Law's 'either-or' thinking to Karl Barth's philosophy 'of crisis, of choice, of dialectical tension'.

his dispensations, to keep his laws, to meditate on his perfection, and to declare our confidence and submission, by profound and frequent adoration, . . . and when we love God with the whole heart, the power of godliness will be shewn by steadiness in temptation, by patience in affliction, by faith in the divine promises, by perpetual dread of sin, by continual aspirations after higher degrees of holiness, and contempt of the pains and pleasures of the world, when they obstruct the progress of religious excellence.[1]

Here Johnson is speaking of Christian perfection, and he is careful to qualify his prescription for it with the observation: 'To give the heart to God, and to give the whole heart, is very difficult; the last, the great effort of long labour, fervent prayer, and diligent meditation.'[2] This apparent softening of Law's exacting and ascetic approach to Christian dedication is characteristic of Johnson's maturity, for, as he grew older, his modifications of Law's doctrines became more marked, as will be demonstrated later in this chapter.

There are many other instances of Johnson's adoption, or adaptation, of Law's ideas, both in the sermons and in the moral essays, particularly the *Rambler*: the human tendency to regard one act of benevolence or charity by oneself as a proof of invariable virtue; the assumption that the act of approving virtuous conduct constitutes a virtue in itself; our proneness to treat acts of intemperance and anger as isolated or merely occasional, and therefore excusable and insignificant; and the habit of rationalizing or minimizing our guilt by comparing ourselves favourably with others whose sins, we believe, are greater than our own: these are some of the failings exposed by Law and Johnson in much the same way. To the last of these, indeed, Law devotes an entire chapter of the *Serious Call* (Chapter 24), his central injunctions being: 'You are not to consider or compare the *outward form*, or *course* of your life, with that of other people's and then think yourself to be less sinful than they, because the outward course of your life is less sinful than theirs.'[3] In Sermon XVI, Johnson observes: 'It is by comparing ourselves with others, that we often make an estimate of our happiness, and

---

[1] *Works*, ix. 410–12 (Sermon XIII).   [2] Ibid., p. 409.
[3] Law, p. 336.

even sometimes of our virtue.'[1] Another sermon underscores the point more heavily (Sermon XIII):

One of the artifices, by which men . . . deceive themselves, is that of comparing their own behaviour with that of men openly vicious, and generally negligent; and inferring that themselves are good, because they suppose that they see others worse. The account of the Pharisee and Publican may shew us that, in rating our own merit, we are in danger of mistake. But though the estimate should be right, it is still to be remembered, that he who is not worst, may yet fall far below what will be required. Our rule of duty is not *the virtue of men*, but *the law of God*, from which alone we can learn what will be required.[2]

This is very close in thought to *Rambler* 28, in which Johnson observes:

The tribe is likewise very numerous of those who regulate their lives, not by the standard of religion, but the measure of other men's virtue; who lull their own remorse with the remembrance of crimes more atrocious than their own, and seem to believe that they are not bad while another can be found worse.[3]

Another version of the same idea appears in *Rambler* 76:

When their hearts are burthened with the consciousness of a crime, instead of seeking for some remedy within themselves, they look round upon the rest of mankind, to find others tainted with the same guilt.[4]

In tracking down such examples of sophistry and self-deception, Johnson is clearly following the path of the *Serious Call*.

Among the various forms of self-deception, or, as Johnson prefers to call it, self-delusion, three are singled out for special attention by both men: the life of fancy and imagination, with its concomitant dangers; the concealment of our faults and weaknesses from others to the point where we also conceal them from ourselves; and the envelopment of our personalities by the passions, and especially by pride. As Miss Balderston comments,

In the operations of the passions, a field of study in which Johnson . . . declared that new discoveries are 'commonly of more curiosity

---

[1] *Works*, ix. 438. [2] *Works*, ix. 411.
[3] *Works*, ii. 139. Yale Edn. iii. 154. [4] *Works*, ii. 358. Yale Edn. iv. 34–5.

than importance', some of Law's observations of the 'minuter parts' were acute enough to be remembered by Johnson. In Chapter 16 of the *Serious Call* Law analyzes the insidious ways in which our passions, particularly pride, lay hold on us. Of pride he says: 'There is no one vice that is more deeply rooted in our nature, or that receives such constant nourishment from almost everything that we think or do. There being hardly anything in the world that we *want* or *use*, or any *action* or *duty* of life, but pride finds some means or other to take hold of it.' He had earlier warned that 'No people have more occasion to be afraid of the approaches of pride, than those who have made *some advances* in a pious life. For pride can grow as well upon our *virtues* as our *vices*, and steals upon us on all occasions.' In the same chapter, his climactic warning against this particular sin is: 'Now how *monstrous* and *shameful* the nature of sin is, is sufficiently apparent from that *great Atonement*, that is necessary to cleanse us from the guilt of it. Nothing less has been required to take away the guilt of our sins, than the sufferings and death of the Son of God.' These ideas taken separately might be met with in other moralists. But when we find Johnson combining them in a single sermon we recognize a debt. The sermon deals with pride and humility. Pride, writes Johnson, 'mingles with all our other vices, and without the most constant and anxious care, will mingle also with our virtues'. He defines the most dangerous source of pride as 'consciousness of virtue'. And, as a deterrent to this sin, he reminds the proud 'that the blood of Christ was poured out upon the cross to make their best endeavours acceptable to God; and that they, whose sins require such an expiation, have little reason to boast of their virtue'. One might justly suspect, in this case, that Johnson had re-read Law's chapter before sitting down, in characteristic haste, to pen a sermon for his friend Taylor.[1]

The parallel to which Miss Balderston has drawn our attention here is certainly impressive, even if the conjunction of ideas is in itself fairly commonplace: in the Litany, for instance, the Deprecation against sin is closely followed by the Obsecration. But I think that she underestimates the power and range of Johnson's formidable memory in suggesting that he had re-read Law's *Serious Call* just before composing the sermon for Taylor. Law's

---

[1] Balderston, p. 387; Law, pp. 216–17, 209, 212; *Works*, ix. 343, 348–9 (Sermon VI).

thought had become a part of Johnson's own ever since the latter's Oxford days.

As Miss Balderston herself admits, 'Many of the ideas which the two men hold in common belong too much to the realm of "general truth" to warrant inclusion in a study of the influence of Law on Johnson. One of these is the all-inclusive theme of Johnson's moral writings—the emptiness of all things mortal, and the paramount concerns of eternity.'[1] There is a remarkable correspondence between their views on self-condemnation, or what Law calls 'the severity of a self-condemning conscience'[2] and Johnson 'the pungency of remorse'.[3] Both are equally concerned about the most effective means by which the moral life may be achieved, the rejection of habits that lead to self-condemnation, and the adoption of a rigorous regimen which includes, in Law's phrase, 'the well-ordering of our time, and the business of our common life',[4] and, in Johnson's private resolutions, such rules as 'to rise early every morning, as an instance of self-denial, as a method of renouncing indulgence, as a means of redeeming your time'.[5] Both men, moreover, enjoin upon their readers, and try to observe in their own lives (Johnson, apparently, less successfully than Law), the loftier disciplines of Christianity: prayer, mortification of the flesh, self-denying love and charity, and regular repentance for sin. Above all, it is in their attitude to charity that the two men reveal almost total identity of views.

Law was strongly opposed to the traditional view that charity was a means of finding favour with the Deity: he regarded it simply as an act of obedience to the commandment to 'love our neighbour as ourselves', even to the extent of ignoring the worthiness of the recipient. In this respect, Law's Miranda in the *Serious Call* is the model of true Christian love: 'It may be . . . that I may often give to those that do not deserve it, or that will make an *ill use* of my alms. But what then? Is not this the very method of divine goodness? Does not God make *his sun to rise on the evil and on the good*? . . . And shall I with-hold a little *money*, or *food*, from my

[1] Balderston, p. 387.   [2] Law, p. 26.
[3] *Rambler*, 110, *Works*, iii. 23. Yale Edn. iv. 223.   [4] Law, p. 332.
[5] Law, pp. 169–70. Cf. *Diaries*, pp. 257–8 *et passim*.

fellow creature, for fear he should not be good enough to receive it of me? . . . Shall I use a *measure* towards him, which I pray God never to use towards me?'[1]

As every reader of Boswell's *Life* knows, Johnson's practice of Christian charity was much the same as that advocated by Law. He gave unstintingly to the worthy and the unworthy alike, and he sheltered in his home a wide variety of human derelicts. 'He loved the poor', wrote Mrs. Thrale, 'as I never saw any one else do. . . . What signifies, says some one, giving halfpence to common beggars? They only lay it out in gin or tobacco. "And why should they be denied such sweeteners of their existence (says Johnson)?" '[2] Hawkins also tells of his unsparing generosity and his tendency 'to be surrounded by . . . necessitous and undeserving people'.[3] Boswell's observation that 'Johnson's charity to the poor was uniform and extensive, both from inclination and principle'[4] is well borne out by all these accounts, and by Johnson's own sermons on charity, in one of which he states:

Some readily find out, that where there is distress there is vice, and easily discover the crime of feeding the lazy, or encouraging the dissolute. To promote vice is certainly unlawful, but we do not always promote vice when we relieve the vicious. It is sufficient that our brother is in want; by which way he brought his want upon him, let us not too curiously inquire . . . no man is so bad as to lose his title to Christian kindness. *If a bad man be suffered to perish, how shall he repent?*[5]

This is a near-echo of the words of Paternus in the *Serious Call*:

Do good, my son, first of all to those that most deserve it; but remember to do good to all. The greatest sinners receive daily instances of God's goodness towards them; He nourishes and preserves them, that they may repent, and return to Him: do you therefore imitate God, and think no one too bad to receive your relief and kindness, when you see that he wants it.[6]

[1] Law, p. 82.   [2] Hester Lynch Piozzi, Bibl. 28, i. 204.
[3] Hawkins, p. 404.   [4] *Life*, iv. 132.
[5] *Works*, ix. 393. See also Aston, *A Sermon Preached at the Cathedral Church of St. Paul*, pp. 25–6; *Rambler* 81, *Works*, ii. 381–2, and Yale Edn. iv. 60–4; and *Idler* 4, Yale Edn. ii. 13–14.
[6] Law, p. 242.

As Robert Voitle has pointed out, in his chapter on 'The Nature of Johnson's Altruism' in *Samuel Johnson the Moralist*, 'the most fervid of Johnson's sermons are those dealing with personal charity'. The impassioned quality of the peroration to the fourth sermon, for instance, is a testimony to the strength of Johnson's conviction on this subject.[1] Although Professor Voitle does not indicate the source of so much of this conviction, it is plainly derived in large measure from Johnson's reading of Law.

In illustrating his argument that 'Law, more than any other single writer, gave the temper to Johnson's religion', Professor Quinlan draws attention to his Latin poem, 'Christianus Perfectus', as an example of 'clear and persuasive evidence of Johnson's concern with the doctrine of perfection'.[2] The poem emphasizes many of the salient points of doctrine which we have already recognized as common to the teachings of both Law and Johnson: the renunciation of things material, the constant direction of our thoughts towards God, the mastering of rebellious impulses, the unswerving determination to imitate Christ. Professor Quinlan observes, however, that

Johnson never renounced the world and never followed the counsels on perfection to the extent or in just the same manner that Law had urged. Far from renouncing the world, he passed much time in society. Although he meditated and prayed, he seldom, it would appear, pursued a regular course of daily devotions. He read many religious works, but read them, not systematically, but as they came to hand. Religion often occupied his thoughts, sometimes because he consciously turned his mind to it, but as frequently, perhaps, because fears and scruples forced his attention. Nevertheless, Boswell makes a telling observation when, after describing Johnson's first introduction to *A Serious Call*, he writes: 'From this time forward, religion was the predominant object of his thoughts; though, with the just sentiments of a conscientious Christian, he lamented that his practice fell far short of what it ought to be.'

Boswell here intimates that Law had a dual influence on Johnson. In the first place, *A Serious Call* awakened in him a lively sense of the importance of religion. In the second place, the acknowledged hortatory message of this work compelled him thereafter to engage in

[1] Bibl. 49, pp. 54–5. [2] Quinlan, pp. 5 and 11.

frequent comparisons between the high ideal that Law had set before him and his own shortcomings. The inevitable result was an intensification of his native fears and scruples.[1]

While this is true in a general way, Professor Quinlan does not, in my view, take sufficiently into account the respects in which Johnson modified his acceptance of Law's doctrines as he matured, and blended with them less austere principles which he derived both from his own experience and reflection and from his readings of the works of other great authorities. As Miss Balderston expresses it,

The undeveloped ideas which he first met in Law's book were expanded, empirically tested, generalized, related, and significantly qualified. They were also vitalized. Johnson has spoken them to generations of men with incomparable authority; Law speaks faintly to us. Mrs. Thrale, who alone among Johnson's contemporaries suspected Johnson's debt to Law in the *Rambler*, put the matter aptly in a metaphor: 'Many of the *Ramblers* apparently took their rise from that little volume, as the Nile flows majestically from a source difficult to be discovered, or even discerned.'

Nothing could more decisively show Johnson's independence of mere discipleship to Law than the fundamental concepts on which they differed. . . .[2]

The truth of the last statement becomes more and more apparent as we examine the sermons composed by Dr. Johnson. While they reveal, as we have indicated, the great and lasting debt to *A Serious Call* which Johnson himself was the first to acknowledge, they also demonstrate the many respects in which the mature religious thinker gradually pruned the branches of Law's tree of doctrine, stripping them of some of the rigidities of theory, and grafting upon them the wisdom that arises from a practical, commonsense view of Christianity.

It has already been shown that, while Law was generally otherworldly in his outlook and devotion, perfectionist in his principles and practice, and idealistic to the point of mysticism, Johnson was an intensely social personality, deeply involved in mankind. As he observes of religious recluses in *Adventurer* 126, 'Piety practised in solitude, like the flower that blooms in the desert, may give its

---

[1] Quinlan, pp. 12–13.   [2] Balderston, p. 392.

fragrance to the winds of Heaven, and delight those unbodied spirits that survey the works of God and the actions of men; but it bestows no assistance upon earthly beings, and however free of the taints of impurity, yet wants the sacred splendour of bene-ficence.'[1] While Law was not a hermit of the kind Johnson is picturing here, he openly and consistently renounced the world as a place of ineradicable evils, and he urged all Christians to do like-wise: 'If you are not thus out of and contrary to the world,' he argued in *A Serious Call*, 'you want the distinguishing mark of Christianity.'[2]

That this was not Johnson's view is easy to prove. In a sermon largely devoted to the criticism of religious hypocrites (Sermon XIII), he points out that

The power of godliness is contained in the love of God and of our neighbour; in that sum of religion, in which, as we are told by the Saviour of the world, the law and the Prophets are comprized. . . .

The power of godliness, as it is exerted in the love of our neighbour, appears in the exact and punctual discharge of all the relative and social duties. He whom this power actuates and directs, will regulate his conduct, so as neither to do injury, nor willingly to give offence. He will neither be a tyrannical governour, nor a seditious subject; neither a cruel parent, nor a disobedient son; neither an oppressive master, nor an eye-servant. But he will not stop at negative good-ness, nor rest in the mere forbearance of evil; he will search out occa-sions of beneficence, and extend his care to those who have no other claim to his attention than the great community of relation to the universal Father of mankind. . . .

. . . One instance of the power of godliness is readiness to help the weak, and comfort the fallen, to look with compassion upon the frail, to rekindle those whose ardour is cooling, and to recall those who, by inadvertency, or under the influence of strong temptation, have wandered from the right way; and to favour all them who mean well, and wish to be better, though their meaning and their wishes have not yet fully reformed their lives.[3]

The emphasis here, as in many other places in Johnson's sermons, is on the redemptive power of Christianity: the evils of this world

---

[1] Yale Edn. ii. 475.

[2] Law, p. 223. The same argument is the backbone of Law's earlier work, *A Prac-tical Treatise upon Christian Perfection*. [3] *Works*, ix. 411–13.

are indeed, in his view, often eradicable, and the true Christian, working in and through society, not apart from it, has the power of godliness to effect their eradication. In the sermon just quoted, Johnson is careful to remind us that the most habitual sinners 'may yet . . . be numbered among the just'.[1] The evils of men do not place them beyond redemption.

Such views represent the triumph of Johnson's humanism over the more ascetic philosophy of Law. As Walter Jackson Bate has convincingly argued,[2] what Johnson saw as ineradicable was the basic dynamism of human nature, which was productive both of good and of evil; this fundamental force could be harnessed as a constructive and creative drive in the reforming of character, and in the management of the mind. The most persistent and lasting qualities of man—his eternal curiosity, his need to assert himself, his love of recognition and of praise, his essential egoism—could become, by careful redirection, the very impulses that would enable him to achieve wider and worthier goals, which 'pure virtue and unassisted reason'[3] could not in themselves accomplish.

To quote Professor Voitle once more,

> The moral life is a life of constant activity. It is this belief that most decisively sets Johnson apart from those moralists who emphasize character and virtue. . . . The cloisterer may be of spotless virtue; he may be wise and know all things, but a truly good man he cannot be, because a good man strives. 'It cannot be allowed, that flight is victory; or that he fills his place in creation laudably, who does no ill, *only* because he does *nothing*. . . .'[4]

Nowhere is this attitude of Johnson's more in evidence than in his sermons on charity, where he repeatedly states his belief that beneficent actions stem from affections or feelings which may be weak in themselves, but which become strong and active through the assistance of reason and the application of religious principles. Talking of compassion for the needy and distressed, he observes:

> If we look into the state of mankind, and endeavour to deduce the will of God from the visible disposition of things, we find no duty,

---

[1] *Works*, ix. 412.   [2] *The Achievement of Samuel Johnson*, pp. 130–1.
[3] *Idler* 69, Yale Edn. ii. 216.   [4] Voitle, p. 135.

more necessary to the support of order, and the happiness of society, nor any, of which we are more often reminded, by opportunities of practising it, or which is more strongly urged upon us, by importunate solicitations, and affecting objects. . . .

From those, to whom large possessions have been transmitted by their ancestors, or whose industry has been blessed with success, God always requires the tribute of Charity; he commands, that what he has given be enjoyed in imitating his bounty, in dispensing happiness, and chearing poverty, in easing the pains of disease, and lightening the burden of oppression; he commands that the superfluity of bread be dealt to the hungry; and the raiment, which the possessor cannot use, be bestowed upon the naked, and that no man turn away from his own flesh.[1]

In the peroration to the same sermon, which was preached at Bath as an appeal to seasonal residents and visitors to support a charity school in that city, Johnson's eloquence becomes impassioned:

. . . Remember thou! that now faintest under the weight of long-continued maladies, that to thee, more emphatically, the night cometh in which no man can work; and therefore say not to him that asketh thee, 'Go away now, and to-morrow I will give;' To-morrow? To-morrow is to all uncertain, to *thee* almost hopeless; to-*day* if thou wilt hear the voice of God calling thee to repentance, and by repentance to Charity; harden not thy heart, but what thou knowest that in thy last moment thou shalt wish done, make haste to do, lest thy last moment be now upon thee.[2]

No clearer example could be afforded of the need, as Johnson conceived it, to translate self-pity into active beneficence. Instead of the saintly perfection so strongly advocated by Law, we have here the practical goodness which comes from the rational redirection of ordinary impulses.

SAMUEL CLARKE

If William Law provided the necessary disciplinary framework for Samuel Johnson's faith, and the steps by which a devout and

[1] *Works*, ix. 319–20 (Sermon IV).
[2] Ibid., p. 330. The 'tincture of enthusiasm' mentioned by Hawkins (see p. 51 above) is in evidence in this peroration. For comment on Johnson's 'enthusiasm' see Donald J. Greene, Bibl. 98, and Richard North, Bibl. 132.

holy life might be attained (as witnessed, for instance, in Sermons IX and XXII, where the self-examination procedures before Communion, advocated by Law, are closely followed by Johnson), it was to the work of Samuel Clarke (1675–1729?) that he turned for what he considered to be the best sermons in the language, 'bating a little heresy'.[1] The 'little heresy' is specified in the *Life*, where Boswell, on behalf of Sir John Pringle, asks Johnson's opinion as to the best English sermons for style: 'I should recommend Dr. Clarke's sermons, were he orthodox. However, it is very well known *where* he was not orthodox, which was upon the doctrine of the Trinity, as to which he is a condemned heretick; so one is aware of it.'[2] In another part of the *Life* there is reported a more qualified view of the 'little heresy'. According to some 'Memorandums' made by William Bowles (1755–1826), 'of Dr. Clarke he [Johnson] spoke with great commendation for his Universality and seemed not disposed to censure him for his Heterodoxy: he held he said the Eternity of the Son, and that was being far from Heretical'.[3]

In spite of his deviation from orthodoxy, which will be discussed later in this chapter, Clarke appealed to Johnson as an eloquent homilist, a sound explicator of the Biblical text, and, most of all, as a thorough interpreter of the propitiatory sacrifice. According to the testimony of William Seward (1747–99), indeed, Johnson 'told a relation of Dr. Clarke that they [the sermons of Samuel Clarke] made him a Christian',[4] and this apparently excessive claim is supported by the Reverend Richard George Robinson, the Chancellor's Vicar of Lichfield Cathedral, who quoted Johnson as saying, some three months before his death, that 'if he was saved, he should be "indebted for his salvation to the sermons of Dr. Clarke" '.[5] In more moderate vein, we have the unequivocal statement of Hawkins that it was Clarke 'whose sermons he valued above all other', and that 'Johnson was ever an admirer of Clarke'.[6]

When we examine the sermons of Samuel Clarke, we find them to be somewhat abstract discussions of theological doctrine,

---

[1] *Johnsonian Miscellanies* (Bibl. 23), ii. 305.   [2] *Life*, iii. 248.

[3] *Life*, iv. 523–4. See also iii. 248; iv. 416; v. 287–8.

[4] 'Anecdotes by William Seward', *Johnsonian Miscellanies* (Bibl. 23), ii. 305.

[5] *Gentleman's Magazine*, LVIII (Jan. 1788), 39.

[6] Hawkins, pp. 365 and 253.

11. Samuel Clarke, D.D.
From Nichols's *Literary Anecdotes*

sometimes deeply philosophical and at other times purely explana-
tory, but always carefully and systematically arranged, with a detailed apparatus of points, sub-points, cross-references from Biblical
texts, and innumerable illustrations. In some of these respects they
provided a model for several of Johnson's own procedures: frequently,
for instance, he begins with a careful explication of the text, then
moves to a practical application of it, and concludes with a reaffirmation, in more abstract terms, of the theme. In Johnson's
sermons, however, there is much less interlacing of textual reference,
and a greater emphasis on the practical usefulness of the doctrine
embodied in the main text.

Apart from the value of Clarke's homilies as models of logical
exactitude, Johnson recognized in his work a quality which he
admired and emulated: a high degree of commonsense, which is
most clearly demonstrated in his affirmation that the fundamental
justification for believing in God is to be found in nature, and in his
definition of faith as 'a rational persuasion and firm belief of His
attributes discovered by nature, and of His promises made known
in the Gospel, so as thereby to govern and direct our lives'.[1]
Scripture, as Clarke sees it, is a clear confirmation of the existence
of the God whom nature reveals to us, and serves as a more detailed
account of God's attributes, wishes, and commands. In his view,
the proof of the reality of God lies in two basic facts: the fact of our
existence as human beings, which implies a creator, and the fact of
'the order and beauty of the world', which implies a first cause.[2]

It may well be observed at this point that there is nothing very
remarkable in this view, which was characteristic of the deists and
of eighteenth-century rationalism as a whole. But where Clarke
differed from many of the deistical free-thinkers was in his emphasis
on scriptural confirmation of the existence of the God that nature
reveals to us, and in his insistence that there is no opposition
between reason and revelation. In an age that prided itself on
scientific accuracy and attempted to reduce all truth to a system,
Clarke's synthesis of natural, scientific law with the aims of morality, by means of an analogy between the natural universe and the

[1] Samuel Clarke, 'Of Faith in God', *Sermons* (Bibl. 82), i. 3.
[2] Ibid., pp. 4–5. See also Samuel Clarke, Bibl. 83, pp. 243–5 and 270.

moral sphere, was bound to appeal to the more intellectual of his
listeners and readers.

This is not to say that Johnson accepted a totally scientific explanation of the universe and human life and morality in terms of
natural law. But he was very much aware of, and deeply interested
in, the various attempts of the empiricists to apply concepts of the
natural law to the study of human morality. To some extent he
appears to have agreed with Locke that 'morality is capable of
demonstration, as well as mathematics',[1] a view which Samuel
Clarke, who maintained that there was nothing mysterious in
Christian morality, enthusiastically endorsed. Clarke contended
that there is, in nature, an observable standard of 'fitnesses' and
'unfitnesses', by perceiving which men are able to ascertain the
correct rule of action and so to recognize and follow what
is good. Failure to comply with this rule is an attempt to 'destroy
the order by which the universe subsists', as well as an act of self-
condemnation:

For the judgment and conscience of a man's own mind, concerning
the reasonableness and fitness of the thing that his actions should be
conformed to such or such a rule or law, is the truest and formallest
obligation; even more properly and strictly so than any opinion whatsoever of the authority of the Giver of a law, or any regard he may
have for its sanction by rewards and punishments. For whoever acts
contrary to this sense and conscience of his own mind is necessarily
self-condemned; and the greatest and strongest of all obligations is
that which a man cannot break through without condemning himself. The dread of superior power and authority and the sanction of
rewards and punishments, however indeed absolutely necessary to
the government of frail and fallible creatures, and truly the most
effectual means of keeping them in their duty, is yet really in itself
only a secondary and additional obligation, or enforcement of the
first. The original obligation of all . . . is the eternal Reason of things:
that Reason which God himself, who has no superior to direct him,
and to whose happiness nothing can be added nor anything diminished from it, yet constantly obliges himself to govern this world by.[2]

---

[1] *Human Understanding* (Bibl. 121), III. xi. 16. Johnson read, among other works of
the kind, William Derham, *Physico-Theology* (Bibl. 87). See *Life*, v. 323.
[2] *Natural Religion* (Bibl. 81), pp. 39 and 43.

Although he does not use quite the same terms, and although he even satirizes Clarke's use of the words 'fitness' and 'unfitness' in *Rasselas*, Johnson appears to be subscribing to a similar view of original obligation in several places. In the first sermon in the Taylor collection, for instance, he discusses the natural disposition of human beings to seek the company of others as a means of achieving happiness, and comments:

How high this disposition may extend, and how far Society may contribute to the felicity of more exalted Natures, it is not easy to determine, nor necessary to enquire; it seems however probable, that this inclination is allotted to all rational Beings of limited excellence, and that it is the privilege only of the infinite Creator to derive all his happiness from himself.

It is a proof of the regard of God for the happiness of mankind, that the means by which it must be attained, are obvious and evident; that we are not left to discover them, by difficult speculations, intricate disquisitions, or long experience, but are led to them, equally by our passions and our reason, in prosperity and distress. . . .[1]

Johnson goes on to argue that marriage, which he regards as an extension of the social compact prescribed by the natural law, is a subdivision of 'the great Society of the World'—a subdivision which 'produces new dependencies and relations', and hence 'gives rise to a particular scheme of duties'.[2] Thus he appears to endorse one of Clarke's basic tenets: conformity to the rule of right action imposes an obligation, the discharge of which produces a good, and the neglect of which produces an evil. To both Clarke and Johnson the law based upon the standard of the natural fitnesses of things is an absolute, or at least a norm. According to this view, God, who has prescribed the natural order, serves merely as the lawgiver whose presence as an authority ensures that 'the eternal Reason of things' is kept in operation.[3]

Does this mean that the will of God has become secondary to the law of nature, as if, as Professor Basil Willey puts it, 'its function were merely to ratify the enactments of the natural legislation'?[4]

[1] *Works*, ix. 289–90.   [2] Ibid., p. 290.
[3] Clarke, op. cit., p. 43.
[4] *The Eighteenth-Century Background* (Bibl. 159), pp. 59–60.

Leslie Stephen has answered this question in part by suggesting that

Clarke does not shrink from maintaining that moral obligation is antecedent even to the consideration of its being the rule of God. . . . Nature, the true metaphysical deity of Clarke and his school, is sometimes identified with God, and sometimes appears to be in some sense a common superior of man and his Creator. The law of nature thus becomes a code of absolutely true and unalterable propositions, strictly analogous to those of pure mathematics.[1]

There is a good deal of justice in this interpretation of Clarke's doctrine, for, as he himself says, it is 'absurd and blameworthy, to mistake *negligently* plain *Right* and *Wrong* . . . or *wilfully to act contrary* to known Justice and Equity . . . as it would be absurd and ridiculous for a Man in Arithmetical Matters, ignorantly to believe that *Twice two is not equal to Four*; or wilfully and obstinately to contend, against his own clear Knowledge, that the *whole is not equal to all its Parts*'.[2] That Johnson accepted Clarke's system of mathematically demonstrable morality *in toto* is impossible to believe, although Hawkins would lend support to such a view: '. . . Dr. Clarke supposes all rational agents as under an obligation to act agreeably to the relations that subsist between such, or according to what he calls the fitness of things. Johnson was ever an admirer of Clarke, and agreed with him in this and most other of his opinions, excepting in that of the Trinity. . . . He therefore fell in with the scheme of fitness. . . .'[3]

He did, but not entirely. An example of Johnson's partial acceptance of Clarke's interpretation of the law of nature will be found in Sermon V of the Taylor collection, where he takes up the eternal problem of human misery. This is a closely reasoned discourse, deserving of special attention. Johnson begins it by saying that 'there is nothing upon which more Writers, in all ages, have laid out their abilities, than the miseries of life'. Some of these writers, he continues, have suggested that 'contemplation of the evils of life' is a means of persuading us to turn our attention to 'an enquiry

---

[1] *History of English Thought in the Eighteenth Century* (Bibl. 148), i. 124.
[2] Samuel Clarke, *Works* (Bibl. 84), ii. 613.   [3] Hawkins, pp. 253-4.

after more certain and permanent felicity'. Others have questioned and criticized the wisdom or justice of an all-wise, all-powerful God who would permit the evils and miseries of life to exist. Johnson attacks this second group of writers for their tendency to betray weak minds into doubts and distrust. 'But', he goes on, 'these doubts may easily be removed, and these arguments confuted, by a calm and impartial attention to religion and to reason; it will appear upon examination, that though the world be full of misery and disorder, yet God is not to be charged with disregard of his creation; that if we suffer, we suffer by our own fault, and that *he has done right, but we have done wickedly.*'[1] In a later part of the sermon, having reminded us that humanity had forfeited its happiness by its own fault, Johnson argues that 'few of the evils of life can justly be ascribed to God':

In examining what part of our present misery is to be imputed to God, we must carefully distinguish that which is actually appointed by him, from that which is only permitted, or that which is the consequence of something done by ourselves, and could not be prevented, but by the interruption of those general and settled laws, which we term the course of nature, or the established order of the universe. Thus it is decreed by God, that all men should die; and therefore the death of each man may justly be ascribed to God, but the circumstances and time of his death are very much in his own power, or in the power of others. . . .

If we examine all the afflictions of mind, body, and estate, by this rule, we shall find God not otherwise accessory to them, than as he works no miracles to prevent them, as he suffers men to be masters of themselves, and restrains them only by coercions applied to their reason. If God should, by a particular exertion of his Omnipotence, hinder murder or oppression, no man could then be a murderer or an oppressor, because he would be with-held from it by an irresistible power; but then that power, which prevented crimes, would destroy Virtue; for Virtue is the consequence of choice. Men would be no longer rational, or would be rational to no purpose, because their actions would not be the result of free-will, determined by moral motives; but the settled and predestined motions of a machine impelled by necessity.

[1] *Works*, ix. 332.

Thus it appears, that God would not act as the Governour of rational and moral agents, if he should lay any other restraints upon them, than the hope of rewards, or fear of punishments; and that to destroy, or obviate the consequences of human actions, would be to destroy the present constitution of the world.[1]

Johnson then blames human beings for most of their own miseries; even illness and disease may often 'proceed from our own laziness, intemperance, or negligence', but he admits that 'There are indeed distempers, which no caution can secure us from, and which appear to be more immediately the strokes of Heaven; but these are not of the most painful or lingering kind, they are for the most part acute and violent, and quickly terminate, either in recovery or death; and it is always to be remembered that nothing but wickedness makes death an evil.'[2] Coming from one who was the victim of a congenital disease and, as he grew older, a multiplicity of afflictions, this statement may seem surprising, but he himself warns us to consider 'how many diseases the vices and follies of our ancestors have transmitted to us, and to beware of imputing to God, the consequences of luxury, riot, and debauchery'.[2]

Thus Johnson, like Clarke, considers evil to be the result, in the main, of man's wilful disregard or defiance of the law of nature —his deliberate violation of the scheme of 'fitnesses' and 'unfitnesses'. He appears to have been impressed particularly by Clarke's argument that the only restraints God placed upon our free will were the hope of rewards and the fear of punishments. In one of his *Discourses* Clarke gives eloquent expression to this argument. Discussing the need, in the minds of men, for 'a good Testimony', he turns to the 'Necessity of some particular Revelation, to discover what *Expiation* God would accept *for Sin*':

There was a Necessity of some particular Revelation, to give Men full assurance of the Truth of those great *Motives* of Religion, the *Rewards and Punishments of a future State*; which, notwithstanding the strongest arguments of Reason, Men could not yet forbear doubting of: In fine, There was a Necessity of some *particular Divine Revelation*, to make the whole Doctrine of Religion *clear and obvious* to all Capacities, to add *weight and Authority* to the plainest Precepts, and to

[1] *Works*, ix. 333–4.   [2] Ibid., p. 335.

furnish Men with extraordinary *Assistances* to enable them to overcome the Corruptions of their Nature. . . .[1]

Clarke then proceeds to claim that the testimony of Christ
concerning the immortality of the soul, and the rewards and
punishments of the future state, has had a greater and more
powerful influence on the lives and actions of men than the reasonings of the philosophers. Christianity, he argues, is superior to any
other creed because it offers, even to untutored minds, 'more just
and right Apprehensions concerning his [God's] Attributes and
Perfections, a deeper Sense of the Difference of Good and Evil, a
greater regard to moral Obligations and to the plain and most
necessary Duties of Life, and a more firm and universal expectation
of a Future State of Rewards and Punishments; than in any
Heathen Country, any considerable Number of Men were ever
found to have had'.[2]

Turning to the Deists, Clarke contends that 'almost all the
Things that are said wisely and truly' by them are obviously
borrowed 'from that Revelation, which they refuse to embrace;
and without which, they could never have been able to have said
the same things'. The fact is, however, that 'the Rewards and
Punishments of another World, the great motives of Religion,
cannot be so *powerfully enforced*, to the influencing the Lives and
Practise of all sorts of Men, by one who shall undertake to demonstrate the reality of them by Abstract Reasons and Arguments; as
by one who, showing sufficient Credentials of his having been
himself in that other State, shall assure them of the Truth and
Certainty of these things'.[3]

Clarke goes on to refute the arguments of those who decry
Christian revelation because it is not universal and therefore not
demonstrably the will of God. God is not bound, in his view, 'to
make all Men capable of the same Degree or the same kind of
Happiness, or to afford all Men the very same *means and opportunities*
of obtaining it'.[4]

Johnson takes up the same subject in Sermon X, in which his
arguments are an eloquent expansion of those of Samuel Clarke.

[1] Bibl. 80, p. 200. [2] Ibid., pp. 208–9. [3] Ibid., pp. 210–13.
[4] Ibid., p. 217.

Using as his text Galatians 6: 7, 'Be not deceived, God is not mocked; for whatsoever a man soweth, that shall he reap', he comments that one of the great blessings of the Christian faith is the certainty of a future state, and of the rewards and punishments that await us after death, adjusted according to our conduct in this world. Discussing the situation of those who are not blessed with this divine revelation, Johnson observes:

The ancient Heathens, with whose notions we are acquainted, how far soever they might have carried their speculations of moral or civil wisdom, had no conception of a future state, except idle fictions, which those who considered them treated as ridiculous; or dark conjectures, formed by men of deep thoughts and great enquiry, but neither, in themselves, capable of compelling conviction, nor brought at all to the knowledge of the gross of mankind, of those who lived in pleasure and idleness, or in solitude and labour; they were confined to the closet of the student, or the school of the lecturer, and were very little diffused among the busy or the vulgar.

There is no reason to wonder, that many enormities should prevail, where there was nothing to oppose them. When we consider the various and perpetual temptations of appetite within, and interest without; when we see, that on every side there is something that solicits the desires, and which cannot be innocently obtained; what can we then expect, but that, notwithstanding all the securities of law, and all the vigilance of magistrates, those that know of no other world will eagerly make the most of this, and please themselves whenever they can, with very little regard to the right of others.

As the state of the Heathens was a state of darkness, it must have been a state, likewise, of disorder; a state of perpetual contest for the goods of this life, and by consequence of perpetual danger to those who *abounded*, and of temptation to those that were in want.[1]

Johnson was, of course, fully aware that there were quite advanced peoples, such as the Jews, who 'enjoyed a very ample communication of the Divine will, and had a religion which an inspired Legislator had prescribed':

But even to this nation, the only nation free from idolatry, and acquainted with the perfections of the *true* God, was the doctrine of

[1] *Works*, ix. 378.

a future state so obscurely revealed, that it was not necessarily conse-
quential to the reception, or observation, of their *practical* religion.
The Sadducees who *acknowledged* the authority of the Mosaical law,
yet *denied* the separate existence of the soul, had no expectation of a
future state. They held that there was no resurrection, neither Angel
nor Spirit.

This was not in those times, the *general* state of the Jewish nation;
the Pharisees held the resurrection, and with them probably far the
greater part of the people; but that any man could be a Jew, and
yet deny a future state, is a sufficient proof that it had not yet
been *clearly revealed*, and that it was reserved for the Preachers of
Christianity to bring life and immortality to light. In such a degree
of light they are now placed, that they can be denied or doubted no
longer. . . .[1]

This is very close to Clarke's reasoning.[2] Both had held that the
light of nature was defective, that the state of the heathens was a
state of darkness, and that the defectiveness and the darkness had
been removed by the divine revelation and by the system of
rewards and punishments. As Clarke expressed it,

. . . by Divine Revelation in the Gospel, this defect of the Light of
Nature *is* now actually supplied in such a manner; Life and Immortality
are so brought to Light; and the Wrath of God is so revealed from
Heaven against all Ungodliness and Unrighteousness of Men; that
this very thing, the clear and distinct and consistent Account which
the Gospel gives us of these final Rewards and Punishments . . . is
itself no contemptible Argument of the Truth and Divine Authority
of the Christian Revelation. By the certain Knowledge of these
Rewards and Punishments it is, that the practise of Virtue is now
established upon a sure Foundation. . . . There is now sufficient
Weight on the side of Virtue, to enable Men to conquer all the
Temptations of the Devil, the Flesh, and the World; and to despise
the severest Threatnings, even Death itself; *This is the victory that
overcometh the World, even our Faith.*[3]

[1] Ibid., pp. 378–9.
[2] The points made by Clarke and Johnson were not, of course, new. They had
been presented eloquently, for instance, by Dryden in *Religio Laici*. But from the
fact that the sequence as well as the combination of these arguments is virtually
identical in the contexts quoted, a connection can be safely inferred.
[3] Clarke, op. cit., pp. 238–9.

If these arguments about the truth of divine revelation impressed Johnson so strongly as to lead him to reproduce them in his own inimitable manner in Sermon X, Clarke's testimony on the subject of the propitiatory sacrifice moved him even more profoundly. 'He pressed me', Dr. Brocklesby told Boswell, 'to study Dr. Clarke and to read his Sermons. I asked him why he pressed Dr. Clarke, an Arian. "Because, (said he,) he is fullest on the *propitiatory sacrifice.*" '[1] In a footnote to this quotation, Boswell reminds us that Johnson had not always held Clarke in such high esteem:

The change of his sentiments with regard to Dr. Clarke is thus mentioned to me in a letter from the late Dr. Adams, Master of Pembroke College, Oxford:—'The Doctor's prejudices were the strongest, and certainly in another sense the weakest, that ever possessed a sensible man. You know his extreme zeal for orthodoxy. But did you ever hear what he told me himself? That he had made it a rule not to admit Dr. Clarke's name in his Dictionary. This, however, wore off. At some distance of time he advised with me what books he should read in defence of the Christian Religion. I recommended Clarke's "Evidences of natural and Revealed Religion", as the best of the kind; and I find in what is called his "Prayers and Meditations", that he was frequently employed in the latter part of his time in reading Clarke's Sermons.'[2]

Before considering the reasons for Johnson's earlier prejudice against Clarke's work, and indeed for his continued recognition of the heretical elements it contained, we might ask why Johnson found him so satisfactory on the subject of the propitiatory sacrifice.

In the *Discourse* already quoted, Clarke asks these questions:

What can be more perfective of the Light of Nature, than to have those great Motives of Religion, the Rewards and Punishments of a Future State which Nature *only obscurely* points at, described to us more *plainly, affectionately,* and *lively*? What can be more perfective of the Light of Nature, than to have the *means of attoning* [sic] *for Sin,* which Nature discovers *only the want of, plainly declared and exhibited* to us? What can be more perfective of the Light of Nature, than such

---

[1] *Life*, iv. 416. Boswell omitted 'and that above all things is necessary to believe as Xians'. MS. Yale C582.   [2] Ibid., n. 2.

a discovery of *the heinousness of Sin* and the *necessity of Holiness*, as the *Death of Christ* and the *Purity of the Gospel* does make unto us?[1]

He then proceeds to discuss the nature of the atonement and of the propitiatory sacrifice; in his 'rational Scheme of Belief' he shows that God

in the fulness of Time; that is, at that time which his infinite Wisdom had fore-appointed, which all the Antient Prophecies had determined, and which many concurrent circumstances in the state of the Jewish Religion, and in the disposition of the Roman Empire, had made a fit season for the reception and propagation of a new Institution of Religion: *that* God (I say) at That Time, should *send his Only-begotten Son.* That *Word* or *Wisdom* of the Father, That Divine Person *by whom* (as has been before shown) He created the World, and by whom he made all former particular Manifestations of himself unto Men; *that* he should send him, *to* take upon him our humane Nature, and therein to make a full and particular Revelation of the Will of God to Mankind, who by Sin had corrupted themselves and forfeited the Favour of God, so that by the bare Light of Nature they could not discover any certain means by which they could be satisfactorily and absolutely secure of regaining that Favour; To preach unto Men Repentance and Remission of Sin, and by giving himself a Sacrifice and Expiation for Sin, to declare the Acceptableness of Repentance, and the Certainty of Pardon thereupon, in a Method evidently consistent with all necessary Vindication of the Honour and Authority of the Divine Laws, and with God's irreconcileable Hatred against Sin; To be a Mediator and Intercessor, between God and Man; To procure the particular Assistance of God's Holy Spirit, which might be in Men a new and effective Principle of a Heavenly and Divine Life; in a word, *To* be the Saviour and Judge of Mankind, and finally to bring them to Eternal Life. . . .[2]

All this, Clarke maintains, is perfectly 'credible to right and true Reason'.[2] In his characteristically methodical way, he goes on to explain every particular of it: first, the revelation of God's will to mankind is consistent with reason; secondly, the nature of Christ's sacrifice is also reasonable, as it symbolizes God's hatred

---

[1] Clarke, op. cit., p. 240.   [2] Ibid., pp. 257 ff.

of sin and relates back in time to the heathen and Hebrew custom of sacrificing, which,

how unreasonable soever an expectation it was, to think that the Blood of Beasts could truly expiate Sin, yet thus much it plainly and undeniably shows, that it has been the common Apprehension of Mankind in all Ages, that God would not be appeased nor pardon Sin without some Punishment and Satisfaction; and yet at the same Time they had good Hopes, that upon the Repentance of Sinners, God would accept some other Satisfaction instead of the Destruction of the Offenders. 'Tis therefore plainly agreeable to right Reason, to believe, that God, in Vindication of the Honour of his Laws, and for a Testimony of his Hatred against Sin, should appoint some Sacrifice or Expiation for Sin, at the same time that he forgives the Sinner upon his true Repentance.[1]

Thirdly, Clarke argues,

It is also reasonable that a Mediator or Intercessor should be appointed between God and Man. . . . The generality of the wisest Heathens thought it agreeable to Reason, to make use of Subordinate Intelligences, Demons or Heroes, by whom they put up their Prayers to the Superior Gods; hoping that by the Mediation of these Intercessors, the unworthiness of their own Persons, and the defects of these Prayers might be supplied; and they might obtain such merciful and gracious Answers to their Prayers, as they could not presume to hope for upon their own Account.[2]

Whereas the pagans had no guarantee that such mediation would be acceptable to the supreme deity, the fact that they thought such mediation possible shows that it accords with right reason. This statement leads Clarke into his fourth argument:

The greatest real Difficulty in this Matter, to the Judgment of right Reason, seems to arise from the consideration of the *Dignity of the Person*, whom we believe to have given himself a Sacrifice and Propitiation for the Sins of Mankind, *viz.* how is it possible, that the *Only-begotten Son of God* should be *Incarnate* and become *Man*; how it is conceivable that *God* should *condescend* so far as to *send*, and the *Son of God* condescend willingly to *be sent*, and do such great things for his Creatures; and above all, how it is consistent with Reason, to suppose

<hr>

[1] Clarke, op. cit., pp. 260–1.   [2] Ibid., p. 261.

God condescending to do so much for such *frail* and *weak* Creatures as Men, who, in all appearance, seem to be but a very small, low, and inconsiderable part of the Creation. And here indeed it must readily be acknowledged, that humane Reason could never have discovered such a method as this, for the reconciliation of Sinners to an offended God, without express Revelation. But then neither on the other Side, when once this Method is made known, is there any such Difficulty or Inconceivableness in it, as can reasonably make a wise and considerate Man call in question the truth of a well-attested Revelation, merely upon that account. . . .[1]

Turning to the question whether Christ's expiation was really necessary, and whether some other method of redeeming mankind might not have been found, Clarke argues that the way chosen was the wisest and fittest, as it gave men a deep sense of 'the heinous nature of Sin': 'Forasmuch as it shows us, that at the same time that God was willing to save the Sinner, yet, least incouragment should be given to Sin by letting it go unpunished, he did not think fit to forgive the Transgressions of Men without great Sufferings in our Nature, and to do away the guilt of our Sins but upon such difficult Terms as the Death of his own Son.'[2] This method of combining and illustrating justice, mercy, and truth Clarke considers to be second to none, and not at all harmful to 'the Dignity of the Person'.[2]

As for the argument that God would surely not condescend to go to all this trouble for such a small creature as man, who, after all, might be only one of many orders of beings in the universe, Clarke contends that

the same Divine *Logos*, the *Word* or *Messenger* of the Father, who in various Dispensations, according to the particular Needs and Exigencies of Mankind, has made various Manifestations of God, and Discoveries of the Divine Will, to us here upon Earth; may also, for aught we know, have to other Beings, in other parts of the Universe, according to their Capacities or Wants, made different Manifestations of God and Discoveries of his Will, in ways of which we can know nothing, and in which we have no Concern. . . .[3]

[1] Ibid., pp. 262 ff.   [2] Ibid., p. 266.
[3] Ibid., pp. 268–9.

In his fifth argument, which follows, Clarke parries the objection that the Christian revelation, not being universal or universally known, is therefore invalid. He points out that rational endowments are unequally spread throughout the world, that there are many varieties of men and animals, and therefore that not all are given the knowledge of Christ's revelation. But, he insists, 'Though the Redemption purchased by the Son of God, is not indeed actually made known unto All Men; yet as no Man ever denied, but that the Benefit of the Death of Christ extended backwards to those who lived *before* his Appearance in the World; so no man can prove, but that the same Benefit may likewise extend itself forwards to those who never heard of his Appearance, tho' they lived *after* it.'[1]

The five arguments which Clarke advances in this way are so simple as to border on the naïve: in summary, he finds nothing unreasonable in any of the central evidences of Christianity—the revelation, the sacrifice, the mediation, the condescension, and the mercy of God, all of which, he suggests, were so calculated as to be consistent with man's experience and his capacity to understand. Was this what Johnson meant when he commended Clarke for being 'fullest on the propitiatory sacrifice'? Was this the interpretation of the Atonement which suited Johnson more than any other? I believe the answer to both these questions to be 'yes'.

Boswell tells us that on 22 August 1773, during their visit to Aberdeen, he entered into a discussion of religion. This discussion, which is carefully recorded in the *Journal of a Tour to the Hebrides*, shows Johnson's views on the atonement to be remarkably close to those just quoted from Clarke's discourse. 'I spoke of the satisfaction of Christ', Boswell tells us:

He said his notion was that it did not atone for the sins of the world. But by satisfying divine justice, by showing that no less than the Son of God suffered for sin, it showed men and innumerable created beings the heinousness of sin, and therefore rendered it unnecessary for divine vengeance to be exercised against sinners, as it otherwise might have been. In this way it might operate even in favour of those who had never heard of it. As to those who did hear of it, the effect it should produce would be repentance and piety, by

---

[1] Clarke, op. cit., p. 270.

impressing upon the mind a just notion of sin. That original sin was the propensity to evil, which no doubt was occasioned by the Fall.

Boswell then adds his own interpretation:

He presented this great subject in a new light to me and rendered much more rational and clear the ideas of what our Saviour has done for us, as it removed the notion of imputed righteousness in the usual sense, and the difficulty of our righteousness co-operating; whereas by his view Christ has done all already that he had to do, or is ever to do, for mankind, by making his great satisfaction, the consequences of which will affect each individual according to the particular conduct of each. I would illustrate this by saying that Christ's satisfaction is like there being a sun placed to show light to men, so that it depends upon themselves whether they will walk the right way or not, which they could not have done without the sun, 'the sun of righteousness.'[1]

Boswell here has apparently missed the point, which was that the sacrifice of Christ satisfied divine justice and so saved mankind, even that part of mankind which had never heard of it—precisely the point of Clarke's fifth argument.

When he reports Johnson as saying that his notion was that the satisfaction of Christ 'did not atone for the sins of the world', Boswell implies that Johnson regarded the sacrifice as exemplary rather than vicarious: that it had not wiped out the sins of mankind, but had shown the heinousness of sin and the need for repentance and piety.

In his commentary on this subject Professor Quinlan has presented the interesting view that Johnson 'for many years, probably during most of his adult life, . . . favoured the interpretation that the Atonement was in the nature of a penal and an exemplary sacrifice',[2] and that he changed his opinion only a few years before his death. Professor Quinlan adduces, as evidence of this change, the conversation recorded by Boswell as having taken place on 3 June 1781. The following are the main points of this conversation:

The great sacrifice for the sins of mankind was offered at the death of the MESSIAH, who is called in scripture, 'The Lamb of God, that

---

[1] *Life*, v. 88–9.   [2] Quinlan, p. 51.

taketh away the sins of the world.' To judge the reasonableness of the scheme of redemption, it must be considered as necessary to the government of the universe, that God should make known his perpetual and irreconcilable detestation of moral evil. He might indeed punish, and punish only the offenders; but as the end of punishment is not revenge of crimes, but propagation of virtue, it was more becoming the Divine clemency to find another manner of proceeding, less destructive to man, and at least equally powerful to promote goodness. The end of punishment is to reclaim and warn. *That* punishment will both reclaim and warn, which shows evidently such abhorrence of sin in God, as may deter us from it, or strike us with dread of vengeance when we have committed it. This is effected by vicarious punishment. Nothing could more testify the opposition between the nature of God and moral evil, or more amply display his justice, to men and angels, to all orders and successions of beings, than that it was necessary for the highest and purest nature, even for DIVINITY itself, to pacify the demands for vengeance, by a painful death; of which the natural effect will be, that when justice is appeased, there is a proper place for the exercise of mercy; and that such propitiation shall supply, in some degree, the imperfections of our obedience, and the inefficacy of our repentance: for, obedience and repentance, such as we can perform, are still necessary. . . . The peculiar doctrine of Christianity is, that of an universal sacrifice, and perpetual propitiation. Other prophets only proclaimed the will and threatenings of God. Christ satisfied his justice.[1]

The argument here is not greatly different from that of the 1773 conversation, which, as was shown, echoed the views expressed in Clarke's *Discourse*, but Professor Quinlan maintains that it evinces an important change:

Johnson no longer believes that it is man alone who must make propitiation for his sins. Christ by his universal sacrifice has made a perpetual propitiation. And this propitiation supplies the imperfections of man's obedience and repentance. True, Johnson qualifies the statement by saying that Christ makes up for man's inadequacy 'in some degree', a qualification that implies . . . a shift in emphasis rather than a complete reversal of opinion. Nevertheless, by 1781 his idea of the Atonement had clearly altered and the former view that it

[1] *Life*, iv. 124–5.

served chiefly as an exemplary act is no longer predominant. Instead, he has now arrived at the more generally held Christian belief that the death on the Cross was truly an expiatory sacrifice.[1]

Professor Quinlan notes that Boswell, alluding to the earlier conversation in 1773, remarked, in a footnote in his *Journal of a Tour to the Hebrides*: 'What Dr. Johnson now delivered, was but a temporary opinion; for he afterwards was fully convinced of the *propitiatory sacrifice*, as I shall shew in my future work, *The Life of Samuel Johnson, LL.D.*'[2]

Unfortunately, as Professor Quinlan admits, the supporting evidence that Johnson changed his view of the Atonement is not quite as specific as that which Boswell supplies. It is true that in Johnson's prayers there are, as Professor Quinlan argues, fewer references to Christ than to the Holy Spirit, but it is difficult to accept this either as an indication of Johnson's unsure belief in the propitiatory nature of the sacrifice or as evidence that Johnson had ignored 'Law's urging that one address his prayers directly to Christ'.[3] In these matters Johnson was more likely to follow the Prayer Book, where all the familiar prayers, such as those in the Order of Service for Morning and Evening Prayer, are addressed, as Johnson's are, to the Father, and conclude with a reference to the mediation of the Son. If there were any significant difference between Johnson's last prayer, dated 5 December 1784, and the earlier statements or prayers which Professor Quinlan quotes (21 April 1764 and 19 April 1778), there might be some merit in his argument that the prayers reveal a strengthening of his belief in the propitiatory nature of the sacrifice; but the difference is very slight indeed. Here are the appropriate extracts from the three in question:

April 21, 1764. 'I will pray to God for resolution, and will endeavour to strengthen my faith in Christ by commemorating his death.'[4]

April 19, 1778. 'Almighty and most merciful Father, suffer me once more to commemorate the death of thy Son Jesus Christ, my Saviour and Redeemer, and make the memorial of his death profitable

---

[1] Quinlan, pp. 55–6.   [2] *Life*, v. 88 n. 2.   [3] Quinlan, p. 56.
[4] *Diaries*, p. 79.

to my salvation, by strengthening my Faith in his merits, and quickening my obedience to his laws.'[1]

December 5, 1784. 'Almighty and most merciful Father, I am now as to human eyes it seems, about to commemorate for the last time the death of Thy Son Jesus Christ our Saviour and Redeemer. Grant, O Lord, that my whole hope and confidence may be in his merits and in thy mercy: forgive and accept my late conversion, enforce and accept my imperfect repentance: make this commemoration available to the confirmation of my wish, the fulfilment of my hope, and the enlargement of my charity, and make the Death of Thy Son Jesus effectual to my redemption.'[2]

It is difficult, moreover, to accept the argument that 'positive and specific allusions to the propitiatory nature of the sacrifice are not evident until the last few years of Johnson's life'. As early as 1738, in a prayer composed on his birthday, Johnson clearly states his hope of salvation to be 'through the *satisfaction* of Jesus Christ'.[3]

One further piece of evidence adduced by Professor Quinlan from Johnson's prayers merits special consideration.

Although his belief in the propitiatory nature of the sacrifice developed gradually over a period of years, one date seems to mark a climax in his thinking on the subject. It was Easter Sunday, 1776. On this day he received the Sacrament, as he had each year since his wife's death. His customary Holy Week preparations included fasting, the forming of good resolutions, and attendance at church on Good Friday. He also followed his usual practice of composing a penitential prayer. This is remarkable chiefly for the opening supplication: 'Almighty and most merciful Father, who hast preserved me by thy tender forbearance, once more to commemorate thy Love in the Redemption of the world, grant that I may so live the residue of my days, as to obtain thy mercy when thou shalt call me from the present State.' Unfortunately the next two lines in the manuscript are deleted, for they might have indicated something unusual. In its mutilated form the prayer differs from earlier ones chiefly in the allusion to God's expression of love for mankind in accepting Christ's sacrifice. Even this reference might not be significant, were it not for Johnson's experience in church on this particular Easter Sunday.

---

[1] *Diaries*, p. 289.   [2] Ibid., pp. 417–18.
[3] Ibid., pp. 37–8. Quinlan, p. 57.

He reports that he read the prayer in his pew, commended his friends and departed relatives, and, at the altar, renewed his resolutions. He continues: 'When I received, some tender images struck me. I was so mollified by the concluding address to our Saviour that I could not utter it.' . . . The words that he could not utter, because they so profoundly moved him, form a regular part of the Communion Service. They are: 'O Lord, the only-begotten Son, Jesu Christ; O Lord God, Lamb of God, Son of the Father, that takest away the sins of the world, have mercy upon us. . . .' This was a familiar supplication. From childhood Johnson must have known this part of the Book of Common Prayer, and most certainly must have recited it whenever he received the Sacrament. Yet never before had this address, containing in essence the doctrine of the propitiatory sacrifice, come home to him in its full significance.[1]

This is hard to believe. While it is true that Johnson records here a deeply emotional experience, it was not the first time that he fully understood the significance of the words of the supplication.

The sermon Johnson composed for his wife's funeral clearly indicates the deep significance he attached to the meaning of Christ's sacrifice. Mrs. Johnson, it will be remembered, died on 17 March 1752. As has been pointed out, long before this melancholy event, indeed in the very first prayer he copied into his diary, Johnson had referred to 'the satisfaction of Jesus Christ',[2] and in other prayers he clearly indicates that both 'the sufferings and the merits of our Lord and Saviour'[3] ensured the conditions for man's redemption. It is interesting to note that one such prayer, composed on Easter Day 1770, follows a reference to the fact that Johnson had just been reading a sermon by Clarke on the death of Christ, and immediately precedes a similar reference to a sermon by the same author on the humiliation of the Saviour.[4] Again, in his *Convict's Address to His Unhappy Brethren*, composed for delivery by Dr. William Dodd, Johnson speaks of 'a sincere reception of the

[1] Ibid., pp. 57–8.   [2] *Diaries*, p. 38.
[3] Ibid., p. 130. See also pp. 63, 75–6.
[4] Ibid., pp. 129, 132. The only sermon in which Johnson discusses in any detail the death and humiliation of Christ is Sermon XI (*Works*, ix. 349–50). The Clarke Sermons referred to are probably LII ('of the Nature of the Sufferings of Christ') and LIII ('of the Humiliation and Sufferings of Christ') in *Sermons on Several Subjects and Occasions* (Bibl. 82), pp. 339–57.

doctrines taught by our blessed Saviour, with a firm assurance that he died to take away the sins of the world, and that we have, each of us, a part in the boundless benefits of the universal Sacrifice'.[1] The sacrifice alluded to here is much more than exemplary: it is the propitiatory sacrifice.

In at least eight of the sermons in the Taylor collection there are references to the propitiatory sacrifice. While we are handicapped by our ignorance of the dates when these sermons were composed, it would seem reasonable to assume that they did not all follow the supposed change in Johnson's thinking on this subject.

The truth is that Johnson, as has been shown, believed all his adult life in the Atonement, but as he grew older he became more and more convinced of the vital importance of it, and, as this chapter has attempted to demonstrate, Samuel Clarke's common-sense interpretation of it impressed and influenced him more profoundly than any other.[2]

There remain to be considered the doctrines propounded by Clarke with which Johnson disagreed, and for which Clarke had been branded a heretic, at least to the extent of being excluded as a source of quotations from Johnson's *Dictionary*.[3] As previously mentioned, the 'little heresy', as Johnson called it, referred to Clarke's views on the Trinity, which had caused something of a stir in ecclesiastical circles.

When Dr. Brocklesby called Clarke an Arian, he was oversimplifying the position, for in his *Scripture-Doctrine of the Trinity* Clarke states that the Bible supports neither the Athanasian nor the Arian point of view. He contends that the Trinity is a subject capable of various interpretations, and proceeds to offer his own, which, briefly stated, is that the Father is superior to the other two members of the Trinity:

The Father (or First Person) Alone, is Self-existent, Underived, Unoriginated, Independent; made of None, begotten of None, Proceeding from None. . . . The Father (or First Person) is the Sole Origin

---

[1] William Dodd, *The Convict's Address to His Unhappy Brethren*, p. 9.

[2] See particularly Sermons VI, VII, IX, X, XI, XX, XXI, XXII, and XXV: *Works*, ix. 349–50, 355, 371–2, 374, 376, 386, 479, 487, 493, 494.

[3] *Life*, i. 189 n. 1.

of all Power and Authority, and is the Author and Principle of what-
soever is done by the Son or by the Spirit. . . . The Father (or First
Person) Alone, is in the highest, strict, and proper Sense, absolutely
Supreme over All. . . . The Scripture, when it mentions the One God,
or the Only God, always means the Supreme Person of the Father. . . .
The Son (or Second Person) is not Self-existent, but derives his Being
or Essence, and All his Attributes, from the Father, as from the
Supreme Cause. . . .[1]

Clarke goes on to say that, since we have no knowledge of the
precise metaphysical manner in which the Son derives his being or
essence from the Father, 'they are therefore equally worthy of
Censure, who either on the one hand presume to affirm, that the
Son was made . . . out of Nothing; or, on the other hand, that He
is the Self-existent Substance'.[2] Pointing out that the Scripture,
in declaring the Son's derivation from the Father, never makes
mention of any limitation of time, Clarke continues:

The Son, before his Incarnation, was with God, was in the Form of
God, and had Glory with the Father. . . . Yet He had not then distinct
Worship paid to him in his Own Person, but appeared only as the . . .
Habitation of the Glory of the Father . . . the Distinctness and Dignity
of his Person, and the True Nature of his Authority and Kingdom,
not being yet revealed. . . . At his Incarnation He emptied himself . . .
of that Glory, which he had had with God before the World was, and
by virtue of which He is described as having been in the Form of
God: And in this State of Humiliation, suffered and died for the Sins
of the World. . . . After the accomplishment of which Dispensation,
He is described in Scripture as invested with distinct Worship in his
Own Person; his original Glory and Dignity being at the same time
revealed, and his Exaltation in the Human Nature to his Mediatorial
Kingdom declared: Himself sitting upon his Fathers Throne, at the
right hand of the Majesty of God; and receiving Prayers and Thanks-
givings from his Church. . . .[3]

Clarke concludes by saying that, while the Scripture directs us
to pay homage to Christ, it is because of Christ's actions relative
to us, not because of any superiority of Christ over the Father, to

---

[1] Samuel Clarke, *The Scripture-Doctrine of the Trinity*, pp. 243–70.
[2] Ibid., p. 276.   [3] Ibid., pp. 290–368.

whom all honour must ultimately redound. He also points out that
there is no clear precept or example in Scripture for addressing
prayers directly and expressly to the person of the Holy Spirit.[1]
Throughout this book the emphasis is on the separateness of the
attributes of the three persons of the Trinity, and away from the
idea of a Godhead of one substance.

This, in brief, was the body of opinions that shocked Clarke's
orthodox readers. He made matters worse for himself when he
omitted the celebration of Holy Communion from the service he
conducted on Trinity Sunday in 1713, probably because he wanted
to avoid reading the Proper Preface, with which he expressed his
disagreement in his *Scripture-Doctrine of the Trinity*. For this sin of
omission he was censured by the Lower House of Convocation, and
the bishops instituted an inquiry into his Trinitarian position. At
this point Clarke partially recanted, and promised to avoid delivering sermons on this sensitive subject thereafter. The damage had
been done, however, and Clarke was never granted high office in
the Church.[2]

Although it took place some sixty years after Clarke's mis-
demeanour, the discussion recorded by Boswell in the *Life* under
Friday, 7 May 1773, appears to include Clarke, at least by implication. Bennet Langton asked Johnson whether it would be 'wrong
in a magistrate to tolerate those who preach against the doctrine
of the Trinity'. After indicating that he found the question offensive, Johnson said: 'I think that permitting men to preach any
opinion contrary to the doctrine of the established church tends, in
a certain degree, to lessen the authority of the church, and, consequently, to lessen the influence of religion.'[3]

In the light of this reply, the extent of Johnson's regard for
Clarke appears the more remarkable: that he could overcome his
prejudice against someone who frankly held and preached opinions
'contrary to the established church' argues a degree of tolerance

---

[1] Samuel Clarke, op. cit., p. 375.

[2] *Life*, iii. 248 n. 2. See also Quinlan, p. 29; and Norman Sykes, *From Sheldon to
Secker* (Bibl. 150), p. 166. In the *D.N.B.* account William Whiston is quoted as saying
that Clarke refused preferment that involved subscription to the Articles; but there
is little evidence to show that he had many opportunities of refusing.

[3] *Life*, ii. 254, and n. 2.

that even such a perceptive commentator as Boswell failed to acknowledge. There is some evidence, too, that Johnson did not always hold Clarke's other doctrines in such high esteem, and that he went so far as to satirize his metaphysics and his rather abstract manner in Chapter XXII of *Rasselas*, where the prince meets a philosopher who preaches that happiness is to be found in living according to Nature, 'in obedience to that universal and unalterable law with which every heart is originally impressed; which is not written on it by precept, but engraven by destiny; not instilled by education but infused at our nativity'.[1] When Rasselas asks what is meant by 'living according to Nature', the philosopher replies: 'To live according to Nature is to act always with due regard to the fitness arising from the relations and qualities of causes and effects; to concur with the great and unchangeable scheme of universal felicity; to co-operate with the general disposition and tendency of the present system of things.'[2] We are not surprised at the reaction of Rasselas to this flood of philosophical gobbledygook: 'The prince soon found that this was one of the sages whom he should understand less, as he heard him longer.'[2]

Whether the philosopher's speech was a deliberate parody of Samuel Clarke in particular is impossible to say; there were many advocates, including Rousseau, of the life according to nature. But the 'nature' Johnson has in mind is not a return to the primitive so much as an obedience to the natural law, which writers like Clarke, Cumberland, and Shaftesbury regarded as a dynamic force that had many of the attributes and performed many of the functions of the deity. As Professor Quinlan observes,

When the sophist in *Rasselas* tells his listeners that 'the way to be happy is to live according to nature, in obedience to that universal and unalterable law with which every heart is originally impressed,' he echoes the sentiments of Richard Cumberland, who remarks, 'The law of nature is a proposition proposed to the observation of, or impress'd upon, the mind, with sufficient clearness by the nature of things, from the will of the first cause, which points out that possible action of a rational agent which will chiefly promote the common good and by which only the entire happiness of particular persons

---

[1] *Works*, i. 248.   [2] Ibid., p. 249.

can be obtained.' When the sophist attempts to answer the query of Rasselas, however, the language seems more like a travesty on the vague metaphysical reasonings of Clarke, especially because of the latter's frequent use of the terms 'fitness' and 'unfitness'. What particularly annoyed Johnson, it would appear, was Clarke's abstruseness in passages such as the following: 'That there are differences of things, and different relations, respects, or proportions of some things towards others; it is evident and undeniable. . . . That from these different relations of different things there necessarily arises an agreement or disagreement of some things with others, or a fitness or unfitness of the application of different things or different relations one to another, is likewise as plain as that there is any such thing as proportion or disproportion in geometry or arithmetic.'[1]

Notwithstanding Johnson's annoyance, presumed or real, over such passages as this, we have the testimony of William Adams and William Seward[2] that his admiration for Clarke was very great. Dr. Adams, in particular, tells us that his prejudices against Clarke 'wore off. At some distance of time he advised with me what books he should read in defence of the Christian Religion. I recommended "Clarke's Evidences of Natural and Revealed Religion," as the best of the kind; and I find in what is called his "Prayers and Meditations," that he was frequently employed in the latter part of his time in reading Clarke's Sermons.'[3] The sermons, as was noted earlier, appealed to Johnson for the very reasons that some of his more abstruse prose did not: their clarity, systematic organization, and commonsense presentation.

There is one remarkable instance of the direct borrowing, by Johnson, of materials from Clarke's sermons. In the end leaves of a copy of the first edition of the *Prayers and Meditations*, the owner of the copy, Edmond Malone, transcribed some notes of Johnson's found among the latter's papers 'together with several prayers composed at Ashbourne in the September before his death'.[4]

[1] Quinlan, p. 36.

[2] *Life*, iv. 416 n. 2, and 'Anecdotes by William Seward', *Johnsonian Miscellanies* (Bibl. 23), ii. 305.

[3] *Life*, iv. 416 n. 2.

[4] From Malone's notes in his copy of *Prayers and Meditations*, at present in the possession of W. R. Batty, Esq., of Southport, Lancs., England.

These notes, which deal with the subject of the Eucharist, have been identified by Professor Quinlan as jottings on four sermons by Samuel Clarke, and some of them, as he demonstrates, closely correspond to details found in Sermon IX of the Taylor collection. Professor Quinlan concludes:

> In view of this parallelism, I believe it must be granted that Johnson had studied Clarke's ideas on the Sacrament. According to Malone, the notations were found with various manuscript materials that Johnson had presumably penned while at Ashbourne during the last few months of his life. But the outline of Clarke's sermons on Communion was probably made earlier. The reasons for so thinking are: the indication that Johnson used these notes in preparing his discussion of Communion in his own ninth sermon: and the inference, based on the test of sentence length, that this sermon belongs to the middle period of his writing career. Furthermore, it does not seem likely that, ill as he was in the last year of his life, Johnson would have been occupied at this late date with composing sermons.[1]

This is a convincing argument, except for the inference based upon the test of the sentence length, which is, in my view, a very unreliable guide.

Enough has been said to prove that Samuel Clarke's impact on Johnson the homilist was very strong indeed, and that Johnson's admiration for Clarke's work, particularly his sermons, increased with the years. Whatever the merits of Clarke as a theologian and a moralist may now appear to be, they were great enough to break through Johnson's avowed prejudice against the unorthodox and to move him to reconsider his own position from time to time. Indeed, in the shaping and composition of his own sermons,

---

[1] Quinlan, p. 95. This author's attempt (pp. 92–100, 209–12) to date the sermons on the basis of their sentence length, although applied with caution to indicate periods rather than actual years, fails to take into account either the occasions for which the three precisely dated sermons were composed, or the putative state of the copy from which the sermons were printed. Finding that the earliest (written for Aston in 1745) averaged 64 words per sentence, the funeral sermon (1752) 56·4 words, and the sermon for Dodd (1777) 25·8, he concludes that the sermons, like Johnson's other prose, permit the association of earlier date and longer sentence. But the occasion, more than the period of Johnson's life, could surely have affected the sentence length. Moreover, since Johnson was not alive to read the proofs of most of the sermons, we cannot be certain that the sentence punctuation is his. It may well have been revised, e.g. by Taylor, for oral delivery.

Johnson was indebted in no small way to the models that Clarke had provided.

RICHARD BAXTER

In discussing some of the effects of the work of Samuel Clarke on Johnson's homiletic thinking and practice, we noted that Johnson was liberal-minded enough to see beyond the unorthodox and the heretical, and to recognize the merits of a great Christian writer with whose position he was not always in sympathy. Another evidence of his broadmindedness in religion is found in his extensive reading and knowledge of the work of such Nonconformist writers as Richard Baxter.

Although Johnson was, as Boswell described him, 'a sincere and zealous Christian, of high Church-of-England . . . principles',[1] he was tolerant of other denominations and creeds to a greater extent than Boswell, or any of his biographers, may have realized. In this respect he shared the view of William Law, who contended: 'We must enter into a Catholic affection for all men, love the spirit of the Gospel wherever we see it, not work ourselves into an abhorrence of George Fox, or an Ignatius Loyola, but be equally glad of the light of the Gospel wherever it shines, or from what quarter it comes; and give the same thanks and praise to God for an eminent example of piety wherever it appears, either in Papist or in Protestant.'[2] In his own words, Johnson explains in Sermon XI, for which his text is 1 Peter, 3: 8, 'Finally be ye all of one mind, having compassion one of another, love as brethren, be pitiful, be courteous':

> By the union of minds which the Apostle recommends, it must be supposed that he means not speculative, but practical union; not similitude of opinions, but similitude of virtues.[3]

Later in the same sermon he adds:

> To suppose that there should, in any community, be no difference of opinion, is to suppose all, of whom that community consists, to be

[1] *Life*, iv. 426.
[2] See R. Newton Flew, Bibl. 92, p. 312. The quotation is from Law's controversial reply to Dr. Joseph Trapp, who had dismissed Law's doctrine of salvation as Quakerism: William Law, *Works* (Bibl. 119), vi. 188.
[3] *Works*, ix. 387.

111. Richard Baxter. After R. White, 1670

wise alike, which cannot happen; or that the understanding of one part is submitted to that of another, which however would not produce uniformity of opinion, but only of profession; and is, in important questions, contrary to that sincerity and integrity, which truth requires; and an infraction of that liberty, which reason allows. But that men, of different opinions, should live at peace, is the true effect of that humility, which makes each esteem others better than himself, and of that moderation, which reason approves, and charity commands. . . .[1]

Similarly, in his *Life of Sir Thomas Browne*, Johnson observes:

Men may differ from each other in many religious opinions, and yet all may retain the essentials of Christianity; men may sometimes eagerly dispute, and yet not differ much from one another; the rigorous prosecutors of error should, therefore, enlighten their zeal with knowledge, and temper their orthodoxy with charity. . . .[2]

Such was his tolerance that he went so far as to express to William Bowles his opinion that Baxter's *Reasons of the Christian Religion* contained 'the best collection of the evidences of the divinity of the Christian system'.[3] One of his last requests to Dilly, the bookseller, in a letter dated 6 January 1784, was for the best printed edition of Baxter's *Call to the Unconverted*.[4] And when Boswell asked him which works of Baxter he should read, Johnson answered: 'Read any of them; they are all good.'[5]

One of the most obvious reasons for Johnson's interest and admiration was the fact that, just as Samuel Clarke had been 'fullest on the propitiatory sacrifice', Baxter was fullest on human doubts concerning the future state, a subject with which Johnson was very frequently preoccupied. As Hawkins tells us in his biography, 'to allay those scruples and terrors which haunted him in his vacant hours, he betook himself to the reading of books of practical divinity, and, among the rest, the writings of Baxter and others of the old puritan and non-conforming divines. Of Baxter, he entertained a very high opinion, and often spoke of him to me as

---

[1] Ibid., p. 388.   [2] Ibid., vi. 502.   [3] *Life*, iv. 237.
[4] Ibid., p. 257; *Letters*, 924.
[5] *Life*, iv. 226. 'All' meant a very large number of works; according to A. G. Matthews's *List* (Bibl. 124), there were at least 141. See also *Life*, iv. 521.

a man of great parts, profound learning, and exemplary piety....'[1]
Although Hawkins was writing of Johnson's last years, it is clear
from references in the *Prayers and Meditations* as early as 29 and 30
March 1766 that Johnson had been moved by the doubts expressed
by Baxter concerning his salvation. 'I had this day a doubt like
Baxter of my State',[2] he wrote; and the second entry reads,
'Troubled with Baxter's scruple, which was quieted, as I returned
home. It occurred to me that the scruple itself was its own
confutation.'[3] This is a reference to the doubt which Baxter had
expressed regarding the adequacy of his faith to merit salvation—
doubt based on such questions as why he found himself still so much
concerned with things of the flesh; why he continued to be dutiful
out of fear rather than love; and why anyone who knew he possessed saving grace could go on sinning, knowingly and deliberately.[4]

In *Reliquiae Baxterianae* Baxter relates how, quite early in his
life, he was afflicted by coughing spasms and the spitting of blood
to such an extent that he believed himself to be close to death. As
a result,

> ... I was yet more awakened to be serious and solicitous about my
> soul's everlasting state; and I came so short of that sense and serious-
> ness which a matter of such infinite weight required, that I was in
> many years' doubt of my sincerity, and thought I had no spiritual
> life at all. ...
>
> Thus was I long kept with the calls of approaching death at one
> ear and the questionings of a doubtful conscience at the other; and
> since then I have found that this method of God's was very wise, and
> no other was so like to have tended to my good. ...[5]

He goes on to list the doubts, fears, and apprehensions that had
troubled him in his youth, and observes that he found 'more fear
than love in all my duties and restraints':

> But I afterward perceived that education is God's ordinary way
> for the conveyance of his grace, and ought no more to be set in opposi-
> tion to the Spirit than the preaching of the Word; and that it was the
> great mercy of God to begin with me so soon. ... And I understood

---

[1] Hawkins, p. 540.   [2] *Diaries*, p. 106.   [3] Ibid., pp. 107–8.
[4] *Reliquiae Baxterianae* (Bibl. 60), Lib. I, Part I, pp. 6–8 and 134–8.
[5] Ibid., p. 5.

that though fear without love be not a state of saving grace, . . . the soul of a believer groweth up by degrees from the more troublesome (but safe) operations of fear to the more high and excellent operations of complacential love. . . .[1]

Thus Baxter's 'scruple' did indeed, as Johnson suggested, prove to be its own confutation: fear is a necessary milestone on the road to salvation. Arguing along similar lines, Johnson in Sermon XIV maintains that anxieties and fears about our future state

are so far from being proofs of reprobation, that though they are often mistaken by those that languish under them, they are more frequently evidences of piety, and a sincere and fervent desire of pleasing God. We are not to imagine, that God approves us because he does not afflict us, nor, on the other hand, to persuade ourselves too hastily that he afflicts us, because he loves us. We are, without expecting any extraordinary effusions of light, to examine our actions by the great and unchangeable rules of Revelation and reason, *to do to others as we would that they should do to us*, and to love God with all our heart, and express that love by keeping his commandments.[2]

When he found his own meditations insufficiently disturbing, Johnson wrote this of his uneasiness:

I perceive an insensibility and heaviness upon me. I am less than commonly oppressed with the sense of sin, and less affected with the shame of Idleness. Yet I will not despair. I will pray to God for resolution, and will endeavour to strengthen my faith in Christ by commemorating his death.[3]

On an otherwise blank page of a journal he wrote the words, 'Faith in some proportion to fear.'[4] And in *Rambler* 110 he commented:

Sorrow and fear, and anxiety, are properly not parts, but adjuncts of repentance; yet they are too closely connected with it to be easily separated; for they not only mark its sincerity, but promote its efficacy.[5]

This view of the usefulness of fear and sorrow is one that Johnson shared with Baxter. Both men came to understand that, as Baxter

---

[1] Ibid., pp. 6–7. [2] *Works*, ix. 422. [3] *Diaries*, pp. 78–9.
[4] *Diaries*, p. 269. [5] *Works*, iii. 23.

expressed it, 'God breaketh not all men's hearts alike';[1] that honest doubts and fears may fit men to understand and answer the doubts of others, and hence procure for themselves 'an increase of quietness of mind';[2] and that probabilities may, in the end, have to be accepted instead of 'full undoubted certainties'.[2]

Neither Johnson nor Baxter could claim at the end of his life 'that I have such a certainty of my sincerity in grace as excludeth all doubts and fears of the contrary'.[2] Both grappled till the last with the problem of reconciling their severe physical sufferings with the notion of a merciful God, and both repeatedly advocated for themselves a regimen of exercise and temperance. In this respect, there is a close similarity between certain passages of Baxter's autobiography and many of the entries in Johnson's *Prayers and Meditations*. More significantly, there is much emphasis, in the writings of both homilists, on the 'duties of Resignation, Obedience and Love to God',[3] to use Baxter's phrase, as a necessary preliminary to spiritual security and peace. To quote again from Johnson's fourteenth sermon, 'Trust in God, that trust to which perfect peace is promised, is to be obtained only by repentance, obedience, and supplication, not by nourishing in our own hearts a confused idea of the goodness of God, or a firm persuasion that we are in a state of grace; by which some have been deceived, as it may be feared, to their own destruction. . . .'[4]

In the past, some commentators have argued that Johnson's fears about death and the hereafter suggest an insecurity in his faith,[5] but if these fears are understood in the context of Baxter's 'scruple' they indicate quite the reverse. His attitude is not so much derived from weakness of conviction as from the spirit of the prayer, 'Lord, I believe; help thou mine unbelief.'[6] In Sermon II, which follows a sequence of argument similar to that of *Rambler* 110, Johnson reveals this attitude quite clearly: in the earlier part

[1] *Reliquiae Baxterianae*, Lib. I, Part I, p. 7.

[2] Ibid., p. 9.

[3] Richard Baxter, *The Reasons of the Christian Religion*, Part I, Ch. XIV (Bibl. 63), ii. 53.

[4] *Works*, ix. 421–2.

[5] See W. B. C. Watkins, *Perilous Balance* (Bibl. 51), pp. 81 ff.; Jean H. Hagstrum, Bibl. 101; Philip Williams, Bibl. 160.

[6] Mark 9: 24.

of the sermon, quoting Psalm 130: 3–4, 'If thou, O Lord, wert extreme to mark what is done amiss, O Lord, who shall abide it? But there is mercy with thee, therefore shalt thou be feared', he comments:

It is reasonable, that we should endeavour to please him, because we know that every sincere endeavour will be rewarded by him; that we should use all the means in our power, to enlighten our minds, and regulate our lives, because our errours, if involuntary, will not be imputed to us; and our conduct, though not exactly agreeable to the divine ideas of rectitude, yet if approved, after honest and diligent enquiries, by our own consciences, will not be condemned by that God, who judges of the heart, weighs every circumstance of our lives, and admits every real extenuation of our failings and transgressions.

Were there not mercy with him, were he not to be reconciled after the commission of a crime, what must be the state of those, who are conscious of having once offended him? A state of gloomy melancholy, or outrageous desperation; a dismal weariness of life, and inexpressible agonies at the thought of death; for what affright or affliction could equal the horrours of that mind, which expected every moment to fall into the hands of implacable Omnipotence?[1]

Later in the sermon, after urging repentance and reformation as the most effective means of obtaining God's mercy, Johnson reminds his readers that 'an amendment of life is the chief and essential part of Repentance', and continues, perhaps with Baxter's 'scruple' in mind: 'He that has performed that great work, needs not disturb his conscience with subtle scruples, or nice distinctions. He needs not recollect, whether he was awakened from the lethargy of sin, by the love of God, or the fear of punishment. The Scripture applies to all our passions; and eternal punishment had been threatened to no purpose, if these menaces were not intended to promote virtue.'[2] The last observation is in keeping with Johnson's earlier comment that God is represented in the Scriptures as 'not more formidable for his power, than amiable for his mercy; and is introduced as expostulating with mankind upon their obstinacy in wickedness; and warning them, with the highest affection, to avoid those punishments, which the laws of his government make

---

[1] *Works*, ix. 301–2.   [2] Ibid., p. 307.

it necessary to inflict upon the inflexible and disobedient'.[1] While 'His mercy is ever made the chief motive of obedience to him',[2] the penalty for disobedience is equally stressed: 'The doom of the obstinate and impenitent sinner is plainly declared; it is a fearful thing to fall into the hands of the living God.'[3]

These arguments have a strong resemblance to the remorselessly logical pronouncements of Baxter's *Call to the Unconverted*. 'Though God have no pleasure in your damnation, and therefore calls upon you to return and live,' writes Baxter, 'yet he hath pleasure in the demonstration of his own justice and the executing of his laws; and therefore he is, for all this, fully resolved, that if you will not be converted, you shall be condemned.'[4] Even more explicitly, in his *Reasons of the Christian Religion*, which Johnson praised in superlative terms, Baxter states:

The Belief of a Hell or endless punishment, being that which is *de facto* the restraint of the Obedient part of the World, and that which proveth too weak with the Disobedient part, it thence followeth, that a Hell or endless punishment will be inflicted.

The Reasons I have given before, 1. Because that Experience sheweth that the *Threatning of Hell* is necessary in the *Law*: therefore *it* self is necessary in the execution. 2. Because God doth not govern the World by deceit.[5]

To the objection that 'God is merciful as well as just', and that his punishment might therefore be mitigated, Baxter replies:

True, and therefore he shewed mercy to sinners in the day of mercy: And it is for the contempt and abuse of mercy that he condemneth them: If the Mercy abused had been less, the sin and punishment had been less. A mercifull King and Judge will hang a Murderer or Traytor. Mercy to the good requireth punishment of the bad. Gods Attributes are not contrary. He is mercifull to the due Objects of Mercy, and hath penal Justice for the Objects of that Justice.[5]

As for the objection that 'Hell is a cruelty which expresseth tyranny rather than wise Justice', Baxter will have none of it: 'That's but

---

[1] *Works*, ix. 300–1.   [2] Ibid., p. 301.   [3] Ibid., p. 318 (Sermon III).
[4] Bibl. 62, p. 69.
[5] *The Reasons of the Christian Religion*, Part I, Ch. XV (*Practical Works*, ii. 68).

the voice of Folly, partiality and guilt. Every thief that is hanged is like enough to think the same of his own Punishment and Judge. . . .'[1]

Both Johnson and Baxter express the view that the fear of death or future punishment is in itself an inadequate motive to true repentance. When repentant sinners 'have done all that possibly can be done by them' to secure their salvation, says Johnson, 'they cannot yet be certain of acceptance, because they cannot know, whether a repentance, proceeding wholly from the fear of death, would not languish and cease to operate, if that fear was taken away'.[2] 'And some think,' observes Baxter, 'if they have been affrighted by the fears of hell, and had convictions of conscience, and thereupon have purposed and promised amendment, and take up a life of civil behaviour and outward religion, that this must needs be true conversion. . . . And therefore it is that Christ told some of the rulers of the Jews who were greater and more civil than the common people, that "publicans and harlots go into the kingdom of God before them". '[3]

'Happy is the man that feareth alway: but he that hardeneth his heart shall fall into mischief.' This is the text of Johnson's third sermon, in which he observes 'that the religion which makes fear the great principle of action, implicitly condemns all self-confidence, all presumptuous security; and enjoins a constant state of vigilance and caution, a perpetual distrust of our own hearts, a full conviction of our natural weakness, and an earnest solicitude for Divine assistance'.[4] The theme is one that appealed to Baxter. 'Faith in some proportion to fear' carried many of the same implications for him as for Johnson. There is, however, an interesting difference of emphasis. In his *Thoughts Concerning the Controversies about the Perseverance of the Saints*, for instance, Baxter appears to go a step farther than Johnson when he asserts that

a known impossibility or non-futurity of evil doth evacuate rational fear: But then he that will be perfectly freed from that fear, must have a perfect knowledge of the impossibility or non-futurity. But Christ

[1] Ibid., p. 69. [2] *Works*, ix. 308 (Sermon II).
[3] *A Call to the Unconverted*, p. 48. The quotation is from Matt. 21: 31.
[4] *Works*, ix. 311.

and his Apostles knew that those whom they wrote to had no such perfect knowledge: Nay more, it is not (at least by any ordinary meanes) to be expected in this life, that this knowledge of our sincerity, justification and perseverance should be so perfect as to have no degree of doubting, habitual or actual, at that time or any other. If no grace be perfect in this life, then the assurance of our sincerity, justification and perseverance are not perfect in this life. . . .[1]

At this point, Baxter interposes the anticipated objection that Paul had no doubt of his salvation, yet said, 'But I keep under my body, and bring it into subjection: lest that by any means, when I have preached to others, I myself should be a castaway.'[2] These words, Baxter observes, do not necessarily express fear, but rather 'the use of a meanes to avoid an evil that without such meanes would not be avoided; and that Paul himself was not yet perfect (Phil. 3:12) and knew only in part (I Cor. 13:9) and therefore might have use for fear'.[3] In any case, Baxter contends, Paul's revelation of his salvation may not have brought him certainty. He then counters the objection that such fears are sinful by saying that they are a duty to sinful man's recovery. He concludes that 'no man's assurance of his perseverance is perfect in this life. Therefore in that measure as his assurance is imperfect, and he is liable to the least doubts, in that measure it is his duty to fear.' If men's assurance of an after-life were perfect, God might be forsaken; and Baxter quotes Jeremiah 32:40: 'I will put my fear in their hearts that they shall not depart from me.'[4]

The differences between the views of Baxter and those of Johnson on this point are small, but significant: Johnson maintains that a man who has repented and amended his life 'needs not disturb his conscience with subtle scruples',[5] whereas Baxter says that, even in the saint, some vestige of doubt or uncertainty may, and perhaps ought to, remain. As this part of Baxter's reasoning evidently troubled Johnson, a closer examination of his associated arguments regarding the life to come is called for. For this purpose Chapter

---

[1] Bibl. 65, p. 31.   [2] Ibid., p. 31. The text is I Cor. 9:27.
[3] Bibl. 65, p. 31-2.   [4] Ibid., p. 39.
[5] *Works*, ix. 307. The 'subtle scruples' include such things as doubts about the motives for amendment: whether they come from filial love or servile fear, etc.

XIV of Baxter's *Reasons of the Christian Religion*,[1] entitled 'That there is a Life of Retribution after this, proved. . . .' is the appropriate authority.

In this chapter Baxter argues that to know whether there is a life after this one, and whether men will receive rewards and punishments in it, is a matter 'upon which dependeth our Comforts, and our Religion, and without which we know not what to expect, to hope for, or to fear; nor what to intend and seek after through our lives, nor how to order our hearts or actions'.[2] He then asks whether the law of nature is not a clear revelation of God's will. Is it a law without any rewards or penalties? Without these, precepts would be 'vain to such as us, and uneffectual as to their ends. But God hath not made his Laws in vain.'[2] Baxter then stresses the paternal nature of divine government, which emphasizes merits and demerits in the hereafter in much the same way as the father metes out such things to his children according to their behaviour.

In Sermon X Johnson begins by observing that

One of the mighty blessings bestowed upon us by the Christian revelation, is, that we have now a certain knowledge of a future state, and of the rewards and punishments that await us after death, and will be adjusted according to our conduct in this world. We, on whom the light of the gospel shines, walk no longer in darkness, doubtful of the benefit of good, or the danger of bad actions; we know, that we live and act under the eye of our Father and our Judge, by whom nothing is overlooked or forgotten, and who, though to try our obedience he suffers, in the present state of things, the same events to happen to the good and to the evil, will, at last, certainly distinguish them, by allotting them different conditions beyond the grave; . . .[3]

Whereas Baxter, in the process of establishing the 'certain knowledge of a future state', carefully delineates all the doubts and objections which are obstacles to this knowledge, Johnson prefers to accept the truths of the gospel. Yet, at the same time, he touches upon the very points which Baxter takes pains to expound. For example, the fact that 'God maketh not a sufficient, differencing

---

[1] Part I, Ch. XIV (*Practical Works*, ii. 48 ff.).   [2] Ibid., p. 49.
[3] *Works*, ix. 377-8.

retribution in this life',[1] to use Baxter's words, is briefly explained by Johnson as a trial of our obedience, but adduced by Baxter, in a lengthy passage of ratiocination, as evidence of the reality of a future state: 'And if God's justice make not a sufficient difference here, it is certain that there is another life where he will do it,' concludes Baxter, 'because, else, he should not be just, his laws would be delusory, and his government would be defective, and successful only by deceit.'[2] He continues:

The nature of man is to be most moved with the hopes and fears of Good and Evil after death: Otherwise death itself would compara-tively seem nothing to us. No other creature hath such hopes and fears: If you ask, how I can tell that? I answer, as I can tell that a Tree doth not hear, and a Stone doth not feel or see, because there is no appearance of such a sense, whose nature is to make itself manifest by its evidences where it is: Bruits show a fear of death, and a love of life, but of nothing further; of which there is evidence enough to quiet a mind that seeketh after truth, though not to silence a prating caviller. . . .[3]

Baxter then suggests that the duties we owe to God—resigna-tion, obedience, and love—would not be performed if we knew that we had no life to live but this one: 'If God himself kindle in the best of men desires to know him, love him, and enjoy him perfectly hereafter, then such desires shall attain their end: But God himself doth kindle such desires in the best of men: Ergo—and consequently there is such a Life to come.'[4] Proceeding to a logical proof of this proposition, Baxter draws two main conclusions:

1. We feel in our natures a capacity of knowing all that of God which I have before laid down, and that it is improvable by further light to know much more: We feel that our hearts are capable of *loving* him, and of delighting in the contemplation of the glory of his perfections: And we find all other things so far below the tendancy of our faculties, and the contentment of our minds, that we know that *this is it* that we were made for, and *this* is the proper use that our *Understandings* and *Wills* were given us for.

---

[1] *The Reasons of the Christian Religion*, Part I, Ch. XIV (*Practical Works*, ii. 49).
[2] Ibid., p. 51.   [3] Ibid., p. 52.   [4] Ibid., p. 54.

2. And we find that we attain not any *such perfection* in *this life* as we are capable of and do desire; but that our increase of virtue and holiness is an increase of our desires after more; and the better any man is, the more he still desireth to *be better*; and the more he knoweth, and loveth, and delighteth in God, the more he desireth it in a far higher degree. And even of our *knowledge of nature* we find, that the more we know, the more we would know; and that he that knoweth the *effect*, would naturally fain *know the cause*; and that when he knoweth the *nearer cause*, he would know the *cause of that*, and so know the *first cause*, God himself. And the little we here attain to of Knowledge, Love and Delight, is far short of the perfection in the same kind which our faculties encline unto.[1]

Dilating on the vast and glorious fabric that God has set man to contemplate, and on the fact that, for all his scientific knowledge and research, man still knows very little of it, Baxter says that there must be a state in which 'these works of God shall be better known of us, and God shall have the honour of them more than now'.[2] As further manifestations of a future state, he points to witchcraft and supernatural apparitions, such as the devil of Mascon, and comments that actions of great good in the world are often held up by an unseen, resistant force, while actions of great evil are seldom prevented in this way: hence a spirit of evil is evidently abroad in the world. He proceeds:

No man that confesseth a Life to come, can question the necessity of a Holy Life: But I have thought meet first to prove, that a Holy Life is our unquestionable duty (as the *prius cognitum*) and thence to prove the certainty of the future state: For indeed, though God hath not hid from us the matter of our Reward and Punishment, Hopes and Fears, yet hath he made our *Duty plainer* in the main, and proposed it *first* to our knowledge and consideration. The *Eternity* of the future state, I have not gone about to prove; because I reserve it for a fitter place, and need the help of more than natural light, for such a task. But that it shall be of so much weight and duration, as shall suffice to the full execution of Justice, and so set all streight, that seemed crooked in Gods present Government, this *Nature itself* doth fully testifie. . . .[3]

[1] Ibid., pp. 56–7.   [2] Ibid., p. 59.   [3] Ibid., p. 61.

In Sermon X, Johnson makes no attempt to prove 'the certainty of the future state'. As he points out, the gospel has made it clear that such a state 'can be denied or doubted no longer':

It is now certain that we are here, not in our total, nor in our ultimate existence, but in a state of exercise or probation, commanded to qualify ourselves, by pure hearts and virtuous actions, for the enjoyment of future felicity in the presence of God; and prohibited to break the laws which his wisdom has given us, under the penal sanction of banishment from heaven into regions of misery.[1]

In other respects, however, Jóhnson's arguments appear to be parallel to those of Baxter, and, interestingly enough, to be arranged in a similar order. Both consider the pre-Christian state of mankind to have been a state of self-indulgence and disorder: Baxter sees it as characterized by intemperance and sensuality, oppression and cruelty, and persecution of the innocent by 'the carnal, wild, rebellious rout';[2] while Johnson pictures it as 'a state of perpetual contest for the goods of this life, and, by consequence, of perpetual danger to those who abounded, and of temptation to those that were in want'.[3] Again, both Baxter and Johnson refer to the fact that, to the Jews, the doctrine of a future state was so obscurely revealed that it was inconsequential to their religious observance and practice. Both discuss various non-Christian sects, Johnson observing that the Sadducees had no expectation of a future state, while the Pharisees, who 'held the resurrection', had no clear revelation of a hereafter;[4] and Baxter noting that, though 'most of the known idolaters . . . number their deceased heroes with their gods' (a point not made by Johnson), 'the power of this belief' in a life to come 'is debilitated with the most, and, therefore, piety and virtue proportionately perish'.[5]

More significantly, both Baxter and Johnson solemnly draw attention to the fact that even Christians are sometimes unmoved by their knowledge of the certainty of a life to come, and both account for their apparent apathy in the same three ways: self-deceit, procrastination, and the workings of the Devil. And both

[1] Works, ix. 379.
[2] The Reasons of the Christian Religion, Part I, Ch. XIV (Practical Works, ii. 50).
[3] Works, ix. 378.   [4] Ibid., pp. 378–9.
[5] The Reasons of the Christian Religion, Part I, Ch. XIV (Practical Works ii. 53).

utter grave warnings to those who delay their repentance and conversion, or who deceive themselves into what Baxter calls 'a denial
or contempt of the dreadful future judgment of God',[1] and Johnson
'a willing negligence' of the hour of death and the day of doom.[2]
'God will not suffer his decrees to be invalidated,' says Johnson;
'he will not leave his promises unfulfilled, nor his threats unexecuted.
God "is not a man that he should repent"; what he has spoken
will surely come to pass.'[3] In Baxter's words, those who ignore
the warnings of God, 'as if he would never call men to account,
nor judge them according to his laws', and those who deny 'the
veracity of God, as if he were a liar and deceiver, and did not intend
the things which he speaketh; as if his precepts were but a false
pretension, and he were, indeed, indifferent what he did, and were
not to be believed in his predictions, promises, or threats', are
inevitably exposed to the consequences of 'the malignity of sin'.[4]

Later in his discourse Baxter discusses a number of propositions
which appear to have had a special impact on Johnson's thinking.
The first is that 'sin doth unquestionably deserve a natural death
and annihilation'.[5] In support of this contention, Baxter argues
that, if treason against a king deserves death, rebellion and sin
against God deserve it much more. 'Life and being is God's free
gift: if he take it away from the innocent, he taketh but his own;
therefore there can be no doubt but he may take it away from the
guilty who abuse it'.[5] The second proposition is related to the
first: 'If such a penalty were inflicted, God is not bound to restore
that sinner to being again whom he hath annihilated, (if it be not a
contradiction): And then the penal Privation would be everlasting:
Therefore an endless Privation of Being and all mercies is the Sinner's due'.[5] The third states: 'God is not bound thus to annihilate
the sinner, but may continue all his natural Being, and leave him
under the deserved privation of well-being, depriving him of all
other Mercies'. On this proposition Baxter comments:

This is undeniable; that it is in God's choice whether he will take
away his Being itself, or only all the Mercies which are necessary to

[1] Ibid., Part I, Ch. XV (*Practical Works*, ii. 63).
[2] *Works*, ix. 380.   [3] Ibid., p. 385.
[4] *The Reasons of the Christian Religion*, Part I, Ch. XV (*Practical Works*, ii. 63).
[5] Ibid., p. 65.

his well-being; for he that had nothing before but by free gift, may be deprived of any thing which was none of his own, if he forfeit it by abuse. Nay, we live upon such a continued emanation from God, as the beams from the Sun, that it is but God's stopping of his streams of bounty, and we perish, without any other taking away of mercies from us.[1]

The fourth proposition comes even closer to the heart of Johnson's own thinking, as he expressed it in the conversation which led to the publication of John Taylor's *Letter to Samuel Johnson on the Subject of a Future State*: 'Nature teacheth man to choose a great deal of . . . pain and misery, rather than not to be at all: even so much as will not utterly weigh down the love of life, and of vital operations.'[2] Elaborating on this, Baxter adds:

I say not (as some) that the *greatest torment* or *misery* is more eligible (or less odious) than *annihilation*. But it is certain, that a *great deal* is. We see abundance [i.e. abundant examples of people] . . . who are blind, or lame, or in grievous pains of the Gout and Stone, and many that are in miserable poverty, begging their bread, or toiling from morning to night like horses, and yet seldom taste a pleasant bit, but joyn distracting cares with labours; and yet they are all unwilling to die: Custom hath made their misery tollerable, and they had rather continue so for ever than be annihilated. . . .[3]

When God chooses between annihilating a sinner and letting him suffer in torment, our reason tells us, says Baxter, that the latter is 'more suitable to the ends of Government', since the sinner will then become a spectacle of God's justice: 'That which *is not*, is not *seen* nor *heard*; the annihilated are out of sight. And the mind of man is apt to think of a state of annihilation as that which is as a state of rest, or ease, and feeleth no harm, and so is not terrible enough, . . . The living sufferer therefore is rationally the fittest monument of God's Justice.'[4] So runs Baxter's fifth proposition, which is followed by a sixth, testifying to the inexorable doom of the unrepentant sinner, and by a seventh which states: 'The Belief of a Hell or endless punishment, being that which is *de facto* the

---

[1] *The Reasons of the Christian Religion*, loc. cit., p. 65.
[2] Ibid. See pp. 33–5 above.   [3] Ibid., pp. 65–6.   [4] Ibid., p. 67.

restraint of the Obedient part of the World, and that which proveth too weak with the Disobedient part, it thence followeth, that a Hell or endless punishment will be inflicted.'[1] The reasons for this argument he offers once more: experience shows that the threat of Hell is necessary in the law, and God does not govern the world by deceit: 'The sum of all here proved is, that all Sin deserveth endless misery, and naturally induceth to it; and that all ungodly impenitent souls shall certainly undergoe it; and that none can be saved from this misery, but by turning to God, and being saved from their Sins.'[2]

Of several conversations recorded by Boswell on the future state, a subject he himself found fascinating, one in particular appears to reflect much of Baxter's thinking. To establish the similarity, I quote the passage at length:

While Johnson and I stood in calm conference by ourselves in Dr. Taylor's garden, at a pretty late hour in a serene autumn night [it was 23 September 1777], looking up to the heavens, I directed the discourse to the subject of a future state. My friend was in a placid and most benignant frame. 'Sir, (said he), I do not imagine that all things will be made clear to us immediately after death, but that the ways of Providence will be explained to us very gradually.' I ventured to ask him whether, although the words of some texts of Scripture seemed strong in support of the dreadful doctrine of an eternity of punishment, we might not hope that the denunciation was figurative, and would not literally be executed. JOHNSON. 'Sir, you are to consider the intention of punishment in a future state. We have no reason to be sure that we shall then be no longer liable to offend against GOD. We do not know that even the angels are quite in a state of security; nay we know that some of them have fallen. It may, therefore, perhaps be necessary, in order to preserve both men and angels in a state of rectitude, that they should have continually before them the punishment of those who have deviated from it; but we may hope that by some other means a fall from rectitude may be prevented. Some of the texts of Scripture upon this subject are, as you observe, indeed strong; but they admit of a mitigated interpretation.' He talked to me upon this aweful and delicate question in a gentle tone, and as if afraid to be decisive.[3]

[1] Ibid., p. 68.   [2] Ibid., p. 69.   [3] *Life*, iii. 199–200.

Dealing with the same point in Part II, Chapter X, of his *Reasons of the Christian Religion*, Baxter answers the objection that 'punishment is to warn others from sinning; but after this life there will be none to warn: therefore, there will be no punishment, because the end of punishment ceaseth': 'It is a false position, that punishment is only or chiefly to be a warning to others. It is chiefly for the ultimate end of government, . . . So that it was necessary to the restraint of sinners in this world, that God should threaten hell in his law; and, therefore, it is necessary that he execute that law, or else it would be delusory and contemptible.'[1] Observing that 'many of the angels fell, and are now devils', Baxter goes on: 'Are not the devils now set out in Scripture for a warning to man? And how know we what other creatures God hath to whom these punished sinners may be a warning? or whether the new earth, wherein righteousness must dwell, according to God's promise, 2 Pet. iii. 12, 13, shall not have use of this warning to keep them in their righteousness?'[1] For Baxter, however, the texts do not 'admit of a mitigated interpretation': 'As long as all these things are probable, and the contrary utterly uncertain, how foolish a thing is it to go from the light of a plain revelation and Scripture, and argue, from our dark uncertainties and improbabilities, against that light; and all because self-love and guilt doth make sinners unwilling to believe the truth! So much for the objection against hell.'[1]

From the writings of Baxter on the subject of death, Johnson could hardly have derived much consolation, however great his admiration for them. Although Baxter frequently contends that salvation and not damnation is his message, and insists that God takes pleasure in man's conversion, he more frequently preaches the religion of fear: fear based upon doubts about the adequacy of our lives and faith, fear about the consequences of our sins, fear about the possibility that we may be taking Christ's sacrifice too much for granted, fear about the future life, fear about the retributive justice of God, and fear about the alternatives of annihilation and eternal punishment. Mercy will be shown, says Baxter time and again, only to those who deserve it.[2] But how can we be sure that we deserve it?

---

[1] *Practical Works*, ii. 143.
[2] e.g. *The Reasons of the Christian Religion*, Part II, Ch. X (*Practical Works*, ii. 145).

If he derived little consolation from Baxter's theology, Johnson obviously found much of homiletic value in it, as has been demonstrated in my discussion of Sermon X. This is not to say that he followed Baxter's reasoning uncritically and slavishly, for there is nothing sequacious in Johnson's sermons, or indeed in any of his writings. The manner in which he appears to have tempered and adapted the Baxterian message, without assuming the lugubriously categorical tone of the Puritan divine, may be illustrated by Sermon III in the Taylor collection, where Johnson addresses himself to the text from Proverbs 28 : 14, 'Happy is the man that feareth alway: but he that hardeneth his heart shall fall into mischief.' The sermon opens with these words:

The great purpose of revealed Religion is to afford Man a clear representation of his dependance on the Supreme Being, by teaching him to consider God as his Creator, and Governour, his Father and his Judge. Those to whom Providence has granted the knowledge of the holy Scriptures, have no need to perplex themselves with difficult speculations, to deduce their duty from remote principles, or to enforce it by doubtful motives. The Bible tells us, in plain and authoritative terms, that there is a way to life, and a way to death; that there are acts which God will reward, and acts that he will punish. That with soberness, righteousness, and godliness, God will be pleased; and that with intemperance, iniquity, and impiety, God will be offended; and that of those who are careful to please him, the reward will be such, as eye hath not seen, nor ear heard; and of those who, having offended him, die without Repentance, the punishment will be inconceivably severe, and dreadful.[1]

In consequence of this general doctrine, Johnson goes on,

the whole system of moral and religious duty is expressed, in the language of Scripture, by the *fear of God*. A good man is characterized, as a Man that feareth God; and the fear of the Lord is said to be the beginning of wisdom; and the Text affirms, that happy is the Man that feareth always.

On the distinction of this fear, into servile and filial, or fear of punishment, or fear of offence, on which much has been superstructed by the casuistical Theology of the Romish Church, it is not necessary

---

[1] *Works*, ix. 310.

to dwell. It is sufficient to observe, that the Religion which makes fear the great principle of action, implicitly condemns all self-confidence, all presumptuous security; and enjoins a constant state of vigilance and caution, a perpetual distrust of our own hearts, a full conviction of our natural weakness, and an earnest solicitude for Divine Assistance.[1]

There is a clear parallel here between Johnson's thoughts and those of Baxter as they are expressed in the latter's *Directions for Getting and Keeping Spiritual Peace and Comfort*. Observing that Christ, 'in wisdom and tender mercy, establisheth a law of grace, and rule of life, pure and perfect, but simple and plain; laying the condition of man's salvation more in the honesty of the believing heart, than in the strength of wit, and subtlety of a knowing head', he stresses the fact that, in its beginnings, the Christian faith 'was a matter of great plainness and simplicity'.[2] The same plainness, argues Baxter, is characteristic of Christian teaching on the subject of fear:

> God commandeth no man to believe more than is true, nor immediately to cast away their doubts and fears, but to overcome them in an orderly, methodical way. . . . Not only, 1. A reverent fear of God's majesty; 2. And a filial fear of offending him; 3. And an awful fear of his judgments, when we see them executed on others, and hear them threatened; 4. And a filial fear of temporal chastisements, are lawful and our duty: but also, 5. A fear of damnation exciting to most careful importunity to escape it; whenever we have so far obscured our evidences in the faith, and so of our salvation. The sum of my speech therefore is this: Do not think that all your fears of God's wrath are your sins; much of them is your great duty. . . .[3]

In the same context Baxter cautions his readers to 'avoid causeless scruples about doctrines, duties, sins, or your own state', and to ignore the 'superadded points' which are 'the peculiar mark of the Romish church'.[4] Rather more harshly than Johnson, he upbraids

---

[1] *Works*, ix. 310–11. Cf. Baxter, 'A Treatise of Conversion', *Practical Works*, ii. 484, where he complains that those who have not learned to fear 'increase their presumption and security' through the redemptive acts of Christ. See also Baxter, 'The Right Method for a Settled Peace of Conscience and Spiritual Comfort', *Practical Works*, ii. 919.

[2] 'The Right Method . . .', *Practical Works*, ii. 943.   [3] Ibid., p. 919.

[4] Ibid., p. 943. Cf. quotation from Johnson's Sermon III, pp. 109–10 above.

that church for deliberately confusing and corrupting the plain scriptural doctrine with its casuistry, which he regards as an instrument of the Devil.

Later in Sermon III, where he is contrasting the fear of God with the opposite attitude, hardness of heart, Johnson, again like Baxter, talks of the usefulness of this kind of fear: 'It is apparent from the Text, that the hardness of heart, which betrays to mischief, is contrary to the fear which secures happiness. The fear of God, is a certain tenderness of Spirit, which shrinks from evil, and the causes of evil; such a sense of God's Presence, and such a persuasion of his Justice, as gives sin the appearance of evil, and therefore excites every effort to combat and escape it.'[1] Hardness of heart, which Johnson defines as 'a thoughtless neglect of the Divine Law' and 'a state of dereliction', occurs in men who are 'negligent of those external duties of Religion, which are instituted to excite and preserve the fear of God'.[2] Thus Johnson appears to be taking away some of the harsh negativism from Baxter's religion of fear, and replacing it with a positive functionality: fear as an antidote to hardness of heart. 'It is a great mistake', wrote Baxter, 'to think that filial fear is only the fear of temporal chastisement, and that all fear of hell is slavish. Even filial fear is a fear of hell; . . .'[3] Johnson, on the other hand, sees 'a constant dread of the Divine displeasure' as a direct means of 'fixing' the heart 'only where true joys are to be found'.[4]

It is interesting to note, however, that Baxter and Johnson advocate the same remedies for hardness of heart: solitary contemplation, exposure to the best Christian preaching and teaching, the right choice of company, the study of exemplary lives, firm resolutions to avoid known sins, and unceasing prayer. It is also interesting that, while both men enjoin their readers to 'let go the world' (Baxter)[5] or to carry about with them in the world 'the temper of the cloister' (Johnson),[6] neither recommends or extols the life of a recluse, and neither advises the practice of excessive

---

[1] *Works*, ix. 315–16.   [2] Ibid., pp. 316–17.
[3] 'The Right Method . . .', *Practical Works*, ii. 957.   [4] *Works*, ix. 314.
[5] 'The Right Method . . .', *Practical Works*, ii. 955, and 'A Treatise of Conversion', *Practical Works*, ii. 487.
[6] *Works*, ix. 314.

fasting and austerity. Self-denial and self-discipline are not ends in themselves, but essential adjuncts to the process of disengaging the mind from sensuality, awakening holy fear, and assisting our progress in a good life. As Johnson says, 'they are considered only as expressions of our love of God, and are not substituted for the love of our neighbours'.[1]

Finally, a parallel study of the writings of Richard Baxter and the sermons of Samuel Johnson helps to throw some light on the latter's apparently obsessive fear of death. It has become fashionable in recent years to treat this difficult subject from a psychiatric point of view, and, as a result, to minimize the doctrinal implications. If we remember that Johnson, working in the solemn traditions of the seventeenth-century Puritans, such as Baxter, considered the fear of death to be a necessary corollary to the filial fear of God, and as an indispensable motivating force in the life of a true Christian, it takes on a somewhat different perspective. Certainly it was not, for him, a 'magnificent obsession' that yielded a special kind of perverse pleasure. 'To consider the shortness, or misery, of life, is not an employment to which the mind recurs for solace or diversion; or to which it is invited by any hope of imme-diate delight.'[2] So he remarks in Sermon XV, adding that this sombre consideration is none the less necessary, as 'it is our duty, in the pilgrimage of life, to proceed with our eyes open, and to see our state; not as hope or fancy may delineate it, but as it has been in reality appointed by Divine providence'.[3]

His own prayers bear testimony to the way in which he dis-charged this duty. Almost all of them incorporate references to death or to the shortness of life. In this respect, as in so many others, Johnson was following the counsels of William Law, who, as was noted earlier, prescribed daily contemplation of death and the fear of God.[4] His real and persistent fear of death is also re-marked upon by Boswell a number of times. To Boswell he confided that 'he never had a moment in which death was not terrible to him'.[5] In a significant exchange with the Quaker, Mrs. Knowles,

---

[1] *Works*, ix. 315.   [2] Ibid., p. 423.   [3] Ibid., p. 424.
[4] See pp. 53-6 above; and William Law, *A Serious Call* . . ., p. 339.
[5] *Life*, iii. 153.

Johnson affirms much of what he said in his prayers and sermons: Boswell had expressed his horror at the thought of death:

MRS. KNOWLES. 'Nay, thou should'st not have a horrour for what is the gate of life.' JOHNSON. (standing upon the hearth at Dilly's house rolling about, with a serious, solemn, and somewhat gloomy air,) 'No rational man can die without uneasy apprehension.' MRS. KNOWLES. 'The Scriptures tell us, "The righteous shall have *hope* in his death."' JOHNSON. 'Yes, Madam; that is, he shall not have despair. But, consider, his hope of salvation must be founded on the terms on which it is promised that the mediation of our SAVIOUR shall be applied to us,—namely, obedience; and where obedience has failed, then, as suppletory to it, repentance. But what man can say that his obedience has been such, as he would approve of in another, or even in himself upon close examination, or that his repentance has not been such as to require being repented of? No man can be sure that his obedience and repentance will obtain salvation.' MRS. KNOWLES. 'But divine intimation of acceptance may be made to the soul.' JOHNSON. 'Madam, it may; but I should not think the better of a man who should tell me on his death-bed he was sure of salvation. A man cannot be sure himself that he has divine intimation of acceptance; much less can he make others sure that he has it.'[1]

This was, substantially, the view expressed by Baxter: 'No man's assurance of his perseverance is perfect in this life.'[2] 'Though he is not free from all the natural fears of death, yet his belief and hope of endless happiness doth abate those fears by the joyful expectation of the gain which followeth.'[3] 'Though death of itself be an enemy, and terrible to nature, yet being the only passage into happiness, he gladly entertaineth it.'[3] It is only 'the hypocrite or seeming Christian' who 'may possibly by his self-deceit have some abatement of his fears, and . . . may by pride and wit seem very valiant and comfortable at his death, to hide his fear and pusillanimity from the world'.[4]

Whether or not Johnson derived his ideas about death and the future life from the writings of Baxter, there seems little doubt that

---

[1] Ibid., pp. 294–5.   [2] Bibl. 65, p. 39.
[3] Baxter, 'The Character of a Sound, Confirmed Christian', *Practical Works*, ii. 1059.
[4] Ibid., p. 1060.

they contributed to his extraordinary ability to see his own lack of religious assurance in the cold light of reason; that same reason which prompted him to believe in the freedom of the will and in man's moral responsibility, and which prevented his indulgence in any form of self-delusion. As a result of this lack of assurance he was often, as has been shown, in a state of spiritual vigilance and anxiety which, in turn, produced an intense preoccupation with religious questions. Out of the tension came some of his most profound and far-reaching pronouncements; and out of the anxiety some of his most eloquent sermons took their meticulously reasoned form.

SANDERSON, HOOKER, JEREMY TAYLOR, TILLOTSON, AND OTHERS

It is clear that Samuel Johnson derived some measure of his strength as a homilist from a number of seventeenth-century divines. The earlier Renaissance preachers, such as John Donne and Lancelot Andrewes, had not made any impact on him, as far as we know, for he makes no mention of their homiletic works, and his attitude to metaphysical wit, of the kind that Donne displayed even in his devotional writings, was such that Johnson would have been unlikely to affect it. His biographers have indicated that one of the strongest influences on his style and moralistic outlook was that of the most erudite of the seventeenth-century men of religion, such as Sanderson, Hooker, Hakewill, and Jeremy Taylor, none of whom could be described as metaphysical stylists.[1]

Bishop Sanderson (1587–1663), whom Johnson admired, Hawkins tells us, for his 'acuteness',[2] wrote sermons of a highly intellectual and allusive quality, conspicuous for their frequent quotations in Latin and Greek from the ancient writers and the early Church Fathers, and for their structural firmness. Sanderson was a believer in close adherence to the Biblical text, careful and logical organization of his arguments, and conclusions that combined moralistic reasoning with fidelity to the text. Whether Johnson consciously emulated his manner would be hard to prove, but there seems to

---

[1] e.g. *Life*, i. 219; Hawkins, pp. 271, 542.   [2] Hawkins, p. 271.

be little doubt that some of Sanderson's methods are reflected in Johnson's own homiletic procedures. In particular, the structure of each of Sanderson's sermons provided a model which Johnson may have modified for his own purposes.[1]

In quite a different way, Johnson was also indebted to Richard Hooker, whose *Laws of Ecclesiastical Polity* he ransacked for illustrations to accompany his definitions of theological terms in the *Dictionary*. Although there is very little reference to Hooker in his recorded conversations, it is obvious that Johnson held him in high esteem as an intellectual, a political thinker, and an authority on religion. As Professor Donald Greene has pointed out, the two basic postulates of Johnson's conception of government come from Hooker, whose views on the subject of divine law he respected equally.[2] Now and again his indebtedness to Hooker in both areas—political and religious—becomes evident in a single context. In the Vinerian lectures he helped to compose for Robert Chambers, for instance, we find this passage:

---

[1] As an example of Sanderson's careful structuring, the outline of Sermon I of his *Fourteen Sermons Heretofore Preached* (Bibl. 141) may be mentioned.

Sections 1–4:	the Occasion, Scope, Coherence, and Division of the Text.
Section 5: Point I.	*Of not Despising Others*:
Section 6:	Be they never so weak
Section 7:	and we never so strong.
Section 8:	Both for the Sin's sake, in the Despisers:
Section 9:	and for the Scandal's sake, to the Despised.
Sections 10 and 11:	Point II. *Of not Judging Others*:
Section 12:	with the true meaning thereof: and four Reasons, viz.
Section 13:	1. the want of commission: ⎫ in us.
Section 14:	2. the want of Skill: ⎭
Section 15:	3. the Uncharitableness, and ⎫ of the thing itself.
Section 16:	4. the Scandalousness ⎭
Section 17: *Application*.	To the case in our church: showing
Section 18:	1. Wherein it agreeth with that of the Romans in this chapter;
Sections 19–21:	2. And how it differeth from it. I. in the matter.
Section 22:	II. in respect of the Persons.
Section 23:	III. in the Practice of the Persons.
Section 24:	IV. in their mutual respective Carriage. And that
Section 25:	1. *in the point of Despising*. Where
Section 26:	The several grievances of our Brethren are pro-
Sections 27–9:	posed; and answered.
Sections 30–7:	2. *in the point of Judging*.
Section 38:	The Conclusion.

Johnson's procedures, which will be discussed later (Ch. IV), were similar to this.
[2] *The Politics of Samuel Johnson*, pp. 194 and 245.

By whatever means political bodies were first *framed*, they are clearly *supported* by these two foundations: 1. a desire of social life, to which both reason and instinct (if I may be allowed the expression) incline men; and 2. a certain rule of obedience established in every State, to which every member of it chooses rather silently to submit than to exchange the protection and pleasures of society for the solitude and horrors of a desert.[1]

Hooker's two bases for a human commonwealth are: 'the one a natural inclination whereby all men desire sociable life and fellowship; the other, an order expressly or secretly agreed upon touching the manner of their living together.'[2]

Johnson carries Hooker's argument a step further:

Society implies in its nature an interest common to many individuals, a pursuit of the highest degree of happiness that can be obtained and enjoyed by any number, great or small, which that society comprises. To the happiness of the whole, it will be frequently necessary to sacrifice the happiness of a part. . . . There is therefore a necessity of some *governing* power, by which those who are inclined to be happy at the cost of others may be compelled to their part of the general task,—and of a *public wisdom*, by which private judgment shall be directed and controlled.[3]

The application of this political argument to a religious context can be seen in Sermon XXIV, one of those dealing with the duties of the governors and the governed, and presumably composed for John Taylor to deliver to a large parliamentary congregation at St. Margaret's in Westminster:

That the institutions of government owe their original, like other human actions, to the desire of happiness, is not to be denied; nor is it less generally allowed, that they have been perverted to very different ends from those which they were intended to promote. This is a truth, which it would be very superfluous to prove by authorities, or illustrate by examples. Every page of history, whether sacred or profane, will furnish us abundantly with instances of Rulers that have deviated from justice, and subjects that have forgotten their allegiance; of nations ruined by the tyranny of Governours, and of

[1] E. L. McAdam, Jr., *Dr. Johnson and the English Law* (Bibl. 126), p. 82.
[2] *The Laws of Ecclesiastical Polity*, Bk. I, Ch. X.   [3] McAdam, p. 82.

Governours overborne by the madness of the populace. Instead of a concurrence between Governour and subjects for their mutual advantage, they seem to have considered each other, not as allies or friends, to be aided and supported, but as enemies, whose prosperity was inconsistent with their own, and who were therefore to be subdued by open force, or subjected by secret stratagems.[1]

The utilitarian trend of this argument becomes even more apparent a little later in the sermon:

Man is, for the most part, equally unhappy, when subjected, without redress, to the passions of another, or left, without controul, to the dominion of his own. . . . By this consideration have all civilized nations been induced to the enaction of penal laws, laws by which every man's danger becomes every man's safety, and by which, though all are restrained, yet all are benefited.

Government is therefore necessary, in the opinion of every one, to the safety of particular men, and the happiness of society; and it may be considered as a maxim universally admitted, that *the people* cannot *rejoice*, except *the righteous are in authority*. . . .[2]

Even with wise and just government, Johnson goes on to argue, the happiness of the people may still be deficient: to remedy this deficiency 'our policy must at last call for help upon religion':

. . . The mere observer of human laws avoids only such offences as the laws forbid, and those only when the laws can detect his delinquency. But he who acts with the perpetual consciousness of the divine presence, and considers himself as accountable for all his actions to the irreversible and unerring judgement of omniscience, has other motives of action, and other reasons of forbearance. He is equally restrained from evil, in public life, and in secret solitude; and has only one rule of action, by which *he does to others what he would that others should do to him*, and wants no other enforcement of his duty, than the fear of future punishment, and the hope of future rewards.

The first duty therefore of a Governour is to diffuse through the community a spirit of religion, to endeavour that a sense of the divine authority should prevail in all orders of men, and that the laws should be obeyed, in subordination to the universal and unchangeable edicts of the Creatour and Ruler of the world.[3]

---

[1] *Works*, ix. 506. The Yale MS. Sermon contains a similar argument.
[2] Ibid., p. 507.   [3] Ibid., pp. 512–13.

In this way Johnson adapts the political argument for a utilitarian basis for society, derived, as has been shown, from Hooker, to his religious context, in which he implies that the model of leadership is that of the universal Law-giver.

Hooker had argued that all laws take their origin from the eternal law that exists in the mind of God.[1] From this archetypal law, all others derive their form: the laws governing the operations of nature, the laws of the angelic order, and the law of reason which applies to men, comprehensible through human reason. He adds two more categories of law: divine law, which is based upon what men know only through Revelation, and human law, which is based upon what men know through a combination of reason and Revelation, and by which they judge what is and what is not expedient for society. The Church, Hooker argues, is duty-bound to legislate on the basis of both these categories of law, though it must be careful to avoid creating laws which are contrary to Revelation. It is the responsibility of the Church to interpret, apply and administer such laws with respect to ecclesiastical doctrine.[2]

Johnson appears to have endorsed these views of Hooker, if we may interpret his inclusion of certain quotations in the *Dictionary* as indicative of such acceptance.[3] First of all, after defining 'Church' as 'the collective body of Christians, usually termed the catholick *church*', he quotes Hooker as follows: 'The *church*, being a supernatural society, doth differ from natural societies in this; that the persons unto whom we associate ourselves in the one, are men, simply considered as men; but they to whom we be joined in the other, are God, angels, and holy men.' Again, under the word 'doctrine' he cites this passage from Hooker: 'To make new articles of faith and *doctrine*, no man thinketh it lawful; new laws of government, what church or commonwealth is there which maketh not either at one time or other?' Yet another quotation from Hooker, following 'canon' in the *Dictionary*, appears to indicate Johnson's agreement with Hooker's view of the Church's responsibility,

[1] Hooker, Bk. I, Chs. II and III.
[2] Ibid. John S. Marshall, *Hooker and the Anglican Tradition* (Bibl. 123), pp. 159 ff., points out that Hooker objected to the view of the theologians of Trent that the Church 'has an infallible character given it by its Lord'.
[3] See W. K. Wimsatt, Bibl. 163, pp. 80–1.

which was mentioned above: 'The truth is, they are rules and *canons* of that law, which is written in all men's hearts; the church had for ever, no less than now, stood bound to observe them, whether the apostle had mentioned them or no.'

Johnson's admiration for Hooker was not confined to matters of substance in the *Laws of Ecclesiastical Polity*. Boswell tells us that Johnson's own prose style was 'much formed' upon that of Hooker, and others.[1] In the Preface to the *English Dictionary* Hooker the stylist is mentioned with approval in the same breath as the Bible, Bacon, Raleigh, Spenser, Sidney, and Shakespeare:

. . . From the authors which rose in the time of Elizabeth, a speech might be formed adequate to all the purposes of use and elegance. If the language of theology were extracted from Hooker and the translation of the Bible; the terms of natural knowledge from Bacon; the phrases of policy, war, and navigation from Raleigh; the dialect of poetry and fiction from Spenser and Sidney; and the diction of common life from Shakespeare, few ideas would be lost to mankind, for want of English words, in which they might be expressed.[2]

Near the end of the same Preface, in an unusually personal and poignant passage, Johnson writes:

. . . The chief glory of every people arises from its authors: whether I shall add any thing by my own writings to the reputation of English literature, must be left to time: much of my life has been lost under the pressures of disease; much has been trifled away; and much has always been spent in provision for the day that was passing over me; but I shall not think my employment useless or ignoble, if, by my assistance, foreign nations, and distant ages, gain access to the propagators of knowledge, and understand the teachers of truth; if my labours afford light to the repositories of science, and add celebrity to Bacon, to Hooker, to Milton, and to Boyle.[3]

Why did Johnson place Hooker in this great company? Because he considered him to be one of the finest intellects and one of the most seminal writers of all time; because he found his writings, particularly his sermons, admirable in their clear, close reasoning, and demanding in their challenge to the alertness of the reader;

---

[1] *Life*, i. 219. [2] *Works*, v. 40. [3] Ibid., pp. 49–50.

and because Hooker was a master of the rich, long sentence and the memorable phrase, the solemn and moving climax, the dignified and eloquent peroration. Witness the close of his sermon on 'The Certainty and Perpetuity of Faith in the Elect':

And then blessed for ever and ever be that mother's child, whose faith hath made him the child of God. The earth may shake, the pillars of the world may tremble under us, the countenance of heaven may be appalled, the sun may lose his light, the moon her beauty, the stars their glory; but concerning the man that trusted in God, if the fire have proclaimed itself unable as much as to singe a hair of his head, if lions, beasts ravenous by nature, and keen with hunger, being set to devour, have as it were religiously adored the very flesh of the faithful man; what is there in the world that shall change his heart, overthrow his faith, alter his affection towards God, or the affection of God to him?[1]

There is nothing quite as emotionally compelling or as sublimely assured as this anywhere in Johnson's own religious writings; but the meticulous choice of words, the closely reasoned, concretely illustrated argument, the carefully graduated sentence, and the majestic movement towards a memorable climax were all qualities that Johnson essayed in the development of his own homiletic style.

Hooker's method of expatiation through precise word-definition was another procedure that Johnson frequently followed. The topic sentence in Hooker is often expanded in this way:

All things which God did create he made them at first true, good, and right. True, in respect of the correspondence unto that pattern of their being, which was eternally drawn in the counsel of God's foreknowledge; good, in regard of the use and benefit which each thing yieldeth unto another; right, by an apt conformity of all parts with that end which is outwardly proposed for each thing to tend unto.[2]

Johnson frequently uses a similar approach:

These changes of conduct or opinion may be considered as the revolutions of human nature, often necessary, but always dangerous. Necessary, when some favourite vice has generally infected the world, or some errour, long established, begins to tyrannize, to demand implicit faith, and refuse examination. But dangerous, lest the mind, incensed by oppression, heated by contest, and elated by victory, should be too far transported to attend to truth, and out of zeal to secure her conquest, set up one errour, to depress another.[1]

At times, too, his explication and expatiation are one:

To sow and to reap are figurative terms. To sow, signifies to act; and to reap, is to receive the product of our actions. As no man can sow one sort of grain, and reap another, in the ordinary process of nature; as no man gathers grapes of thorns or figs of thistles, or when he scatters tares in the furrows, gathers wheat into his garners; so, in the final dispensations of providence, the same correspondence shall be found in the moral system; every action shall at last be followed by its due consequences; we shall be treated according to our obedience or transgressions; the good shall not miss their reward, nor the wicked escape their punishment; but when men shall give account of their own works, they that have done good shall pass into everlasting life, and they that have done evil into everlasting fire.[2]

Like Hooker, Johnson could not resist the temptation to seize upon a word or a phrase, to expound it with a lexicographer's exactness and a rhetorician's skill, and so draw out of it every ounce of significance.

It was in the work of another Anglican preacher, however, that Johnson found the quality of poetic eloquence: Jeremy Taylor, the lyrical homilist of Golden Grove, whom Johnson admired, as Hawkins tells us, for his 'amazing erudition'.[3] There is a colourful, almost novel-like, attractiveness about the titles of some of Taylor's sermons, which Johnson, whose approach was more abstract and austere, did not attempt to reproduce: 'The House of Feasting; or, the Epicure's Measures', 'The Marriage Ring; or, the Mysteriousness and Duties of Marriage', 'Apples of Sodom; or, the Fruits of Sin' are some examples. Taylor was fond, too, of interlarding his sermons with classical allusions, quotations from the Church Fathers, and purple passages, all of which Johnson used sparingly.

---

[1] *Works*, ix. 350–1 (Sermon VII).
[2] Ibid., pp. 385–6 (Sermon X). For Johnson's lexicographic explanation of terms in the Sermons see pp. 213–15 below.
[3] Hawkins, p. 271.

But many of their themes are similar, and their methods of attack are closely parallel: the textual explication, followed by the exploration and exposition of the theme, and then by the practical application and exhortation. Both are richly aphoristic, and both lead up to their aphorisms with long, carefully balanced periods. More particularly, both Jeremy Taylor and Samuel Johnson believed firmly in the value of a spiritual regimen, and their devotionalism is characterized by an adherence to regular practices and exercises. And both were at their most majestic when dealing with the sombre realities of death and the last judgement, with the vanity of earthly things and the transitoriness of this life. There are more than merely verbal echoes, for instance, between the first chapter of Taylor's *Holy Dying* and the hortatory conclusion of Sermon XXV, which Johnson composed for the funeral of his wife. Taylor insistently reminds his readers that the fact of death is less awesome than the judgement to follow:

It is not the most terrible part of death to leave the life of this world, but to give an account of it unto the Creator of the world; especially in such a time wherein he is to use no mercy: this is a thing so terrible, that it made holy Job to tremble, notwithstanding he had so good an account to make. . . .[1]

Johnson uses the solemn occasion of his wife's decease to issue a similar warning:

But let us not be thus shamefully deluded! Let us not thus idly perish in our folly, by neglecting the loudest call of Providence; nor, when we have followed our friends, and our enemies, to the tomb, suffer ourselves to be surprised by the dreadful summons, and die, at last, amazed and unprepared! Let every one whose eye glances on this bier, examine what would have been his condition, if the same hour had called him to judgement, and remember, that, though he is now spared, he may, perhaps, be to-morrow among separate spirits. The present moment is in our power; let us, therefore, from the present moment, begin our repentance![2]

On the subject of repentance Taylor and Johnson held similar views. In his 'Doctrine and Practice of Repentance' Taylor had

---

[1] Jeremy Taylor, 'Holy Dying', in *Works* (Bibl. 151), i. 368.
[2] *Works*, ix. 524–5 (Sermon XXV).

expressed the opinion that, while attrition—sorrow for sin not based upon the love of God but motivated by mere fear of the consequences—is the first step towards true repentance or 'perfect contrition', it is not enough in itself to merit salvation. At the same time, he cautions against unnecessary anxiety on the part of the repentant sinner who undergoes agonies of self-questioning as to whether his motivation is negative or positive. A genuine desire to keep God's commandments is, to his mind, a clear indication of a positive love of God, provided that it is consistent and profoundly felt.[1] In Sermon II, where Johnson writes that the genuinely contrite man 'needs not recollect whether he was awakened from the lethargy of sin by the love of God, or the fear of punishment',[2] he appears to be following the same line of reasoning. He goes one step further, however, by contending that 'The Scripture applies to all our passions, and eternal punishments had been threatened to no purpose, if these menaces were not intended to promote virtue.'[2]

It would, of course, be quite wrong to claim that Johnson followed Taylor, or indeed any of the homilists whose works he admired, slavishly and uncritically. There is evidence in Boswell's *Life* to show that he had some reservations about Taylor's tendency to poetize and to exaggerate:

I mentioned Jeremy Taylor's using, in his forms of prayer, 'I am the chief of sinners', and other such self-condemning expressions. 'Now, (said I) this cannot be said with truth by every man, and therefore is improper for a general printed form. I myself cannot say that I am the worst of men; I *will* not say so.' JOHNSON. 'A man may know, that physically, that is, in the real state of things, he is not the worst man; but that morally he may be so. Law observes, that "Every man knows something worse of himself, than he is sure of in others." You may not have committed such crimes as some men have done; but you do not know against what degree of light they have sinned. Besides, Sir, "the chief of sinners" is a mode of expression for "I am a great sinner." So St Paul, speaking of our SAVIOUR's having died to save sinners, says, "of whom I am the chief;" yet he did not think himself so bad as Judas Iscariot.' BOSWELL. 'But, Sir, Taylor means it literally, for he founds a conceit upon it. When praying for the

[1] Jeremy Taylor, 'The Doctrine and Practice of Repentance', *Works*, ix. 239–40.
[2] *Works*, ix. 307.

conversion of sinners, and of himself in particular, he says, "LORD, thou wilt not leave thy *chief* work undone." ' JOHNSON. 'I do not approve of figurative expressions in addressing the Supreme Being; and I never use them. Taylor gives a very good advice: "Never lie in your prayers; never confess more than you really believe; never promise more than you mean to perform." ' I recollected this precept in his 'Golden Grove'; but his *example* for prayer contradicts his *precept*.[1]

Apart from the testimony that this passage provides to Johnson's remarkable memory, it is interesting for its criticism of Taylor's use of figurative expressions in addressing the deity. In his own religious writing Johnson avoided extravagances of expression, as the evidence of his prayers, meditations, and sermons clearly shows. That he did not avoid figurative expressions altogether, however, and that he sometimes expressed himself poetically in a homiletic context, will be demonstrated later.[2]

Both in his choice of themes and in the manner of his presentation of them, Johnson clearly belongs to the Puritan homiletical tradition, and to an even older tradition of Christian morality. For him, as has already been suggested, the more lush and affective styles of the Elizabethan preachers, and the more profoundly philosophical and discursive qualities of the Cambridge Platonists and Latitudinarians, were not sufficiently direct, dignified, or comprehensive to be considered appropriate to the needs of an eighteenth-century congregation. The speculative Platonism of humanists such as Henry More was too remote from common understanding and from ascertainable truth. As Hawkins tells us, 'Dr. Henry More, of Cambridge, he did not much affect: he was a platonist, and, in Johnson's opinion, a visionary. He would frequently cite from him, and laugh at, a passage to this effect:—"At the consummation of all things, it shall come to pass, that eternity shall shake hands with opacity."[3] A passage from Boswell's *Life* also indicates that Johnson considered More's philosophical probings inferior to the teachings of scripture, at least on the subject of the future state. When Boswell asked whether there was any harm in 'forming to ourselves conjectures as to the particulars of our happiness' in the hereafter, Johnson replied, 'Sir, there is no

---

[1] *Life*, iv. 294–5.   [2] See pp. 210 ff. below.   [3] Hawkins, p. 542.

harm. What philosophy suggests to us on this topick is probable: what scripture tells us is certain. Dr. Henry More has carried it as far as philosophy can. You may buy both his theological and philosophical works in two volumes folio, for about eight shillings.'[1]

The type of preaching which Johnson preferred was evidently that of the seventeenth-century divines who, no doubt influenced by (and themselves contributing to) the reform of prose style associated with the work of Sprat, Dryden, and the Royal Society, practised a plain, direct, unadorned expression of theological truths. Of this style, Robert South (1634–1716) and John Tillotson (1630–94) were exponents *par excellence*. It was South's view that 'wit in divinity is nothing but sacred truths suitably expressed'.[2] At times this desire for 'suitable' expression led him into a rather rugged aggressiveness, upon which Johnson commented to Boswell: 'South is one of the best, if you except his peculiarities, and his violence, and sometimes his coarseness of language.'[3] In his *Sermons Preached upon Several Occasions* this quality of forthrightness verging on violence is much in evidence. One example will serve to illustrate it. Pointing out that even the most sensual of sinners has an immortal spirit, South declaims:

And for the sensual epicure, he also will find, that there is a certain living spark within him, which all the drink he can pour in will never be able to quench or put out; nor will his rotten abused body have in its power to convey any putrefying, consuming, rotting quality to the soul: no, there is no drinking, or swearing, or ranting, or fluxing a soul out of its immortality.[4]

This forceful manner, even with its tendency to excessive piling up of colourful epithets, evidently appealed to Johnson, who quotes South in the *Dictionary* almost as often as Hooker, and who once presented a copy of South's sermons to Philip Metcalfe, a friend of Sir Joshua Reynolds.[5]

---

[1] *Life*, ii. 162 and n. 1.

[2] *Works* (Bibl. 145), iii. 33 (Sermon XXXVII). See W. Fraser Mitchell, *English Pulpit Oratory from Andrewes to Tillotson* (Bibl. 130), p. 315.

[3] *Life*, iii. 248.   [4] *Sermons Preached upon Several Occasions* (Bibl. 144), i. 178.

[5] *Life*, iv. 205. Chester F. Chapin, *The Religious Thought of Samuel Johnson*, pp. 110–12, suggests that Johnson's stress on prayer as 'the great sign of our dependence on God' may be an echo of a similar emphasis in the work of South.

Archbishop Tillotson's sermons were just as direct and practical as those of South, but less vigorous and less colourful. Tillotson, who practised the kind of clarity advocated by the reformers of prose style, perhaps went too far in the process of stripping his expression of all embellishment. At any rate Johnson was a little hesitant about recommending Tillotson's sermons as models of style, although he admired them for their emphasis on what was reasonable in religion, for their carefully controlled arguments, and for their total lack of affectation.

Tillotson's 'normality' of style was the pattern followed by many preachers of the eighteenth century, who, except for the 'enthusiasts', played down the emotions and concentrated on a fairly temperate, moderately eloquent form of plain speaking, avoiding alike the dramatic richness of the Elizabethans and the Metaphysicals and the excessive austerity of the Puritans. As a result, many sermons became ponderous and dull, lapsing into what Vicesimus Knox describes as a 'dull, dry, torpid, languid, soporific style'.[1] Johnson, partly deliberately, partly intuitively, returned to the seventeenth century in his search for a livelier idiom, adding to it, of course, his own special brand of authoritative eloquence.

Although there is nothing to show that he had read the advice given to contemporary preachers by the author of *Christian Eloquence in Theory and Practice* (1722), Johnson certainly applied to the writing of his sermons precepts similar to those found there:

The Light of Reason is pure, but something dim: Truth, which is always serious, should be a little enlivened, that it may be the more pleasing; but too much Sprightliness would lessen its Effect and Credit. As Truth of no Kind whatever, so particularly no Christian Truth, should ever be deliver'd in a too ludicrous and sportive manner: On the contrary, care should be taken that it appear always with an Air of Modesty and Gravity. . . .

---

[1] Vicesimus Knox, *Winter Evenings or Lucubrations on Life and Letters* (Bibl. 113), i. 180. Knox is referring particularly to sermons delivered at Westminster Abbey before a parliamentary congregation—'mere water-gruel' he calls them. The preachers on such occasions fear to say anything political. 'It is safer to talk about good old King Charles and King David, the Jews and the Samaritans, the Scribes and the Pharisees, the Greeks and the Romans' (p. 181).

If you would please, study to do so by the Excellency and Importance of the Truths you treat of; by solid and convincing Arguments; by a proper Application and clear Exposition of the Passages in Scripture; by well chosen Citations from the Fathers, and, when the subject requires it, from Councils and the Constitutions of the Church; by the orderly Disposition of Figures; by the Elevation and Propriety of Expression; by a Sublimity, Exactness, and Novelty of Thoughts: Hence, without doubt, you may draw abundant matter to delight and please. But for the glittering Objects, which are propos'd to common Hearers, they are of no other Use, but to dazzle and amuse, to inveigle them with an empty Shew, that vanishes immediately, without leaving any Footsteps of Virtue in the mind: These are false Ornaments, and vain Beauties, which are never used to set off true Eloquence. Shall a Preacher make it his great Care to divert the Imagination, when it is his Business to set the Truths of Christianity in the clearest Light, to represent them in all their Majesty, to give them their full Weight and Force upon the Mind, and to persuade Men to the Practice of them against all the Reluctancy of Nature? This were childish, and a very ill Compliment to his Hearers, whom he treats thus like so many Infants, that are delighted with little Images and Puppets.[1]

The author then draws a sharp distinction between country and city preaching, contending that the former appeals primarily to the senses and the imagination, the latter to the intellect. He praises the city preachers:

Their Terms are pure and simple, their Style noble and elevated, their Thoughts and Reflections just and reasonable, their Sentiments acute and delicate. They seem very cautious to preserve in every thing the Dignity of the Pulpit, and to keep up the Greatness of the Matters there propos'd by them: Their Discourses are not too figurative or florid; without any of the little sparkling Prettinesses, affected by many, but avoided studiously by them, as the Marks of a weak Understanding. You never see them lay themselves out in Descriptions, Narrations and Similitudes, which become rather a Rhetorician than a Christian Orator. If they find it necessary to produce Facts, they do but just touch upon them; and for all the Turns of Wit, that look like Raillery or Pleasantry, and have any thing of a comick

[1] Samuel D'Oyley, op. cit., pp. 14–17.

Air in them, they utterly detest them; being persuaded that they are prophane Liberties, inconsistent with the Gravity of Religion, and such as cannot be admitted, without dishonouring the sacred Ministry of God's word.[1]

These observations come very close to Johnson's celebrated statement in his *Life of Waller*, in which he contends that 'contemplative piety, or the intercourse between God and the human soul, cannot be poetical',[2] and goes on to apply this view to the criticism of poetry on sacred subjects:

Of sentiments purely religious, it will be found that the most simple expression is the most sublime. Poetry loses its lustre and its power, because it is applied to the decoration of something more excellent than itself. All that pious verse can do is to help the memory, and delight the ear, and, for these purposes, it may be very useful; but it supplies nothing to the mind. The ideas of Christian Theology are too simple for eloquence, too sacred for fiction, and too majestick for ornament; to recommend them by tropes and figures, is to magnify, by a concave mirror, the sidereal hemisphere.[3]

It was this strong opinion which tempered Johnson's admiration for Milton's achievement in *Paradise Lost*: 'The good and evil of Eternity are too ponderous for the wings of wit; the mind sinks under them in passive helplessness, content with calm belief and humble adoration.'[4]

It is significant that Johnson's sermons are barren of quotations from sacred poetry. Indeed, his allusions to works of literature in general are remarkably few, in keeping with his conception of the sermon as an independent literary genre, a practical discourse to which the productions of poetical wit and fancy were almost totally alien. To contaminate it with such irrelevant matter was to commit one of the 'grosser faults' for which he so memorably censured *Lycidas*:

. . . With these trifling fictions are mingled the most awful and sacred truths, such as ought never to be polluted with such irreverend com-

---

[1] Samuel D'Oyley, op. cit., p. 17.
[2] *Works*, vii. 213; *Lives of the English Poets* (Bibl. 11), i. 291.
[3] *Works*, vii. 214; *Lives*, i. 292–3.
[4] *Works*, vii. 135; *Lives*, i. 182. G. B. Hill, the editor, notes: 'There was little calmness in Johnson's belief.'

binations. The shepherd, likewise, is now a feeder of the sheep, and afterwards an ecclesiastical pastor, a superintendent of a Christian flock. Such equivocations are always unskilful; but here they are indecent, and, at least approach to impiety, of which, however, I believe the writer not to have been conscious.[1]

For a variety of reasons, then, Johnson found in the work of many of the seventeenth-century Puritan divines those qualities of sermon-writing which were most appealing to him: simplicity and directness, close adherence to the scriptural text, careful and reasoned expatiation and argument, and freedom from spurious emotionalism and histrionic or rhapsodical embellishment. To say this, of course, is not to imply that he followed them unreservedly or that he accepted all their interpretations of doctrine. As a strong Anglican, indeed, he is often at odds with their precepts and critical of their tenets. But for their plain speaking, and their logical, balanced arguments, their emphasis upon what he considered to be the crucial themes, such as death and the last judgement, and their championship of common sense in religious devotion, he admired them very greatly.

On this point Professor Maurice Quinlan may have done an injustice to Johnson in that section of his book in which he comments upon Johnson's unfavourable attitude to the Protestant Dissenting sects. While it is true that Johnson refused to enter the churches of the Nonconformists,[2] it is also true, as has been shown, that he held many of the Dissenters, such as Richard Baxter and Isaac Watts, in very high esteem. To say, as Professor Quinlan has said, that 'perhaps he thought of all Puritans as Calvinistic'[3] is to distort Johnson's whole religious position. The Church of England in the eighteenth century numbered many Calvinists in its ranks. Moreover, when we recall that Johnson considered Milton, one of the greatest of the seventeenth-century Puritans, as apparently 'untainted by any heretical peculiarity of opinion',[4] and that he frequently quoted him in his *Dictionary* in illustration of theological terms, we should not assume that Puritanism was as distasteful to

[1] *Works*, vii. 120; *Lives*, i. 165.
[2] Quinlan, op. cit., pp. 159 ff.   [3] Ibid., p. 159.
[4] *Works*, vii. 115; *Lives*, i. 155.

him as Professor Quinlan implies.[1] At any rate, the examples of such avowed distaste which Professor Quinlan supplies, and which he apparently had some difficulty in finding, are scarcely convincing. Much more relevant to any discussion of Johnson's attitude to the Dissenting sects than quotations from the *Dictionary* under 'predetermination' and 'election', which Quinlan offers, is his wise and tolerant statement in the *Life of Sir Thomas Browne*:

Men may differ from each other in many religious opinions, and yet all may retain the essentials of Christianity; men may sometimes eagerly dispute, and yet not differ much from one another; the rigorous prosecutors of error should, therefore, enlighten their zeal with knowledge, and temper their orthodoxy with charity; that charity, without which orthodoxy is vain; charity that 'thinketh no evil', but 'hopeth all things', and 'endureth all things'.[2]

The important thing for Johnson was not that a man was a Puritan or a Roman Catholic or a Jew, but that his devotions should be directed towards a common moral end; and he happened to find, in the tradition of Christian morality as interpreted by the seventeenth-century Puritans, the views and precepts most congenial to his own thinking and way of life: in many ways an austere tradition, central to which are a *contemptus mundi*, a need for the frequent contemplation of death and the last judgement, and the prescription of an exacting regimen based on the solemn truth that 'the night cometh when no man can work'.[3] Such were the grave themes that occupied Johnson's thoughts as he composed his own sermons.

[1] Nor should we assume that Roman Catholicism was repugnant to him. See Chester F. Chapin, op. cit., pp. 32–51, for an interesting discussion of Johnson's earlier attitudes to the Portuguese Jesuits described by Father Lobo in his *Voyage Historique d'Abissinie* (1728), which Johnson had translated into English. Chapin draws attention to what appears to have been a youthful prejudice against the Roman Catholic faith, but he suggests that Johnson, as he matured, reduced the essentials of Christianity to a few simple truths, unaffected by sectarian differences. In his next chapter, pp. 52–70, Chapin discusses Johnson's relationship to the Puritan tradition and to the contemporary evangelical movement, of which Johnson's close friend, Hill Boothby, was an enthusiastic supporter. See also Robert Bracey, Bibl. 69.

[2] *Works*, vi. 502. See also ix. 388 (Sermon XI) for a similar statement.

[3] John 9: 4. See *Life*, ii. 57, and n. 5.

III

The Main Themes and Ideas of Johnson's Sermons

HIS APPROACH TO RELIGIOUS ARGUMENT

SAMUEL JOHNSON's deep and admiring interest in writers like Law, Clarke, and Baxter, who taught him so much about Christian perfection, sacrifice, and conversion, is the more remarkable when we remember that the natural bent of his mind was scrupulously and obstinately rationalistic: to such an extent, indeed, that some commentators have described him as a 'sceptic' in the sense of 'one who questions the validity or authenticity of something purporting to be knowledge; one who maintains a doubting attitude'. As one scholar has put it, 'for Johnson all mental action, whether rational or imaginative, is always secondary to the direct experience of reality and is, apart from experience, seriously suspect', and even faith 'was not mysticism or inward light but acceptance of testimony and . . . sense-evidence upon the highest possible authority'.[1]

In most things, certainly, Johnson insisted on systematic, empirical observation. The mystical heights to which Law, for instance, attained, were beyond Johnson's range. In ordering his own thoughts on religious belief and dogma, therefore, Johnson naturally avoided matters that seemed to him to go beyond believable, demonstrable evidence, and sought a systematic creed that could be contained within the bounds of human reason and credulity. In expressing this creed, moreover, he chose to subordinate the ethical and affective means of persuasion, to use the Aristotelian terms, in favour of the logical and rational.[2]

---

[1] J. H. Hagstrum, *Samuel Johnson's Literary Criticism* (Bibl. 42), pp. 7, 69.
[2] *Rhetoric*, i. 2. The translation consulted is that of John Henry Freese, Bibl. 94.

By the same token, he sedulously avoided metaphysical speculation. His references to the 'speculatists'[1] in the sermons and moral
essays are invariably critical, for the scientist and the lawyer in
him would not tolerate for long the futility, as he saw it, of probing
hidden causes and abstruse connections that lay outside human
perception. What makes him especially interesting as a religious
seeker after truth, indeed, is his insistence upon Christian evidences
that come from the testimony of eye-witnesses and upon logical
inferences from that testimony. This rational approach he found in
the work of Samuel Clarke, whom he esteemed more as a homilist
than as a metaphysician, and in the writings of Hugo Grotius,
whom he greatly admired and whose *De Veritate Religionis Christi*
he had attempted to read when he was very young.[2]

It may be objected that, in seeking a reasoned, soundly based
statement of Christian belief, Johnson was no different from other
apologists in the Age of Reason, during which commentators
strove to reduce to a few simple, basic propositions the entire
concept of revealed religion; an age, moreover, in which little was
said by Protestant theologians about such mysteries as the Virgin
Birth, the baptism of the Holy Spirit, the Second Coming, the
Assumption, and the union of two natures in Jesus Christ. After
all, Dr. Robert South, whom Johnson described as one of the best
stylists in theology, had contracted the whole question of Christian
conduct into two simple precepts:

Now he who guides his actions by the rules of piety and religion,
lays these two principles as the great ground of all that he does:

1. That there is an infinite, eternal, all-wise mind governing the
affairs of the world, and taking such an account of the actions of men,
as, according to the quality of them, to punish or reward them.

---

[1] In the eighteenth century 'speculation' meant the theory or study of an art or
science, without regard to the practice of it. In Sermon VI (*Works*, ix. 344) Johnson
draws a sharp distinction between 'speculation' and 'real life', although in Sermon VII
(ibid., p. 358) he concedes that 'there is a much closer connexion between practice
and speculation than is generally imagined'. In Sermon XXIII (ibid., p. 497) he
suggests that 'speculative wisdom' deals in 'illusion' which is soon dissipated by
experience. In Sermon XXV 'the fallacious and uncertain glimmer of philosophy'
(ibid., p. 517) is said to shine on 'speculations' useless to 'the gross body of mankind'
(ibid., p. 519). See also *Adventurer* 45.

[2] *Johnsonian Miscellanies*, i. 157–8. See also *Life*, i. 68–9 n. 3.

2. That there is an estate of happiness or misery after this life, allotted to every man, according to the quality of his actions here.[1]

These two principles, incidentally, form the core of Johnson's own religious message.

If other thinkers and writers had already taken this approach, what makes Johnson's contribution so unusual? This question will be taken up from the stylistic point of view later, but here it may be answered very simply: Probably never since the Reformation had a layman, with such a frankly incredulous frame of mind, and with such a formidable arsenal of knowledge, insight, and wisdom, investigated the whole area of religious truth. Even Milton, whose championship of Christianity was also based upon a rational disposition of mind and character, had not faced, at least to the same degree, the agonies of doubt and self-searching that Johnson suffered.

It appears that Johnson's interest in religion went back to the infidelity of his boyhood and youth, a lapse to which Boswell refers in the *Life*:

SEWARD. 'I wonder that there should be people without religion.' JOHNSON. 'Sir, you need not wonder at this, when you consider how large a proportion of almost every man's life is passed without thinking of it. I myself was for some years totally regardless of religion. It had dropped out of my mind. It was an early part of my life. Sickness brought it back, and I hope I have never lost it since.'[2]

The original draft of this part of the *Life* (Yale Boswell Papers, XV. 207) specifies the period of this lapse as being from ten to twenty-two years of Johnson's age. Mrs. Piozzi's account, which Boswell supplies in a footnote, and which he describes as 'strange fantastical', reads as follows:

At the age of ten years his mind was disturbed by scruples of infidelity, which preyed upon his spirits, and made him very uneasy, the more so, as he revealed his uneasiness to none, being naturally (as he said) of a sullen temper, and reserved disposition. He searched, however, diligently but fruitlessly, for evidences of the truth of revelation; and, at length, recollecting a book he had once seen . . . in

---

[1] *Sermons* (Bibl. 144), i. 269.   [2] *Life*, iv. 215.

his father's shop, intitled *De Veritate Religionis*, etc., he began to think himself highly culpable for neglecting such a means of information, and took himself severely to task for this sin, adding many acts of voluntary, and, to others, unknown penance. The first opportunity which offered, of course, he seized the book with avidity. . . . He redoubled his diligence to learn the language that contained the information he most wished for; but from the pain which guilt had given him, he now began to deduce the soul's immortality . . . which was the point that belief first stopped at; and from that moment resolving to be a Christian, became one of the most zealous and pious ones our nation ever produced.[1]

Although Boswell discredits this statement, we can, after making due allowance for some Thralian exaggeration, deduce from it that Johnson was drawn to the study of the Christian faith from a somewhat sceptical, or at least neutral, position; and a thread of this scepticism or neutrality, slender but none the less visible, continues to run through the fabric of his own faith in the years of his maturity and old age.

Professor Robert Voitle, in an interesting if rather inconclusive part of his book, *Samuel Johnson the Moralist*, considers the evidence adduced by scholars for Johnson's alleged scepticism:

These scholars usually depend on one of four different arguments, or some combination thereof. A few resort to probing deeply into Johnson's psyche; one cites the hints of Johnson's contemporaries; some reason that his faith would have been more placid had it been strong; and others argue by extrapolation that, because Johnson was a sceptic in some areas, he must have been one in religion, too. To the first sort of argument there is no satisfactory reply. . . . All that can be considered here is whether the other three arguments invalidate the general impression which has persisted up to our time, that Johnson was as pious as the average Anglican of his day, if not more so. I do not think they do.[2]

The scholars to whom Professor Voitle alludes are not all named by him, but no doubt he has in mind several of those whom he has mentioned earlier, including W. B. C. Watkins, the author of

---

[1] *Life*, i. 68–9 n. 3. An interesting discussion of what I have called Johnson's 'scepticism or neutrality' appears in C. F. Chapin, op. cit., Chs. IV, V, and X.
[2] Voitle, p. 168.

Perilous Balance; Walter Jackson Bate, who wrote *The Achievement of Samuel Johnson*, one of the most thoughtful books on Johnson from the psychological and philosophical points of view; Jean H. Hagstrum, the writer of a perceptive essay on 'Dr. Johnson's Fear of Death'; Philip Williams, whose article on 'Samuel Johnson's Central Tension: Faith and Fear of Death' is a sensitive interpretation of the subject; and Joseph Wood Krutch, whose *Samuel Johnson* is probably the most comprehensive of recent biographies, with the possible exception of that by James L. Clifford, only one part of which has as yet been published.[1] Professor Voitle does, however, mention specifically in this immediate context Ernest C. Mossner, Stuart Gerry Brown, and Bertrand H. Bronson, and appears to imply that the work of these three scholars illustrates the different arguments to which he has been alluding.

Mossner, in a book called *The Forgotten Hume*, contends that 'Johnson hated Hume because he recognized in him a kindred spirit', and because Johnson himself was troubled by a 'religious scepticism, subdued but never extinguished'.[2] This is, of course, speculative thinking, unsupported, as far as one can see, by any substantial evidence from Johnson's contemporaries. Bronson, in *Johnson Agonistes and Other Essays*, offers a more convincing line of argument:

It is hard to believe, in the face of his intellectual habit and what he says about reasons, that Johnson was naturally religious, or that it would not have been much easier, temperamentally, for him to have been a sceptic. His violence about it is the measure of the desperate fight which it cost him to hold fast his religion. The mind that is predisposed to religion feels itself adrift until it comes to anchor in the harbour of a firm and happy faith.[3]

That Johnson was not 'naturally religious' in the sense in which Bronson appears to use the phrase—temperamentally disposed to accept religious truths without careful inquiry—has already been demonstrated by a reference to his own admission;[4] and that he never really came to anchor in the way that Bronson suggests is a matter of common knowledge. But we should also bear in mind

[1] See Bibl. 51, 34, 101, 160, 24, and 17.   [2] Bibl. 131, p. 206.
[3] Bibl. 36, p. 41.   [4] See p. 133 above.

that Johnson, as we showed in the previous chapter, did not believe that a sure faith was possible in this world, any more than Richard Baxter had done.[1] In Sermon XIV he reminds us that trust in God,

that trust to which perfect peace is promised, is to be obtained only by repentance, obedience, and supplication, not by nourishing in our own hearts a confused idea of the goodness of God, or a firm persuasion that we are in a state of grace; by which some have been deceived, as it may be feared, to their own destruction. We are not to imagine ourselves safe, only because we are not harrassed with those anxieties about our future state, with which others are tormented; but which are so far from being proofs of reprobation, that though they are often mistaken by those that languish under them, they are more frequently evidences of piety, and a sincere and fervent desire of pleasing God. . . .[2]

As we have already argued, Johnson regarded anxiety as inseparable from true piety, since ultimate assurance of salvation is unattainable in this world.[3] Indeed, he considered it spiritually healthier to have doubts about one's own salvation than to be one of those who, as he expresses it in Sermon XIII, 'pacify their consciences with an appearance of piety, and live and die in dangerous tranquillity and delusive confidence'.[4] Again, in Sermon XX, he says

It is astonishing that any man can forbear enquiring seriously, whether there is a GOD; whether God is just; whether this life is the only state of existence; whether God has appointed rewards and punishments in a future state; whether he has given any laws for the regulation of our conduct here; whether he has given them by revelation; and whether the religion publickly taught carries any mark of divine appointment. These are questions which every reasonable Being ought undoubtedly to consider with an attention suitable to their importance. . . .

Let it be remembered, that the nature of things is not alterable by our conduct. We cannot make truth; it is our business only to find it. No proposition can become more or less certain or important, by being considered or neglected. It is to no purpose to wish, or to suppose, that to be false, which is in itself true; and therefore to acquiesce in our own wishes and suppositions, when the matter is of eternal

---

[1] See pp. 95–6 above.   [2] *Works*, ix. 421–2.   [3] See pp. 94–6 above.
[4] *Works*, ix. 405–6.

consequence, to believe obstinately without grounds of belief, and to determine without examination, is the last degree of folly and absurdity. . . .[1]

While this sermon is directed particularly against those who scoff at religion, it seems to me to contain the important touchstone by which Johnson tested his own religious views: 'We cannot make truth; it is our business only to find it.' In other words, he remained open-minded until he arrived at the truth, and he considered it his duty to discover the correct grounds of belief.

Professor Voitle argues that Johnson's 'scepticism', which he is careful to distinguish from freethinking, manifests itself in two main ways, both of which typify his empirical habit of thought: 'an inquiring sort of incredulity' and 'a more general scepticism directed against those forms of knowledge which Johnson considers to be the products of human presumption'.[2] The first he illustrates by quoting Johnson's warning to Joseph Warton, contained in his review of an *Essay on the Writings and Genius of Pope*:

I cannot forbear to hint to this writer, and all others, the danger and weakness of trusting too readily to information. Nothing but experience could evince the frequency of false information, or enable any man to conceive, that so many groundless reports should be propagated, as every man of eminence may hear of himself. Some men relate what they think, as what they know; some men, of confused memories and habitual inaccuracy, ascribe to one man, what belongs to another; and some talk on, without thought or care.[3]

Having, as Professor Voitle says, 'an insatiable appetite for accurate particulars',[4] Johnson found unsubstantiated reports or rumours especially distasteful.

The second kind of scepticism amounts to an almost total distrust of human speculation, whether religious, scientific, or metaphysical. Even speculative readings or interpretations of the text of Shakespeare became repugnant to him,[5] and the metaphysical

---

[1] Ibid., pp. 476–7. This passage, interestingly enough, appears to contradict the view quoted, on p. 133 above, from *Life*, iv. 215.

[2] Voitle, p. 176.   [3] *Works*, vi. 42.   [4] Voitle, p. 176.

[5] See *Johnson on Shakespeare*, Yale Ed., vii. 108–10. Of his own editorial procedures Johnson wrote, 'As I practised conjecture more, I learned to trust it less' (p. 108). At the same time, he admits, 'conjectural criticism has been of great use in the learned world' (p. 109).

presumptions of Soame Jenyns were equally indefensible.[1] When he caught himself speculating about divine mysteries, he recorded his sense of guilt in his *Prayers and Meditations*.[2] The only knowledge which was acceptable to him was that which could be apprehended by the senses or that which had come to man by divine revelation. All the rest was uncertain.

To matters of religious knowledge, he almost always applied the same principle. If there could have been a fool-proof system of mathematically established morality and empirically ascertained theology, as has already been hinted in the passage of this book on Clarke (pp. 68–70), he would have received it gladly. As it was, he sought support for his beliefs in the evidences of the senses, and from historically and scientifically demonstrable fact. In this respect he was again a child of the Age of Reason, in which philosophers sought, for instance, to explain morality in terms of observable natural phenomena. Locke's endeavour to enunciate a psychological theory of happiness, it will be remembered, was partly related to the Christian emphasis on rewards and punishments—another example of the rational desire to wed science and apologetics. To achieve this end, Locke defined good and evil as ultimately pleasure and pain, two experiences which were universal and which were verifiable by the senses:

Things then are good and evil, only in reference to pleasure or pain. That we call *good*, which is apt to cause or increase pleasure, or diminish pain in us. . . . And, on the contrary, we name that *evil* which is apt to produce or increase any pain, or diminish any pleasure in us. . . .[3]

Thus Locke relates the notion of rewards and punishments to the sensations of pleasure and pain:

Good and evil, as hath been shown, are nothing but pleasure or pain, or that which occasions or procures pleasure or pain to us. *Moral*

[1] See Johnson's review of *A Free Enquiry into the Nature and Origin of Evil*, in *Works*, vi. 52 ff.

[2] See, e.g. *Diaries*, pp. 383–4, in which he prays for help 'to withdraw my Mind from unprofitable and dangerous enquiries, from difficulties vainly curious, and doubts impossible to be solved'.

[3] *Human Understanding*, II. xx. 2.

good and evil, then, is only *the conformity or disagreement of our voluntary actions to some law, whereby good or evil is drawn on us, from the will and power of the law-maker*; which good and evil, pleasure or pain, attending our observance or breach of the law by the decree of the law-maker, is that we call *reward* and *punishment*.[1]

The evidence of the senses was adduced in verification of religious as well as psychological teachings. Here, the age had a strong precedent in the Bible, especially in the writings of St. John, who had testified from sense observation to the incarnation of Christ:

> That which was from the beginning, which we have heard, which we have seen with our eyes, which we have looked upon, and our hands have handled, of the Word of life. . . . That which we have seen and heard declare we unto you . . . (1 John 1: 1, 3).

Archbishop John Tillotson, the preacher whose work Johnson rightly described as having been 'applauded by so many suffrages', had defined faith as 'a degree of assent, inferiour to that of sense',[2] and stated that revelation had been supported both by rational evidence and sense observation: 'And to assure us, that these reasonings are true, we have a most credible revelation of these things, God having sent his Son from heaven to declare it to us, and given us a *sensible* demonstration of the thing, in his resurrection from the dead, and his visible ascension into heaven. . . .'[3]

Johnson, in the sermon he wrote for the funeral of his wife (Sermon XXV), using the text from John 11: 25, 'Jesus said unto her, I am the Resurrection, and the Life: he that believeth in me, though he were dead, yet shall he live', discusses the complicated arguments of 'some of the Philosophers' regarding the immateriality of the soul, but doubts whether the majority of people would ever be able to understand them. He continues:

> To persuade common and uninstructed minds to the belief of any fact, we may every day perceive, that the testimony of one man, whom they think worthy of credit, has more force than the arguments of a thousand reasoners, even when the arguments are such as they may be imagined completely qualified to comprehend. Hence it is

---

[1] Ibid., II. xxviii. 5.   [2] *Works*, 4th edn. (London, 1728), ii. 67, 69.
[3] Ibid., p. 69.

plain, that the constitution of mankind is such, that abstruse and intellectual truths can be taught no otherwise than by positive assertion, supported by some sensible evidence, by which the assertor is secured from the suspicion of falsehood; and that if it should please God to inspire a teacher with some demonstration of the immortality of the soul, it would far less avail him for general instruction, than the power of working a miracle in its vindication, unless God should, at the same time, inspire all the hearers with docility and apprehension, and turn, at once, all the sensual, the giddy, the lazy, the busy, the corrupt and the proud, into humble, abstracted and diligent Philosophers.[1]

The important phrase here is 'supported by some sensible evidence', for Johnson an indispensable element of demonstrable fact. In *Rasselas* Imlac is given a similar speech, in which he argues for immortality on the grounds of the immateriality of the soul and the nature of matter, and goes on to reply to the hypothesis of the materialist that matter 'may have qualities with which we are unacquainted',[2] a theory Johnson had discussed briefly in an earlier part of the funeral sermon.[3] Imlac's argument is notable for its insistence on demonstrable evidence, backed by the senses and acceptable to the intellect:

He who will determine against that which he knows, because there may be something which he knows not; he that can set hypothetical possibility against acknowledged certainty, is not to be admitted among reasonable beings. All that we know of matter is, that matter is inert, senseless, and lifeless; and, if this conviction cannot be opposed but by referring us to something that we know not, we have all the evidence that the human intellect can admit. If that which is known may be overruled by that which is unknown, no being, not omniscient, can arrive at certainty.[4]

Here once more we have a manifestation of the scrupulously rational mind of Samuel Johnson, unwilling to accept anything which was not absolutely evident to the senses and to the mind.

This scrupulosity led him to reject the doctrine of transubstantiation, which, in his view, could not be supported by 'sensible

[1] *Works*, ix. 519–20.   [2] Ibid., i. 307.   [3] Ibid., ix. 519.
[4] Ibid., i. 307.

evidence'.[1] Mrs. Thrale tells us in her *French Journals* that, when he was at Douay, Johnson refused to kneel during the elevation of the Host.[2] The reasons for his failure to accept the doctrine are mentioned by Boswell:

Upon the road we talked of the Roman Catholick faith. He mentioned (I think) Tillotson's argument against transubstantiation: 'That we are as sure we see bread and wine only, as that we read in the Bible the text on which that false doctrine is founded. We have only the evidence of our *senses* for both.' 'If, (he added,) God had never spoken figuratively, we might hold that he speaks literally, when he says, "This is my body." '[3]

In the two Communion sermons in the Taylor collection (Sermons IX and XXII) Johnson observes that the doctrines of the blessed Sacrament have been greatly perverted and misrepresented, thus giving rise to many disputes among men of learning; and he argues that the scriptural texts, in Luke and Corinthians, show that the Sacrament is 'a representation of the death of our Saviour' and 'a kind of repetition of baptism, the means whereby we are readmitted into the communion of the church of Christ'.[4] In the second Communion sermon, he is more explicit about the symbolism of the Sacrament:

The Corinthians fell into this enormous sin [that of eating and drinking unworthily], says the Apostle, *not discerning the Lord's Body*, for want of discerning the importance and sanctity of the institution, and of distinguishing the Lord's Body, from the common elements of bread and wine, exhibited on common occasions of festive jollity. It is therefore the first duty of every Christian to discern the Lord's Body, or to impress upon his mind a just idea of this act of commemoration, of the commands by which it is enforced, of the great sacrifice which it represents, and of the benefits which it produces.[5]

In other words, Johnson's interpretation of the text (1 Corinthians 11: 27) is that the 'enormous sin' of the Corinthians lay in their

---

[1] Quinlan, p. 175, observes: '. . . to subscribe to the doctrine of transubstantiation demands that one believe that a change takes place in the elements. Because this change is not confirmed by perception, Johnson was unable to accept the doctrine of transubstantiation. . . .'

[2] M. Tyson and H. Guppy, *The French Journals* (Bibl. 32), p. 156.

[3] *Life*, v. 71.   [4] *Works*, ix. 371, 372.   [5] Ibid., pp. 493-4.

failure to recognize the *symbolic* significance of the bread and the wine. Here he is following the Catechism he had learned as a child:

Quest. What is the inward part, or thing signified?

Answ. The Body and Blood of Christ, which are verily and indeed taken and received by the faithful in the Lord's Supper.[1]

In Sermon IX, moreover, Johnson points out that the Sacrament, properly observed, is effective 'not only by the new strength which every idea acquires by a new impression; and which every persuasion attains by new recollections, approbation, and meditation, but likewise by the supernatural and extraordinary influences of Grace, and those blessings which God has annexed to the due use of means appointed by himself'.[2] Thus the Sacrament is more than a mere commemorative rite: it is the divinely appointed means by which the communicant receives 'the supernatural and extraordinary influences of grace'.[2] In saying this, Johnson goes further than Clarke, on whose ideas he had depended, in some respects, for his discussion of the Sacrament. Clarke had, it will be remembered, played down the supernatural in his argument for the reasonableness and credibility of the divine sacrifice;[3] Johnson concedes that, in this context, there is an element of mystery, transcending the evidence of the senses.

Where Johnson took exception to the Roman Catholic doctrine of transubstantiation was in its insistence that the sacramental bread and wine become in substance the body and blood of Christ. In the *Dictionary* he makes this point clear in his definition of 'transubstantiation': 'a miraculous operation believed in the Romish Church, in which the elements of the eucharist are supposed to be changed into the real body and blood of Christ'. He illustrates the use of the word with a single quotation, from Locke: 'How is the Romanist prepared easily to swallow, not only against all probability, but even the clear evidence of his senses, the doctrine of *transubstantiation?*' This quotation does not, in my view, indicate

---

[1] A Catechism: that is to say, An Instruction to be learned of every Person, before he be brought to be confirmed by the Bishop, in *The Book of Common Prayer* (Oxford: Clarendon Press, 1787), unpaginated.

[2] *Works*, ix. 371.

[3] See pp. 67–8 above. This is one of the rare exceptions to Johnson's 'obstinate rationality'.

that Johnson endorsed the opprobrious intent of Locke's question, but it does seem to suggest that he did not wish to provide a more sympathetic interpretation of the doctrine in the *Dictionary*, for he adds nothing to it in subsequent editions. This is a little surprising, for two reasons: elsewhere Johnson shows a marked disposition to understand and to appreciate the Roman Catholic faith, and his attitude to other miracles is not quite as intolerant. He did, however, admit that what prevented him from becoming a Roman Catholic was 'an obstinate rationality'.[1]

There are two passages in Boswell's *Life* that deal with the subject of Johnson's attitude to miracles, and both are associated with Hume's argument against them, which Boswell dutifully quoted on both occasions, carefully baiting the trap. The first, which is preceded by Johnson's comment that 'every thing which Hume has advanced against Christianity had passed through my mind long before he wrote', reads as follows:

I mentioned Hume's argument against the belief of miracles, that it is more probable that the witnesses to the truth of them are mistaken, or speak falsely, than that the miracles should be true. JOHNSON. 'Why, Sir, the great difficulty of proving miracles should make us very cautious in believing them. But let us consider; although GOD has made Nature to operate by certain fixed laws, yet it is not unreasonable to think that he may suspend those laws, in order to establish a system highly advantageous to mankind. Now the Christian religion is a most beneficial system, as it gives us light and certainty where we were before in darkness and doubt. The miracles which prove it are attested by men who had no interest in deceiving us; but who, on the contrary, were told that they should suffer persecution, and did actually lay down their lives in confirmation of the truth of the facts which they asserted. Indeed, for some centuries the heathens did not pretend to deny the miracles; but said they were performed by the aid of evil spirits. This is a circumstance of great weight. Then, Sir, when we take the proofs derived from prophecies which have been so exactly fulfilled, we have most satisfactory evidence. Supposing a miracle possible, as to which, in my opinion, there can be no doubt, we have as strong evidence for the miracles in support of Christianity, as the nature of the thing admits.'[2]

---

[1] *Life*, iv. 289. See also ii. 105–6.   [2] Ibid., i. 444–5.

The second passage, relating to a conversation which took place some fourteen years later, when Johnson was in his sixty-eighth year, is in some ways more revealing:

Talking of Dr. Johnson's unwillingness to believe extraordinary things, I ventured to say, 'Sir, you come near Hume's argument against miracles, "That it is more probable witnesses should lie, or be mistaken, than that they should happen".' JOHNSON. 'Why, Sir, Hume, taking the proposition simply, is right. But the Christian revelation is not proved by the miracles alone, but as connected with prophecies, and with the doctrines in confirmation of which the miracles were wrought.'

He repeated his observation, that the differences among Christians are really of no consequence. 'For instance, (said he,) if a Protestant objects to a Papist, "You worship images;" the Papist can answer, "I do not insist on *your* doing it; you may be a very good Papist without it: I do it only as a help to my devotion." ' I said, the great article of Christianity is the revelation of immortality. Johnson admitted it was.[1]

Those commentators on Johnson who have accused him of bigotry and excessive single-mindedness would do well to ponder this passage, and to remember other instances of his tolerance of the creeds and opinions of others. In the previous chapter we noted how, in spite of Samuel Clarke's allegedly heretical views on the Trinity, Johnson appreciated him for what he was, a perceptive and lucid theologian.[2] As Boswell rather shrewdly remarked, 'Johnson at all times made the just distinction between doctrines *contrary* to reason, and doctrines *above* reason'.[3] This distinction explains his acceptance of some miracles and his rejection of others. As for beliefs that were neither above nor contrary to reason, he was open-minded enough to admit them, at least as possibilities. Such, for instance, was his attitude to the doctrine of Purgatory, which he described to Boswell as 'a harmless doctrine', about which there was 'nothing unreasonable';[4] and in his own prayers, in which he commends his deceased relatives and friends to God, he implies

---

[1] *Life*, iii. 188.   [2] See pp. 65 ff. above.
[3] *Life*, iv. 329. The distinction was not, of course, new. Richard Hooker, Robert Boyle, Thomas Browne, *et al.* had referred to 'doctrines above reason'.
[4] Ibid., ii. 104–5.

the possibility of a middle state,[1] although he nowhere explicitly mentions it. In any case, the Book of Common Prayer, in the Order for the Burial of the Dead, includes the petition 'that we, with all those that are departed in the true faith of thy holy Name, may have our perfect consummation and bliss, both in body and soul, in thy eternal and everlasting glory',[2] and prayers for the departed were commonly offered in churches of the Anglican communion.

We may conclude, then, that Johnson's 'obstinate rationality' made him as wary of unprovable assumptions in theology as in any other branch of human inquiry. His insistence upon factual accuracy in other things, and even upon exactitude of observation on the part of poets, characterized his lifelong search for religious truth and his inveterate hatred of errors and false suppositions. One of his plainest and most forthright statements about religious belief is found in Sermon VII, for which he chose as his text Jeremiah 6: 16: 'Thus saith the Lord, Stand ye in the ways, and see, and ask for the old paths, where is the good way, and walk therein, and ye shall find rest for your souls. But they said, We will not walk therein.' Every age, Johnson observes, has its own peculiar character and its special mode of thinking. The conduct and opinions of one generation give way to those of the next, and these revolutions of human nature have usually been accompanied by danger and discord. Religion is no exception to this generalization:

That no change in Religion has been made with that calmness, caution, and moderation, which Religion itself requires, and which common prudence shews to be necessary in the transaction of any important affair, every nation of the earth can sufficiently attest. Rage has been called in to the assistance of zeal, and destruction joined with reformation. Resolved not to stop short, men have generally gone too far, and, in lopping superfluities, have wounded essentials.[3]

Zeal for a particular faith or creed, even when it produces turbulent revolutions of this kind, may be pardoned, says Johnson, but a calculated and deliberate deviation from the path of truth can have

---

[1] See, e.g., *Diaries*, pp. 289, 304.
[2] See also the Prayer for the Church Militant, where the dead are mentioned. See *Diaries*, p. 52 and n.
[3] *Works*, ix. 351.

more insidious and evil effects. 'The prevailing spirit of the present age', he continues, 'seems to be the spirit of scepticism and captiousness, of suspicion and distrust, a contempt of all authority, and a presumptuous confidence in private judgement; a dislike of all established forms, merely because they are established, and of old paths, because they are old.'[1] This is not to deny the right of people to judge for themselves, but when that right is exercised ignorantly and indiscreetly, error is multiplied by error, until 'the Church become[s] a scene of confusion, a chaos of discordant systems of worship, and inconsistent systems of faith'.[2]

What is Johnson's remedy for this chaotic state of affairs, and how would he stem the rising tide of controversies and altercations, made the more turbulent by emotional outbursts of argument and uncontrolled uproars of disputation? Not 'by denying, or disputing, the right of private judgement, but by exhorting all men to exercise it in a proper manner, according to each man's measure of knowledge, abilities and opportunities. And by endeavouring to remove all those difficulties, which may obstruct the discovery of truth, and exposing the unreasonableness of such prejudices, as may perplex or mislead the enquirer.'[3]

The chief obstacle to the discovery of religious truth, Johnson maintains, apart from infidelity, superstition, and enthusiasm, is 'an overfondness for novelty',[3] and he proceeds to lay before his readers the dangers of reaching conclusions about religion without a long and diligent examination. Honest error, when accompanied by sincerity, may be thought by many to be just as good as truth, but this is a dangerous fallacy: '. . . if we do not carry on our search without regard to the reputation of our teachers, our followers, or ourselves, and labour after truth with equal industry and caution, let us not presume to put any trust in our sincerity'.[4] Much more than sincerity is required. Diligent pursuit of religious truth demands more time and energy than most people care to reserve for the purpose; and yet many try to answer theological questions of the most complex and intricate kind after very brief reflection and examination. On the other hand, those who have devoted their

[1] *Works*, ix. 351–2.   [2] Ibid., p. 352.   [3] Ibid., p. 353.
[4] Ibid., p. 355.

whole attention to such matters, through prolonged study and meditation, would hesitate to deliver their opinions with complete assurance.[1]

Surely the most reliable way to pursue the truth, says Johnson, is through the study of the writings of old:

> With regard to the order and government of the Primitive Church, we may doubtless follow their authority with perfect security; they could not possibly be ignorant of laws executed, and customs practised, by themselves, nor would they, even supposing them corrupt, serve any interests of their own, by handing down false accounts to posterity. We are therefore to enquire from them, the different orders established in the ministry from the Apostolick ages; the different employments of each, and their several ranks, subordinations, and degrees of authority. From their writings we are to vindicate the establishment of our church, and by the same writings are those who differ from us, in these particulars, to defend their conduct.[2]

Thus Johnson arrives at the core of his argument, which is that those who

> lived in the ages nearest to the times of the Apostles undoubtedly deserve to be consulted. The oral doctrines, and occasional explications of the Apostles, would not be immediately forgotten, in the churches to which they had preached, and which had attended to them, with the diligence and reverence which their mission and character demanded. Their solutions of difficulties, and determinations of doubtful questions, must have been treasured up in the memory of their audiences, and transmitted for some time, from father to son. Every thing, at least, that was declared by the inspired teachers, to be necessary to salvation, must have been carefully recorded, and therefore what we find no traces of in the Scripture, or the early fathers, as most of the peculiar tenets of the Romish church, must certainly be concluded to be not necessary. Thus, by consulting first the Holy scriptures, and next the writers of the Primitive Church, we shall make ourselves acquainted with the will of God; thus shall we discover the good way, and find that rest for our souls which will amply recompense our studies and enquiries. . . .[3]

---

[1] Ibid., p. 356.   [2] Ibid., p. 357.   [3] Ibid., pp. 357–8.

In these words we have much of the essence of Johnson's religious philosophy. Perhaps, since the publication of Professor Donald Greene's *The Politics of Samuel Johnson*, it has become hazardous to apply the term 'conservative'—even with a small 'c'—to Johnson's outlook; but in matters of religion, if not in politics, he was both conservative and orthodox. Yet he took nothing for granted, and his stubbornly rational mind always preferred the testimony of ancient authority to the novelty of untried theory. If he made mistakes in his theological pronouncements, at least he had the consolation of knowing that he had searched for the truth by the light of reason, and through an exhaustive intellectual journey along the old paths. If, as a result, his theology is old-fashioned, we should remember that the epithet is one of which he would not have been in the least ashamed.

THE WEDDING OF RELIGION AND MORALITY

'The first qualification of a writer', contended Samuel Johnson, 'is a perfect knowledge of the subject which he undertakes to treat, since we cannot teach what we do not know, nor can properly undertake to instruct others, while we are ourselves in want of instruction.'[1] In the foregoing chapters much has been said about Johnson's qualifications for the task of sermon writing: his extensive acquaintance with homiletic literature from the Elizabethan age onwards; his broad tolerance and deep understanding of preachers whose doctrinal and denominational positions were in many ways different from those of the Church of England, of which he was, nevertheless, a staunch adherent; his lifelong preoccupation with questions of moral conduct and moral philosophy; and the qualities of his mind—obstinately rational, incredulous, inquiring, and perspicacious. That he possessed in full measure 'the first qualification of a writer' would be hard to deny.

'The next requisite', Johnson went on, 'is, that he be a master of the language in which he delivers his sentiments: if he treats of science and demonstration, that he has attained a stile clear, pure, nervous and expressive; if his topics be probable and persuasory,

---

[1] *Adventurer* 115, Yale Edn. ii. 460.

that he be able to recommend them by the superaddition of elegance and imagery, to display the colours of varied diction, and pour forth the music of modulated periods.'[1]

To achieve these two qualifications, mastery of the subject and ability to discuss it in the appropriate manner, a man must have 'read and compared the writers that have hitherto discussed it, familiarised their arguments to himself by long meditation, consulted the foundations of different systems, and separated truth from error by a rigorous examination'; and he must have 'carefully perused the best authors, accurately noted their diversities of stile, diligently selected the best modes of diction, and familiarised them by long habits of attentive practice'.[1] On all these counts, too, Johnson has an undoubted claim to be considered one of the best prepared sermon writers of his age.

In the composition of his sermons, as in the composition of nearly all his other works, Johnson stressed truth, utility, and application to the purposes of life. His aim was the promotion of piety, just as it was in his *Lives of the Poets*,[2] and his approach was that of the practical moralist who offered a Christian solution to the social and moral problems which confront humanity. His comments on the place of ethics in a scheme of education, provided in his Preface to *The Preceptor*, contains what might be considered his sermon philosophy as well. 'Ethicks, or morality', he writes there,

is one of the studies which ought to begin with the first glimpse of reason, and only end with life itself. Other acquisitions are merely temporary benefits, except as they contribute to illustrate the knowledge, and confirm the practice of morality and piety, which extend their influence beyond the grave, and increase our happiness through endless duration.

This great science, therefore, must be inculcated with care and assiduity, such as its importance ought to incite in reasonable minds; and for the prosecution of this design, fit opportunities are always at hand. As the importance of logick is to be shown by detecting false arguments, the excellence of morality is to be displayed by proving the deformity, the reproach, and the misery of all deviations from it.

[1] Ibid.
[2] See *Works*, viii, p. vii (Advertisement to *The Lives of the Poets*), *Lives*, i, p. xxvi.

Yet it is to be remembered, that the laws of mere morality are of no coercive power; and, however they may, by conviction, of their fitness please the reasoner in the shade, when the passions stagnate without impulse, and the appetites are secluded from their objects, they will be of little force against the ardour of desire, or the vehemence of rage, amidst the pleasures and tumults of the world. To counteract the power of temptations, hope must be excited by the prospect of rewards, and fear by the expectation of punishment; and virtue may owe her panegyricks to morality, but must derive her authority from religion.

When, therefore, the obligations of morality are taught, let the sanctions of Christianity never be forgotten; by which it will be shown that they give strength and lustre to each other; religion will appear to be the voice of reason, and morality the will of God.[1]

Thus Johnson believed religion and morality to be inextricably united, and his sermons were firmly based upon this premise.

An example of this union of religion and morality is to be found in Sermon I, which deals, appropriately enough, with the theme of marriage. After arguing that 'Society is necessary to the happiness of human nature', Johnson shows that marriage is 'an Institution designed only for the promotion of happiness, and for the relief of the disappointments, anxieties, and distresses, to which we are subject in our present state'. Marriage was 'appointed by God himself, as necessary to happiness, even in a state of innocence',[2] and, like every other divinely ordained state, it is systematically regulated by rules and obligations, one of which is the indispensable condition of male authority and female obedience. Johnson is careful, however, to qualify this condition:

But though obedience may be justly required, servility is not to be exacted; and though it may be lawful to exert authority, it must be remembered, that to govern and to tyrannize are very different, and that oppression will naturally provoke rebellion.

The great rule both of authority and obedience is the law of God; a law which is not to be broken for the promotion of any ends, or in compliance with any commands; and which indeed never can be violated without destroying that confidence, which is the great

---

[1] *Works*, v. 243–4.   [2] Ibid., ix. 289, 292, 298.

source of mutual happiness; for how can that person be trusted, whom no principles oblige to fidelity?

Thus Religion appears, in every state of life, to be the basis of happiness, and the operating power which makes every good institution valid and efficacious. And he that shall attempt to attain happiness by the means which God has ordained; and *shall leave his Father and his Mother, and shall cleave unto his Wife*, shall surely find the highest degree of satisfaction that our present state allows; if, in his choice, he pays the first regard to virtue, and regulates his conduct by the precepts of religion.[1]

It is interesting to note that, in the less directly homiletic context of *Rasselas*, Chapters XXVIII and XXIX, where the Prince and Nekayah debate the advantages and disadvantages of the marital state, Johnson advances similar arguments, and concludes, in the words of Rasselas, that 'prudence and benevolence will make marriage happy',[2] without, however, supporting this contention by invoking divine rather than natural law. 'Marriage', says Rasselas, 'is evidently the dictate of nature; men and women are made to be companions of each other; and, therefore, I cannot be persuaded, but that marriage is one of the means of happiness.'[3]

The bridge Johnson so often constructs between morality and religion always has the same keystone, which is best denoted by the word *system*. In the marriage sermon just quoted, for instance, he maintains that the system of nature ordains and produces 'connubial felicity', and it is only when the system is flouted and its obligations ignored that unhappiness sets in.[4] In more sweeping terms, he argues in Sermon VIII that

Every condition has, with regard to this life, its inconveniences, and every condition has likewise its advantages; though its position to the eye of the beholder may be so varied, as that at some times the misery may be concealed, and at other times the happiness; but to judge only by the eye, is not the way to discover truth. We may pass

---

[1] Ibid., pp. 299–300.   [2] Ibid., i. 260.

[3] Ibid., p. 258. While I am aware of the argument that *Rasselas* is in some respects patterned after the Book of Ecclesiastes and Bishop Simon Patrick's paraphrase thereof, the passages on marriage do not appear to me to have any such connection. See Thomas R. Preston, Bibl. 136.

[4] *Works*, ix. 298.

by men, without being able to distinguish whether they are to be numbered among those whose felicities, or whose sorrows, preponderate; as we may walk over the ground, without knowing, whether its entrails contain mines of gold, or beds of sand.

Nor is it less certain, that, with respect to the more important prospects of a future state, the same impartiality of distribution may be generally remarked; every condition of humanity, being exposed on one side, and guarded on the other; so that every man is burthened, though none are overwhelmed; every Man is obliged to vigilance, but none are harassed beyond their strength. The great business therefore of every man is to look diligently round him, that he may note the approaches of the enemy; and to bar the avenues of temptation, which the particular circumstances of his life are most likely to lay open; and to keep his heart in perpetual alarm against those sins which constantly besiege him. If he be rich, let him beware, lest when he is *full*, he *deny God*, and say, *who is the Lord*? If he be poor, let him cautiously avoid to *steal*, and, *take the name of his God in vain*.[1]

Once again, Johnson is arguing that the system of life imposes rules, duties, and obligations. Every station, every circumstance, every opportunity has its attendant rights and wrongs, and the great responsibility of the Christian is to learn to discriminate between them and to make his choice with courage and conviction. What he is preaching, here and elsewhere, is a resolute and positive commitment to life, not an escape from it.

But the main purpose of Sermon VIII, which is based upon the text from Romans 12: 16, 'Be not wise in your own conceits', is to consider the particular temptations which assail the men of learning, the scholar-teachers who, 'as they are themselves appointed the teachers of others . . . very rarely have the dangers of their own state set before them'.[2] That such men of learning are clearly self-deceived is the burden of Johnson's next argument. They are prone 'to fail in the direction of life',[2] to neglect the regulation of their own conduct, and, as they have grown in knowledge, to decrease in virtue. They have 'failed of the wisdom which is the gift of the Father of lights, because they have thought it unnecessary to seek it, with that anxiety and importunity, to which only it is granted;

---

[1] *Works*, ix. 359–60.   [2] Ibid., p. 361.

they have trusted to their own powers, and were *wise in their own conceits*.[1]

Now this argument has a special interest for Johnsonian scholars, and indeed for all readers of Boswell's *Life*, as it seems to take up some of the very temptations to which the Great Cham was himself so often exposed and to which he not infrequently succumbed. It is with full understanding of what he is saying that Johnson continues:

> There is perhaps no class of Men, to whom the precept given by the Apostle to his converts against too great confidence in their understandings, may be more properly inculcated, than those who are dedicated to the profession of literature; and are therefore necessarily advanced to degrees of knowledge above them who are dispersed among manual occupations, and the vulgar parts of life; whose attention is confined within the narrow limits of their own employments, and who have not often leisure to think of more than the means of relieving their own wants, by supplying the demands of others.[2]

The man of letters, then, is peculiarly inclined to belief in his own superiority, and to become inflated, authoritarian, and vain. Here Johnson refers to 'the insolent triumphs of intellectual superiority'[3] with which a man of this kind may indulge himself, and which lead to an exaggerated opinion of the value of his own utterances. This 'pernicious conceit of wisdom'[4] is particularly deplorable in those whose minds become closed by it, for

> ... he that neglects the improvement of his own mind, will never be enabled to instruct others. Light must strike on the body, by which light can be reflected. The disposition therefore, which best befits a young man, about to engage in a life of study, is patience in enquiry; eagerness of knowledge; and willingness to be instructed; a due submission to greater abilities and longer experience; and a ready obedience to those, from whom he is to expect the removal of his ignorance, and the resolution of his doubts.[5]

The state of the scholar requires 'submission to authority',[6] unusual self-discipline, unremitting devotion of time and energy,

---

[1] Ibid.   [2] Ibid., pp. 361–2.   [3] Ibid., p. 362.   [4] Ibid., p. 363.
[5] Ibid., pp. 363–4.   [6] Ibid., p. 364.

and unwearied patience; but these qualities are associated with modesty, not with ostentation: '. . . pride grasps at the whole, and what it cannot hold, it affects to despise; it is rather solicitous to display, than encrease, its acquisitions; and rather endeavours, by fame, to supply the want of knowledge, than by knowledge to arrive at fame'.[1] Turning to the teaching profession, Johnson, again speaking with the authority of personal experience, observes:

> There is no employment in which men are more easily betrayed to indecency and impatience, than in that of teaching; in which they necessarily converse with those, who are their inferiours, in the relation by which they are connected, and whom it may be sometimes proper to treat with that dignity which too often swells into arrogance; and to restrain with such authority as not every man has learned to separate from tyranny. In this state of temporary honour, a proud man is too willing to exert his prerogative; and too ready to forget that he is dictating to those, who may one day dictate to him. . . .[2]

Johnson then reminds his audience that teaching goes far beyond the schools, for '. . . The end of learning, is to teach the publick, to superintend the conduct, watch over the morals, and regulate the opinions of parishes, dioceses, and provinces; to check vices in their first eruption, and suppress heresies in the whispers of their rise. And surely this awful, this arduous task, requires qualities, which a man, *wise in his own conceit*, cannot easily attain. . . .'[2]

How is this 'pernicious conceit of wisdom' to be suppressed? By recognizing how vain and inadequate human judgement really is, and by reflecting that 'one great purpose of knowledge is to shew us our own defects, follies, and miseries';[3] in short, by realizing our vast ignorance and resting humble. A searching self-analysis will 'soon drive back the pedant to his college, with juster conceptions, and with humbler sentiments'.[4]

In the end, however, the most effective method of achieving humility is to apply himself 'to the duties of Religion, and the word of God, that sacred and inscrutable word, which will shew him the inefficacy of all other knowledge, and those duties which

[1] *Works*, ix. 365.   [2] Ibid., p. 366.   [3] Ibid., p. 367.
[4] Ibid., p. 368.

will imprint upon his mind, that he best understands the Sacred Writings who most carefully obeys them. Thus will humility fix a firm and lasting basis, by annihilation of all empty distinctions and petty competitions, by shewing, that *one thing only is necessary*, and that *God is all in all*.'[1] In this way, Johnson neatly and succinctly amalgamates morality and religion in the peroration of his sermon. Just as the marital state imposed certain duties and obligations which were consonant with the will of God, so the profession of teaching derives its ultimate sanction from the system enunciated in the scriptures, which demands obedience and humility. Drawing much the same conclusion as he drew in *Rambler* 154, which closely parallels Sermon VIII in many of its arguments, and in which he states that 'no estimate is more in danger of erroneous calculations than those by which a man computes the force of his own genius',[2] Johnson adds to it this religious truth, that the only absolute knowledge is the knowledge possessed by God.[3]

What he applies to systems within society, such as the state of marriage or the profession of teaching, Johnson also applies, in some of his sermons, to society as a whole, which he regarded as a complex macro-organism, with its appropriate rules and obligations, framed and defined by men interpreting the will of God. When any one of the rules was broken, or any one of the obligations left unhonoured, the whole code or system was breached, just as in legal matters a crime committed by one man against another was construed as detrimental to all. In Sermon XVII, dealing with the text from Exodus 20: 16, 'Thou shalt not bear false witness against thy neighbour', Johnson arrives at a characteristic synthesis of the legal, social, and divine aspects of human obligation.

Beginning with the observation that many men 'make partial and absurd distinctions between vices of equal enormity',[4] and treat some of the commandments of God with deference and others with contempt, he observes that 'it is a very dangerous mistake, to conceive that any man, by obeying one law, acquires the liberty of breaking another; or that all sins, equally odious to God, or hurtful to men, are not, with equal care, to be avoided'.[5] As an

[1] Ibid., p. 369.   [2] Ibid., iii. 230, Yale Edn. v. 55.   [3] *Works*, ix. 369.
[4] Ibid., p. 440.   [5] Ibid., p. 441.

illustration of human inconsistency in these matters, he points out that men who would sedulously avoid theft are not so conscientious in abstaining from calumny, despite the fact that 'Thou shalt not steal' and 'Thou shalt not bear false witness against thy neighbour' are commandments enjoined by the same authority. He then explains what is meant by 'bearing false witness': 'The highest degree of guilt forbidden by this law of God, is false testimony in a literal sense, or deliberate and solemn perjury in a court of justice, by which the life of an innocent man is taken away, the rightful owner stripped of his possessions, or an oppressor supported in his usurpations. . . .'[1] A lower degree of the same crime consists in attacking the reputation of another person by calumny or defamation, which is practised almost universally in society, often as a form of sport. Even if it is based on a partial truth, such defamation, in Johnson's view, constitutes a malicious falsehood. Those who spread or pass on such defamatory lies or half-truths are also guilty of a crime; and those who listen to them with expressed or silent approval are 'chargeable with conniving at wrong'.[2]

In precise, legal terms, Johnson then examines the sin of calumny, guiding himself by the principle that 'the malignity of an offence arises, either from the motives that prompted it, or the consequences produced by it'. Both the motives and the consequences, he finds, are 'of the worst kind'.[3]

The most usual incitement to defamation is envy, or impatience of the merit, or success, of others; a malice raised not by any injury received, but merely by the sight of that happiness which we cannot attain. This is a passion, of all others most hurtful and contemptible; it is pride complicated with laziness; pride which inclines us to wish ourselves upon the level with others, and laziness which hinders us from pursuing our inclinations with vigour and assiduity. Nothing then remains but that the envious man endeavour to stop those, by some artifice, whom he will not strive to overtake, and reduce his superiours to his own meanness, since he cannot rise to their elevation. To this end he examines their conduct with a resolution to condemn it; and, if he can find no remarkable defects, makes no scruple to aggravate smaller errours, 'till, by adding one vice to another, and

<hr>

[1] *Works*, ix. 442.   [2] Ibid., p. 446.   [3] Ibid., p. 447.

detracting from their virtues by degrees, he has divested them of that reputation which obscured his own, and left them no qualities to be admired or rewarded.[1]

Other motives for calumny are personal or professional resentment, and the mere desire 'to gratify the levity of temper and incontinence of tongue'.[2] Those who defame others for the sheer fun of it may mean no harm, but, Johnson contends, in an emphatically simple sentence, 'to deserve the exalted character of humanity and good-nature, a man must mean *well*; it is not sufficient to mean *nothing*'.[2]

The consequences of the crime of defamation are just as pernicious as the motives which give rise to it. 'He that attacks the reputation of another', argues Johnson, 'invades the most valuable part of his property, and perhaps the only part which he can call his own.'[2] When a good man is slandered, moreover, society as a whole is the loser:

Nothing can so much obstruct the progress of virtue, as the defamation of those that excel in it. For praise is one motive, even in the best minds, to superiour and distinguishing degrees of goodness; and therefore he that reduces all men to the same state of infamy, at least deprives them of one reward which is due to merit, and takes away one incitement to it. But the effect does not terminate here. Calumny destroys that influence, and power of example, which operates much more forcibly upon the minds of men, than the solemnity of laws, or the fear of punishment. Our natural and real power is very small; and it is by the ascendant which he has gained, and the esteem in which he is held, that any man is able to govern others, to maintain order in society, or to perform any important service to mankind, to which the united endeavours of numbers are required. This ascendant, which, when conferred upon bad men by superiority of riches, or hereditary honour, is frequently made use of to corrupt and deprave the world, to justify debauchery, and shelter villainy, might be employed, if it were to be obtained only by desert, to the noblest purposes. It might discountenance vanity and folly; it might make the fashion co-operate with the laws, and reform those upon whom reason and conviction have no force.[3]

---

[1] Ibid.   [2] Ibid., p. 448.   [3] Ibid., pp. 448–9.

The gravity of the sin of calumny, then, lies in its destructiveness to society as a whole, and in the irreparable harm it causes, for 'a false report may spread, where a recantation never reaches; and an accusation must certainly fly faster than a defence, while the greater part of mankind are base and wicked'.[1]

Johnson goes on to show how this vicious practice may be avoided. The suppression of those passions of envy and resentment which conduce to it is one way. A rational attitude to it is another: '. . . Let the envious man consider, that by detracting from the character of others, he in reality adds nothing to his own; and the malicious man, that nothing is more inconsistent with every law of God, and institution of men, than implacability and revenge.'[2] His next observation is a clever appeal to enlightened self-interest, followed by a call for compassion and charity:

If men would spend more time in examining their own lives, and inspecting their own characters, they would have less leisure, and less inclination, to remark with severity upon others. They would easily discover, that it will not be for their advantage to exasperate their neighbour, and that a scandalous falsehood may be easily revenged by a reproachful truth.

It was determined by our blessed Saviour, in a case of open and uncontested guilt, that *he who was without fault*, should *cast the first stone*. This seems intended to teach us compassion even to the failings of bad men; and certainly that religion which extends so much indulgence to the bad, as to restrain us from the utmost rigour of punishment, cannot be doubted to require that the good should be exempted from calumny and reproach.

Let it be always remembered, that charity is the height of religious excellence; and that it is one of the characteristicks of this virtue, that it *thinketh no ill of others*.[2]

In this sermon Johnson employs his legalistic and homiletic talents to unusual effect. His heart is obviously in the task, and the careful disposition of his arguments suggests an exceptional degree of forethought. The keen legal mind, the philosophical acumen of the dedicated moralist, and the ability to relate both the legalities and the moralities to the scriptural text are all

---

[1] *Works*, ix. 449.   [2] Ibid., p. 450.

apparent in this performance, which shows once again that Johnson was most at home with sermon themes that afforded a direct, practical application to the society he knew best.

An unusual opportunity for making a sermon of practical utility and application to society as a whole out of a contemporary situation of intense and widespread public interest was that provided by the trial and condemnation to death of the Reverend William Dodd, the forger, in 1777. In composing this sermon for the unhappy prisoner, who delivered it in the chapel of Newgate prison on 6 June, just three weeks before his execution, Johnson selected the text from Psalm 51: 3, 'I acknowledge my faults: and my sin is ever before me', and concentrated on the theme of repentance, which he had tackled, but without the same sense of immediacy, in two other sermons, V and VI. But he also used the occasion of Dodd's impending doom to make an appeal for confidence in his country's judicial processes. Just as in the sermon on false witness, in which he suggests that the withholding of relevant testimony is a serious crime in itself, since silence may contribute to calumny, so in Dodd's *Address to His Unhappy Brethren* he contends that a prisoner's reticence or equivocation on the eve of his punishment would prove injurious to the public good:

There is yet another crime possible, and, as there is reason to believe, sometimes committed in the last moment, on the margin of eternity. —Men have died with a stedfast denial of crimes, of which it is very difficult to suppose them innocent. By what equivocation or reserve they may have reconciled their consciences to falsehood, if their consciences were at all consulted, it is impossible to know. But if they thought, that when they were to die, they paid their legal forfeit, and that the world had no farther demand upon them; that therefore they might, by keeping their own secrets, try to leave behind them a disreputable reputation; and that the falsehood was harmless, because none were injured;—they had very little considered the nature of society. One of the principal parts of national felicity arises from a wise and impartial administration of justice. Every man reposes upon the tribunals of his country the stability of possession, and the serenity of life. He therefore who unjustly exposes the courts of judicature to suspicion, either of partiality or error, not only does an injury to those who dispense the laws, but diminishes the public confidence in the laws themselves, and shakes the foundation of public tranquillity.

For my own part, I confess, with deepest compunction, the crime which has brought me to this place; and admit the justice of my sentence, while I am sinking under its severity. And I earnestly exhort you, my fellow prisoners, to acknowledge the offences which have been already proved; and to bequeath to our country that confidence in public justice, without which there can be neither peace nor safety.[1]

That Johnson, who had—as Boswell and his other biographers have testified[2]—worked very hard to obtain a pardon for Dodd, should see fit, in this public *Address*, to stress the need for popular recognition of the justice of the sentence imposed upon him, is characteristic of the man. Well aware of the wave of public sympathy for Dodd's plight, as shown by the many petitions which had been drawn up on his behalf, Johnson none the less thought it prudent that Dodd himself should go on record as putting the public security before his private concern. Even in the letter which he composed for Dodd, petitioning the King's pardon, a similar note is struck:

I confess the crime, and own the enormity of its consequences, and the danger of its example. Nor have I the confidence to petition for impunity; but humbly hope, that publick security may be established, without the spectacle of a clergyman dragged through the streets, to a death of infamy, amidst the derision of the profligate and profane; and that justice may be satisfied with irrevocable exile, perpetual disgrace, and hopeless penury.[3]

In a wise and authoritative *Rambler* essay (114), composed a quarter of a century earlier, Johnson had expressed the view that 'A slight perusal of the laws by which the measures of vindictive and coercive justice are established, will discover so many disproportions between crimes and punishments, such capricious distinctions of guilt, and such confusion of remissness and severity, as can scarcely be believed to have been produced by publick

---

[1] Bibl. 8, pp. 19–20.

[2] *Life*, iii. 139–48. See also R. W. Chapman (ed.), *Papers Written by Dr. Johnson and Dr. Dodd in 1777* (Bibl. 12), pp. v–xvi.

[3] Chapman, op. cit., pp. 18–19. The letter is dated 22 June 1777. See also *Life*, iii. 144–5.

IV. 'The Revd. Dr. Dodd. Taken from the Life in Newgate the Morning of his Execution . . . by A. Hamilton Junr. . . . Aug. 1, 1777'

wisdom, sincerely and calmly studious of publick happiness.'[1] In the same essay, he discusses the deterrent value of capital punishment, pointing out that the lawgiver 'exercises the right which societies are supposed to have over the lives of those that compose them, not simply to punish a transgression, but to maintain order, and preserve quiet; he enforces those laws with severity, that are most in danger of violation, as the commander of a garrison doubles the guard on that side which is threatened by the enemy'.[2] He argues, moreover, that such severity can defeat its own ends: to mete out the death penalty for theft, for instance, is to reduce the currency of capital punishment:

To equal robbery with murder is to reduce murder to robbery; to confound in common minds the gradations of iniquity, and incite the commission of a greater crime to prevent the detection of a less. If only murder were punished with death, very few robbers would stain their hands in blood; but when, by the last act of cruelty, no new danger is incurred, and greater security may be obtained, upon what principle shall we bid them forbear?[3]

The effect on the public mind of disproportionate punishment is to excite sympathy for the unfortunate offender, and thus to impair the strength of the judicial process:

The obligations to assist the exercise of publick justice are indeed strong; but they will certainly be overpowered by tenderness for life. What is punished with severity contrary to our ideas of adequate retribution, will be seldom discovered; and multitudes will be suffered to advance from crime to crime, till they deserve death, because, if they had been sooner prosecuted, they would have suffered death before they deserved it.[4]

It is interesting to observe that, in writing the *Address* for the unfortunate Dr. Dodd, Johnson gave precedence to the condemned man's 'obligations to assist the exercise of publick justice',[4] and made no reference to the inequitability of the laws. Yet in another sermon (the Yale Manuscript Sermon),[5] which was addressed to

---

[1] *Works*, iii. 39, Yale Edn. iv. 242.   [2] *Works*, iii. 40, Yale Edn. iv. 243.
[3] *Works*, iii. 41, Yale Edn. iv. 244.   [4] *Works*, iii. 43, Yale Edn. iv. 246.
[5] Hereafter referred to as Sermon XXVI.

M

governors, and also concerned with the legal and moral codes, Johnson reverts to the arguments of *Rambler* 114: just as there are degrees or gradations of guilt, so there ought to be degrees or gradations of punishment, and capital punishment ought to be restricted to the most serious crimes.[1] We are justified in concluding that the immediate occasion of the Dodd sermon was such as to impel Johnson to defend public justice, however inequitable in that particular case, in the interests of society as a whole: another indication that, for him, a sermon should contain the utmost practical utility, even at the expense of personal interest. The moralist in him is more pertinacious than the defender of individual rights.

In the *Dictionary* Johnson defined the moralist as 'one who teaches the duties of life', and who knows 'the exact bounds, and different shades, of vice and virtue'. With respect to the public he is one who gives 'ardour to virtue, and confidence to truth'. He conceived the role of the preacher in similar terms: the preacher expounds and interprets the great truths of Christian morality, using as his raw material the experiences of life, and drawing from them the lessons already placed before us in the scriptures. Just as the pitiable plight of Dr. Dodd provided a sobering reminder to us to acknowledge our faults and to practise repentance, the death of a near and dear one calls us to the contemplation of our own mortality. The funeral sermon (XXV), to which brief reference has already been made, shows as clearly as any in the Taylor collection the manner in which the moralist and the man of religion combine to enunciate the duties which are implicit in the higher morality. Johnson begins by asserting that it is 'the privilege only of revealed religion' to 'afford adequate consolations to the last hour, to chear the gloomy passage through the valley of the shadow of death',[2] and to relieve the anxiety of the bereaved. Those who have not been favoured with 'the supernatural light of heavenly doctrine' have either died in the darkness of ignorance or tried 'to solace their passage with the fallacious and uncertain glimmer of philosophy'.[3] Some, however, 'appear to have sought a nobler, and a more certain,

---

[1] Sermon XXVI, pp. 7–8, 11–12.   [2] *Works*, ix. 517.
[3] Ibid., pp. 518–19.

remedy, and to have endeavoured to overpower the force of death by arguments, and to dispel the gloom by the light of reason. They inquired into the nature of the soul of man, and shewed, at least probably, that it is a substance distinct from matter, and therefore independent on the body, and exempt from dissolution and corruption.'[1]

But the arguments of these philosophers, however dispassionate, 'were such as required leisure and capacity, not allowed in general to mankind; they were such as many could never understand, and of which, therefore, the efficacy and comfort were confined to a small number without any benefit to the unenlightened multitude'.[1] Although philosophy may eventually establish the immateriality, and hence the immortality, of the soul, 'there never can be expected a time, in which the gross body of mankind can attend to such speculations, or can comprehend them; and therefore there never can be a time, in which this knowledge can be taught in such a manner, as to be generally conducive to virtue, or happiness, but by a messenger from God, from the Creator of the World, and the Father of Spirits'.[1] The 'peculiar excellence' of the Christian Gospel is that it teaches this knowledge in such a way as to 'influence the most narrow mind, and fill the most capacious intellect', as well as 'to supply a refuge and support to the mind, amidst all the miseries of decaying nature'.[2]

So much is the sting of death rebated by the Gospel, Johnson continues,

that we may now be invited to the contemplation of our mortality, as to a pleasing employment of the mind, to an exercise delightful and recreative, not only when calamity and persecution drive us out from the assemblies of men, and sorrow and woe represent the grave as a refuge and an asylum, but even in the hours of the highest earthly prosperity, when our cup is full, and when we have laid up stores for ourselves; for, in him who believes the promise of the Saviour of the World, it can cause no disturbance to remember, that this night his soul may be required of him; and he who suffers one of the sharpest evils which this life can shew, amidst all its varieties of misery; he that has lately been separated from the person whom a long participation

[1] Ibid., p. 519.   [2] Ibid., p. 520.

of good and evil had endeared to him; he who has seen kindness snatched from his arms, and fidelity torn from his bosom; he whose ear is no more to be delighted with tender instruction, and whose virtue shall be no more awakened by the seasonable whispers of mild reproof, may yet look, without horror, on the tomb which encloses the remains of what he loved and honoured, as upon a place which, if it revives the sense of his loss, may calm him with the hope of that state in which there shall be no more grief or separation.[1]

Having thus shown the means by which human sorrow may be converted into Christian hope, at the very moment when his heart was heavy with grief, Johnson proceeds to demonstrate that the celebration of funeral rites was established by the Christian Church for the consolation of grief and the enforcement of piety. In particular, contemplation of the mercy of God may afford some consolation, 'even when the office of burial is performed to those who have been snatched away without visible amendment of their lives', but —and here he is thinking of his own bereavement—'with more confident hope of pardon and acceptance, may we commit those to the receptacles of mortality, who have lived without any open or enormous crimes; who have endeavoured to propitiate God by repentance, and have died, at last, with hope and resignation.'[2] At this point in the sermon, he mentions his late wife's virtues, maintaining that 'her wit was never employed to scoff at goodness, nor her reason to dispute against truth. In this age of wild opinions, she was as free from scepticism as the cloistered virgin. She never wished to signalize herself by the singularity of paradox. She had a just diffidence of her own reason, and desired to practise rather than to dispute.'[3] Devout, charitable, patient in her sufferings, she was not entirely without fault:

That she had no failings, cannot be supposed: but she has now appeared before the Almighty Judge; and it would ill become beings like us, weak and sinful as herself, to remember those faults which, we trust, Eternal Purity has pardoned.

[1] *Works*, ix. 520–1. The fact that Johnson did not always treat the subject of death with such equanimity has already been noticed. See pp. 112–13 above.
[2] Ibid., pp. 522–3.   [3] Ibid., p. 523.

Let us therefore preserve her memory for no other end but to imitate her virtues; and let us add her example to the motives to piety which this solemnity was . . . instituted to enforce.[1]

It is characteristic of the author of *Rasselas* that he should utilize the hour of his sharpest grief to preach repentance and to inculcate virtue, however frail and unsuitable the example of his wife's life and character might have seemed to his contemporaries. It will be remembered that his friend, John Taylor, refused to preach the funeral sermon, reportedly on the grounds that the late Mrs. Johnson was unworthy of the panegyric it contained.[2] In this regard, the notice which appeared in *The Critical Review* for May 1788, on the occasion of the publication of the sermon by the Reverend Samuel Hayes, is quite illuminating:

This is, in many respects, an admirable discourse: it displays a pure, unaffected piety, little tinctured with the native, the constitutional gloom which hung over the author's mind. The opinions and the ideas are exact and discriminated, and the language has all Johnson's energy and vigour, without his peculiarities. If tradition has not conveyed to us the excellencies of Mrs. Johnson, this sermon shows us that she possessed some, or that her husband thought she did. From his character, we ought to conclude, that these were his sentiments at that time, though it may be allowed that in the period of mourning for a recent loss, the value of good qualities is often enhanced.[3]

This is not the place to discuss the appropriateness, or otherwise, of Johnson's praises of his much-criticized wife. The carefully chosen phrases of the reviewer make it plain that 'tradition' did not hold her in very high esteem. The important point is that, estimable or not, her character provided the kind of example best suited to his homiletic purpose: far from perfect, perhaps, yet devoid of 'any open or enormous crimes'. As he said in *Rambler* 60, in a discussion of the value of biography, even a humble and imperfect life

---

[1] Ibid., pp. 523–4.

[2] Hawkins, p. 314. See also Arthur Murphy, 'Essay on the Life and Genius of Dr. Johnson', *Works*, i, pp. lxxviii–lxxix; and Thomas Taylor, *A Life of John Taylor*, p. 53.

[3] LXV (1788), 397.

may afford a useful point of departure for the contemplation of our own:

I have often thought that there has rarely passed a life of which a judicious and faithful narrative would not be useful. For, not only every man has, in the mighty mass of the world, great numbers in the same condition with himself, to whom his mistakes and miscarriages, escapes and expedients, would be of immediate and apparent use; but there is such a uniformity in the state of man, considered apart from adventitious and separable decorations and disguises, that there is scarce any possibility of good or ill, but is common to human kind. . . . We are all prompted by the same motives, all deceived by the same fallacies, all animated by hope, obstructed by danger, entangled by desire, and seduced by pleasure.[1]

This was not only Johnson's philosophy of biography; it was also the basis of his homiletic practice. Even a funeral has its usefulness in terms of its moral application, both to those who are grief-stricken and to those who are indifferent:

Let those who came hither weeping and lamenting, reflect, that they have no time for useless sorrow; that their own salvation is to be secured, and that the day is far spent, and the night cometh, when no man can work; that tears are of no value to the dead, and that their own danger may justly claim their whole attention! Let those who entered this place unaffected and indifferent, and whose only purpose was to behold this funeral spectacle, consider, that she, whom they thus behold with negligence, and pass by, was lately partaker of the same nature with themselves; and that they likewise are hastening to their end, and must soon, by others equally negligent, be buried and forgotten![2]

THE THEME OF HAPPINESS

Of all the themes, apart from mortality, the vanity of human wishes, and the passing preciousness of time, which reminded him of the common lot of humanity, the most compelling for Johnson was happiness. The subject of the search for happiness is no less apparent in his sermons than in the rest of his writings and in his conversation. There is scarcely a sermon of his in which 'happiness'

[1] *Works*, ii. 286–7, Yale Edn. iii. 320.   [2] Ibid., ix. 525.

or 'felicity' or some variant thereof does not appear. It is the word, the idea, the concernment which binds the entire canon of his sermons together. As has just been shown, the theme of the funeral sermon (XXV) is the happiness or consolation which is to be derived from the Gospel even in the face of death itself. Likewise, the theme of the very first sermon, on marriage, is that religion, which 'appears, in every state of life, to be the basis of happiness', recommends marriage as a means by which 'the highest degree of satisfaction that our present state allows'[1] may be obtained.

Johnson approaches this theme of happiness in six different, if not mutually exclusive, ways in the sermons. In some of them, and most notably in Sermons I, XXI, and XXV, he shows how God, both through the Gospel and by other means, is disposed to produce and encourage human happiness. In others, such as Sermon II, he indicates how lost happiness may be restored through repentance. In a third group, and particularly in Sermon XIV, he demonstrates that man is always influenced by the prospect of happiness. In a fourth category, as exemplified by Sermons VIII, X, XIII, XVII, and XX, he describes some of the obstacles and barriers to happiness. In a fifth division, comprising mainly Sermons XII, XVI, XVIII, and XXIII, he discusses our illusions about happiness. And in the sixth and final group, by far the largest (Sermons III to VII, IX, XI, XV, XIX, XXII, XXIV, and XXVI), he is concerned with the many ways in which the practice of virtue leads to the attainment of happiness.

In the first of these groups *happiness* generally means domestic bliss, creature comfort, and the satisfaction of legitimate desires; in the second, peace of mind arising from the quieted conscience; in the third, and to some extent in the fourth, that elusive and often illusory joy, the chance of attaining which spurs us to action and gives us the strength to overcome hurdles; in the fifth, the recognition that true felicity is not of this world at all; and in the sixth, the ultimate reward of virtuous conduct. Once again, these categories are not rigidly separated, and indeed frequently overlap.

The first kind of happiness is the closest to pleasure. Marriage, as it is discussed in Sermon I, for instance, is 'the basis of happiness'

---

[1] Ibid., p. 300.

because it gratifies both the mind and the senses, and relieves disappointments, anxieties, and distresses—at least in theory. 'It is a proof of the regard of God for the happiness of mankind', argues Johnson, that the means, such as marriage, by which it may be attained are 'obvious and evident'.[1] In Sermon XXI this argument is carried a step further, and the theme of happiness interwoven with a discussion of the benevolent attributes of the deity. The 'eternal parent', we are told, is 'truly disposed' to promote the welfare of his creatures and 'to conduct them, through the greatest variety of circumstances, to the noblest perfection, and the highest degree of felicity', both in this world and in the next:

Were the mercies of the Lord limited to the tenure of our present existence, great and glorious as they are, the human mind would be clouded by the consciousness that a very few years must exclude us for ever from the participation of them. But since the glorious rays of life and immortality have dissipated the gloom that hung upon futurity, since, by the propitiatory sacrifice of the Son of God, death is disarmed of his sting, and the grave deprived of its victory, Divine goodness hath received its perfect consummation.[2]

The happiness we enjoy in this world, the writer contends, springs in large measure from the justly proportioned mechanisms by which man may gratify his temporal wishes safely, moderately, and adequately: this is but one of the manifestations of 'the divine providence and government of the creation', which also ensures that we may 'finally exchange' the pleasures of this world 'for those purer and incorruptible treasures reserved for the righteous in the kingdom of heaven'.[3] If the happiness theme is carried to unusually optimistic lengths in this sermon, which, as has been shown, may be only partially attributed to Johnson, the findings are not inconsistent with the definition of 'creature happiness' which he provides elsewhere.[4]

The second kind of happiness, the tranquillity of mind and spirit which proceeds from a settled conscience, is much more difficult to attain than the first. It comes only after plain, unhypocritical repentance, and unwavering reformation. These alone are

---

[1] *Works*, ix. 289.   [2] Ibid., pp. 481, 487.   [3] Ibid., p. 487.
[4] See Voitle, pp. 144 ff.

the means, Johnson instructs us in Sermon II, by which sinners 'may be restored to those hopes of happiness, from which they have fallen by their own fault'.[1] The condition of mind which prepares the way for such hopes is also the basis for the third kind of happiness, which Johnson never clearly defines, but which is envisaged always in prospect. Every man, he declares in Sermon XIV, is conscious

that he neither performs, nor forbears any thing upon any other motive than the prospect, either of an immediate gratification, or a distant reward; that whether he complies with temptation, or repels it, he is still influenced by the same general regard to his own felicity: but that when he yields to the solicitation of his appetite, or the impulse of his passions, he is overborn by the prevalence of the object before him; and when he adheres to his duty, in opposition to his present interest, he is influenced by the hopes of future happiness.[2]

The search for this kind of happiness, he continues, is almost bound to end in disappointment, because men

seek it where it is not to be found, because they suffer themselves to be dazzled by specious appearances, resign themselves up to the direction of their passions, and, when one pursuit has failed of affording them that satisfaction which they expected from it, apply themselves with the same ardour to another equally unprofitable, and waste their lives in successive delusions, in idle schemes of imaginary enjoyment; in the chase of shadows which fleet before them, and in attempts to grasp a bubble, which, however it may attract the eye by the brightness of its colour, is neither solid nor lasting, but owes its beauty only to its distance, and is no sooner touched than it disappears.[3]

The only solid and lasting form that this elusive happiness can take, then, is 'the perfect peace' which is found by one who has his mind 'stayed on God' and devoutly practises the injunction to love his neighbour.[4]

The fourth kind of happiness, which is closely allied to this, is the reward of eternal bliss, which lies beyond the barriers of self-esteem, procrastination, pretentiousness, calumny, and the mockery

---

[1] *Works*, ix. 302.   [2] Ibid., p. 414.   [3] Ibid., p. 415.
[4] Ibid., p. 423.

of religion. A man of learning who is 'wise in his own conceits', as Sermon VIII shows, for instance, achieves only a transitory form of self-satisfaction, 'for he will find that those whom he imagined so much below his own exaltation, often flourish in the esteem of the world, while he himself is unknown; and teaching those arts, by which society is supported, and on which the happiness of the world depends; while he is pleasing himself with idle amusements, and wasting his life upon questions, of which very few desire the solution'.[1] Procrastination is an equally formidable barrier to eternal happiness: Sermon X, on the text from Galatians, 6: 7, 'for whatsoever a man soweth, that shall he reap', points out that someone who postpones a devout regimen until it is too late may forfeit eternal bliss and expose himself to divine wrath:

As men please themselves with felicities to be enjoyed in the days of leisure and retreat; so among these felicities, it is not uncommon to design a reformation of life, and a course of piety. . . . Such men answer the reproaches of conscience with sincerity and intention of performance, but which they consider as debts to be discharged at some remote time. . . . Projects of future piety are, perhaps, not less common than of future pleasure, and are, as there is reason to fear, not less commonly interrupted; with this dreadful difference, that he who misses his intended pleasure, escapes a disappointment; but he who is cut off before the season of repentance, is exposed to the vengeance of an angry God.[2]

Again, in Sermon XIII, Johnson observes that there are some hypocrites who, perhaps recognizing that happiness is not to be found in this world, indulge 'the pleasures of sin for a season, and the hopes of happiness to eternity' by eating, drinking, and being merry, and following 'only a specious practice of religious duties', with the result that 'even the Christian religion has been depraved by artificial modes of piety, and succedaneous practices of reconciliation. Men have been ever persuaded, that by doing something, to which they think themselves not obliged, they may purchase an exemption from such duties as they find themselves inclined to violate: that they may commute with heaven for a temporal fine, and make rigour atone for relaxity'.[3] Sometimes this rigour leads men

---

[1] *Works*, ix. 368–9.   [2] Ibid., p. 383.   [3] Ibid., p. 407.

to false judgement of others. In Sermon XVII, where he expatiates on the commandment, 'Thou shalt not bear false witness against thy neighbour', Johnson observes that the spreading of a false report about someone else, however strong the suspicion may be, affects the happiness of those concerned: 'For, if suspicion be admitted for certainty, every man's happiness must be entirely in the power of those bad men, whose consciousness of guilt makes them easily judge ill of others, or whom a natural, or habitual jealousy inclines to imagine frauds or villainies, where none is intended.'[1] Furthermore, a false report 'may check a hero in his attempts for the promotion of the happiness of his country, or a saint in his endeavours for the propagation of truth'.[2]

At times Johnson approaches the subject of human happiness from a slightly different vantage point: that of the forces in life which are inimical to the best interests of society. One of these, which he discusses with unwonted heat in Sermon XX, is the force that expresses itself in contempt of religion. Addressing himself to the text from 2 Peter, 3:3, 'Knowing this first, that there shall come in the last days scoffers, walking after their own lusts', he sharply attacks both those who deride religion and those who seriously question the existence of God:

What delusion, what bigotry, is equal to this! Men neglect to search after eternal happiness for fear of being interrupted in their mirth. If others have been misled, they have been misled by their reverence for great authorities, or by strong prejudices of education. Such errours may be extenuated, and perhaps excused. They have at least something plausible to plead, and their assertors act with some show of reason. But what can the most extensive charity allege in favour of those men who, if they perish everlastingly, perish by their attachment to merriment, and their confidence in a jest?[3]

Later in the same sermon he describes the act of reviling and insulting God as 'an infatuation incredible, a degree of madness without a name',[4] and those who commit this act as enemies to society, guilty of an offence worse than robbery, perjury, and even murder, 'the crime of decoying our brother into the broad way of

---

[1] Ibid., p. 444.   [2] Ibid., p. 449.   [3] Ibid., pp. 476–7.
[4] Ibid., p. 478.

eternal misery, and stopping his ears against that holy voice that recalls him to salvation'.[1] Such men, indeed, commit a crime of Faustian proportions, by selling 'that soul which God has formed for infinite felicity' and hence defeating 'the great work of their redemption'.[2]

In the fifth group of sermons, in which Johnson describes the various illusions we entertain on the subject of a happiness which is not to be found, the homilist conceives of man as the victim of his own envy, unreasonable expectations, resentment, and self-interest. Envy, he contends, sometimes persuades a person to believe that others have found the felicity for which he himself has sought in vain. But, he notes in Sermon XII, the ambition to achieve a similar goal of happiness is never really satisfied:

... Every one wants something to happiness; and when he has gained what he first wanted, he wants something else; he wears out life in efforts and pursuits, and perhaps dies, regretting that he must leave the world, when he is about to enjoy it.

So great is our interest, or so great we think it, to believe ourselves able to procure our own happiness, that experience never convinces us of our impotence; and, indeed, our miscarriages might be reasonably enough imputed by us, to our own unskilfulness, or ignorance; if we were able to derive intelligence from no experience but our own. But surely we may be content to credit the general voice of mankind, complaining incessantly of general infelicity: and when we see the restlessness of the young, and peevishness of the old; when we find the daring and the active combating misery, and the calm and humble lamenting it; when the vigorous are exhausting themselves in struggles with their own condition, and the old and the wise retiring from the contest, in weariness and despondency; we may be content, at last, to conclude, that if happiness had been to be found, some would have found it, and that it is vain to search longer for what all have missed.[3]

This argument is strongly reminiscent of the words of Imlac in Chapter XVI of *Rasselas*: 'We are long before we are convinced, that happiness is never to be found, and each believes it possessed by others, to keep alive the hope of obtaining it for himself. . . .'[4]

[1] *Works*, ix. 478.   [2] Ibid., p. 479.   [3] Ibid., pp. 395–6.
[4] Ibid., i. 237.

The futility of the search for happiness often leads to the direct and deliberate contemplation of unhappiness, which, in turn, carries with it the temptation to 'charge God foolishly'. This temptation is the theme of Sermon XVI:

There is no crime more incident to those whose life is imbittered with calamities, and whom afflictions have reduced to gloom and melancholy, than that of repining at the determinations of providence, or of 'charging God foolishly'. They are often tempted to unseemly inquiries into the reasons of his dispensations, and to expostulations about the justice of that sentence which condemns them to their present sufferings. They consider the lives of those whom they account happier than themselves, with an eye of malice and suspicion, and if they find them no better than their own, think themselves almost justified in murmuring at their own state.[1]

Johnson stresses the falsity of such thoughts. In particular, he points out, any comparisons we may make between the lot of other people and our own are likely to be founded on ignorance: 'we admit conjectures for certainties, and chimeras for realities':

To determine the degrees of virtue and wickedness in particular men, is the prerogative only of that Being that searches the secrets of the heart, that knows what temptations each man has resisted; how far the means of grace have been afforded him, and how he has improved or neglected them; that sees the force of every passion, knows the power of every prejudice, attends to every conflict of the mind, and marks all the struggles of imperfect virtue. . . . Nor are we able to decide, with much greater certainty, upon the happiness of others. We see only the superficies of men, without knowing what passes within. Splendour, equipage, and luxury, are not always accompanied by happiness; but are more frequently the wretched solaces of a mind distracted with perplexities, and harassed with terrours. . . .[2]

He goes on to observe that prosperity and happiness are very different from one another, 'though by those who undertake to judge of the state of others they are always confounded'.[3] The surface appearance of riches and success may simply cloak unhappiness. Instead of envying the imagined happiness of others, then, we

---

[1] *Works*, ix. 433.   [2] Ibid., pp. 438-9.   [3] Ibid., p. 439.

should apply ourselves to 'the great work of self-examination and repentance': 'Let this instant begin a new life! and every future minute improve it! Then, in exchange for riches, honours, or sensual delights, we may obtain the tranquillity of a good conscience and that "peace of God which passeth all understanding".'[1]

If envy supports human illusions about happiness, the irascible passions, the passions of resentment, are both obstructive and destructive. In the opening passages of Sermon XVIII Johnson notes that the moralists have divided the passions into two categories, the irascible and the concupiscible: the direct aim of the first is to make other people miserable, of the second to promote our own good. He continues,

> The desire of happiness is inseparable from a rational being, acquainted, by experience, with the various gradations of pain and pleasure. The knowledge of different degrees of happiness seems necessary to the excitement of desire, and the stimulation of activity. He that had never felt pain, would not fear it, nor use any precaution to prevent it. He who had been always equally at ease, would not know that his condition admitted any improvement, and, therefore, could have no end to pursue, or purpose to prosecute. But man, in his present state, knowing of how much good he is capable, and to how many evils he is exposed, has his mind perpetually employed, in defence, or in acquisition, in securing that which he has, or attaining that which, he believes, he either does, or shall, want.
>
> He that desires happiness must necessarily desire the means of happiness, must wish to appropriate, and accumulate, whatever may satisfy his desires. It is not sufficient to be without want. He will try to place himself beyond the fear of want; and endeavour to provide future gratifications for future wishes, and lay up in store future provisions for future necessities.[2]

The universal desire to obtain the means of happiness, Johnson argues, has led to the 'opinion of the civilized world, that he who would be happy must be rich'.[2] This view has produced much corruption, ranging from the petty crimes of the poor to the usurpation of kingdoms by power-hungry conquerors. One of its most pernicious products is fraud, which 'obstructs the happiness

---

[1] *Works*, ix. 440.   [2] Ibid., p. 452.

of the world'.[1] Thus Johnson has produced a variation on the old homiletic text, so adroitly manipulated by Chaucer's Pardoner, *radix malorum est cupiditas*: the root cause of unhappiness is the desire for happiness itself.

It is interesting to note that Johnson takes up this theme once again in Sermon XXIII, which was written to be preached on 30 January, the anniversary of the martyrdom of Charles I. Here he points out that, since the unhappiness of man is self-evident, writers of every shade of opinion have dilated upon it, ranging from 'the inspired teachers of religion' who 'admonish us of our frailty and infelicity, that they may incite us to labour after a better state' to 'the vainest and loosest author' who advises us to 'eat and drink, for to-morrow we die'.[2] You would think, says Johnson, that, with all this talk of unhappiness about, men 'would join in a perpetual confederacy against the certain, or fortuitous, troubles to which they are exposed', and 'universally co-operate in the proportion of universal felicity'.[2] Yet this highly desirable expectation is doomed to disappointment, for

A slight survey of life will show that, instead of hoping to be happy in the general felicity, every man pursues a private and independent interest, proposes to himself some peculiar convenience, and prizes it more, as it is less attainable by others.

When the ties of society are thus broken, and the general good of mankind is subdivided into the separate advantages of individuals, it must necessarily happen, that many will desire what few can possess, and consequently, that some will be fortunate by the disappointment, or defeat, of others, and, since no man suffers disappointment without pain, that one must become miserable by another's happiness.[3]

Such a conflict of self-interests produces strife, confusion, and national disunity of the kind that led to the execution of the king.

The sermons discussed so far in this chapter might well appear to be little more than a repetition and enlargement of the themes of *The Vanity of Human Wishes* and *Rasselas*. Certainly, the 'celestial wisdom' that 'calms the mind, And makes the happiness she does not find'[4] appears to be the solution recommended by the homilist

---

[1] Ibid., p. 454. [2] Ibid., p. 496. [3] Ibid., p. 497.
[4] *The Vanity of Human Wishes*, ll. 367–8, in *Works*. i. 22; Yale Edn. vi, p. 109, ll. 367–8.

as well as by the poet. The only possible happiness is that of the next world, and the only true path to it is virtue in this. Even fear of the Lord, as Sermon III instructs us, is the instrument by which we 'may be prepared for everlasting happiness'.[1] That there is 'no duty more necessary to the support of order, and the happiness of society'[1] than charity is the primary argument of Sermon IV. Again, in Sermon V, which deals with the miseries of life, the question of happiness in relation to virtue is carefully explored:

> We are informed by the Scriptures, that God is not the author of our present state; that when he created man, he created him for happiness; happiness indeed dependent upon his own choice, and to be preserved by his own conduct: for such must necessarily be the happiness of every reasonable being; that this happiness was forfeited by a breach of the conditions to which it was annexed; and that the posterity of him that broke the covenant were involved in the consequences of his fault. Thus religion shows us, that physical and moral evil entered the world together; and reason and experience assure us, that they continue for the most part so closely united, that, to avoid misery, we must avoid sin, and that, while it is in our power to be virtuous, it is in our power to be happy, at least, to be happy to such a degree, as may leave little room for murmur and complaints.[2]

While admitting that there are disasters and 'distempers' which 'no caution can secure us from, and which appear to be more immediately the strokes of heaven', Johnson suggests, somewhat rationalistically, that 'these are not of the most painful or lingering kind; they are for the most part acute and violent, and quickly terminate, either in recovery or death; and it is always to be remembered, that nothing but wickedness makes death an evil'.[3] Later in the same sermon he contends that pride is 'the general source of our infelicity',[3] as it inflates us with exaggerated expectations of our own powers, expectations which are seldom realized. Then he puts his whole argument into a nutshell: 'We fail of being happy, because we determine to obtain felicity by means different from those which God hath appointed.'[4]

---

[1] *Works*, ix. 319.   [2] Ibid., pp. 332–3.
[3] Ibid., p. 335.   [4] Ibid., p. 336.

Extending the argument that 'unhappiness will be diffused, as virtue prevails' into Sermon VI, which deals at length with the sin of pride, Johnson concentrates his attack on what he calls 'the pride of prosperity':

To consider this motive to pride more attentively, let us examine what it is to be prosperous. To be prosperous, in the common acceptation, is to have a large, or an increasing, fortune, great numbers of friends and dependents, and to be high in the esteem of the world in general. But do these things constitute the happiness of man? of a being accountable to his Creator for his conduct, and, according to the account he shall give, designed to exist eternally in a future state of happiness, or misery? What is the prosperity of such a state, but the approbation of that God, on whose sentence futurity depends? But neither wealth, friendships, or honours, are proofs of that approbation, or means necessary to procure it. They often endanger, but seldom promote, the future happiness of those that possess them. And can pride be inspired by such prosperity as this?[1]

Just as the pride of prosperity is illusory and vain, so are newfangled ideas and ill-founded creeds: this, at any rate, is the argument of Sermon VII, which strongly recommends the 'old paths' in philosophy and religion:

The serenity and satisfaction at which we arrive by a firm and settled persuasion of the fundamental articles of our religion, is very justly represented by the expression of finding rest for the soul. A mind restless and undetermined, continually fluctuating betwixt various opinions, always in pursuit of some better scheme of duties, and more eligible system of faith, eager to embrace every new doctrine, and adopt the notions of every pretender to extraordinary light, can never be sufficiently calm and unruffled, to attend to those duties which procure that peace of God which passeth all understanding.[2]

One of the main aims of this sermon is to show 'the happiness which attends a well-grounded belief, and steady practice of religion'.[2] While the theme of happiness is not always as obviously woven into the fabric of the sermons, almost invariably we find some reference to the conjunction of virtue and felicity. Sermon IX,

<hr />

[1] Ibid., pp. 347–8.   [2] Ibid., p. 358.

for instance, one of Johnson's Communion sermons, reminds us that a man who practises his devotions regularly, and partakes of the sacraments, 'will be able to persevere in a steady practice of virtue, and enjoy the unspeakable pleasures of a quiet conscience'.[1] Again, in Sermon XI, which discusses the virtues of compassion, sympathy, charity, and courtesy, Johnson singles out sympathy as 'the great source of social happiness', pointing out that the term connotes not only 'mourning with those that mourn', but also 'rejoicing with them that rejoice'—an activity which is not always easy to perform:

> To feel sincere and honest joy at the success of another, though it is necessary to true friendship, is perhaps neither very common, nor very easy. There is in every mind, implanted by nature, a desire of superiority, which counteracts the pleasure, which the sight of success and happiness ought always to impart. . . . As cruelty looks upon misery without partaking pain, so envy beholds increase of happiness without partaking joy.[2]

Extending this argument for a self-disciplined attitude to the lot of others, Johnson suggests in Sermon XV that contemplation of the shortness and misery of life is a salutary and important practice. Taking as his text Job 14: 1, 'Man that is born of woman, is of few days, and full of trouble', he explains that such an austere form of meditation 'is one of those intellectual medicines, of which the nauseous essence often obstructs the benefit, and which the fastidiousness of nature prompts us to refuse'.[3] None the less, to take a straight look at the miserable condition of men is as much a duty as to alleviate their distress.

In Sermon XIX the relationship between the alleviation of distress and 'the general happiness of society' is carefully explored:

> If we cast our eyes over the earth, and extend our observations through the system of human beings, what shall we find but scenes of misery and innumerable varieties of calamity and distress, the pains of sickness, the wounds of casualty, the gripings of hunger, and the cold of nakedness; wretches wandering without an habitation, exposed to the contempt of the proud, and the insults of the cruel,

---

[1] *Works*, ix. 374   [2] Ibid., p. 389.   [3] Ibid., p. 423.

goaded forward, by the stings of poverty, to dishonest acts, which perhaps relieve their present misery, only to draw some more dreadful distress upon them? And what are we taught, by all these different states of unhappiness? What, but the necessity of that virtue by which they are relieved; by which the orphan may be supplied with a father, and the widow with a defender; by which nakedness may be clothed, sickness set free from adventitious pains; the stranger solaced in his wanderings, and the hungry restored to vigour and to ease?[1]

Johnson then argues that charity is a duty which we are pressed to practice 'by every principle of secular, as well as religious wisdom'.[2] It is wise to be charitable when our circumstances are comfortable, for the time may come when we, too, are in need. He continues: 'If we endeavour to consult higher wisdom than our own, with relation to this duty, and examine the opinions, of the rest of mankind, it will be found, that all the nations of the earth, however they may differ with regard to every other tenet, yet agree in the celebration of benevolence, as the most amiable disposition of the heart, and the foundation of all happiness.'[2] Both the holy scriptures and 'the common prudence of mankind' have prescribed for us the rules to be observed in the practice of charity:

It is necessary that, in bestowing our alms, we should endeavour to promote the service of God, and the general happiness of society, and, therefore, we ought not to give them without inquiry into the ends for which they are desired; we ought not to suffer our beneficence to be made instrumental to the encouragement of vice, or the support of idleness; because what is thus squandered may be wanted by others, who would use our kindness to better purposes, and who, without our assistance, would perhaps perish.[3]

This argument is in keeping with the view which Johnson expressed in his Preface to the *Proceedings of the Committee Appointed to Manage the Contributions for Cloathing French Prisoners of War*, published in 1760: 'That charity is best, of which the consequences are most extensive: the relief of enemies has a tendency to unite mankind in fraternal affection. . . .'[4] But whether it is consistent with Johnson's own practice, which was the apparently

[1] Ibid., p. 463.
[2] Ibid., p. 464.
[3] Ibid., pp. 466–7.
[4] Ibid., vi. 148.

indiscriminate dispensation of charity to whatever beggars and derelicts applied to him for it, is a debatable question.[1]

The promotion of the general happiness of society is not only the work of charity. The persistent desire by society for happiness, Johnson contends in Sermon XXIV, resulted in the institutions of government in the first place. That these very institutions 'have been perverted to very different ends from those which they were intended to promote'[2] is easy to demonstrate. One such perversion is dictatorship, and another is anarchy, and both of them lead to unhappiness:

Man is, for the most part, equally unhappy, when subjected, without redress, to the passions of another, or left, without control, to the dominion of his own. . . .

Government is, therefore, necessary, in the opinion of every one, to the safety of particular men, and the happiness of society. . . .[3]

The rest of this sermon is concerned with three aspects of social happiness:

FIRST: How much it is the duty of those in authority to promote the happiness of the people.

SECONDLY: By what means the happiness of the people may be most effectually promoted.

THIRDLY: How the people are to assist and further the endeavours of their governours.[4]

The happiness of the people is promoted by the governors' close attention to their 'wants and petitions', and to the maintenance of their security, the protection of their liberty, and the extension of commerce. 'To be happy we must know our own rights; and we must know them to be safe.'[5] Yet Johnson is the first to admit that security, freedom, and prosperity do not, in themselves, guarantee happiness:

The husbandman may plough his fields with industry, and sow them with skill; he may manure them copiously, and fence them carefully; but the harvest must depend at last on celestial influence; and all his diligence is frustrated, unless the sun sheds its warmth, and the clouds pour down their moisture.

---

[1] See Voitle, pp. 117–23.   [2] *Works*, ix. 506.   [3] Ibid., p. 507.
[4] Ibid., pp. 507–8.   [5] Ibid., p. 510.

Thus, in all human affairs, when prudence and industry have done their utmost, the work is left to be completed by superiour agency; and in the security of peace, and stability of possession, our policy must at last call for help upon religion.[1]

The first duty of the governor, then, is 'to diffuse through the community a spirit of religion, to endeavour that a sense of the Divine authority should prevail in all orders of men'.[2] In return for just rule, the people must respect and obey the laws, even when they recognize imperfections in their government. 'The happiness of a nation', Johnson concludes, 'must arise from the combined endeavours of governours and subjects.'[3]

In Sermon XXVI, which deals with a similar theme, and which is addressed to 'that Class of Men whose Province it is to super-intend others', Johnson begins by illustrating the text from Proverbs 20: 8, 'A King that sitteth in the Throne of Judgement, scattereth away all Evil with his Eyes':

Among the Precepts delivered by Solomon for the Conduct of Life, and the Attainment of Happiness, some relate to moral duties and general obligations, and therefore are equally to be observed by Men of all Conditions and all Employments, but there are likewise many admonitions directed to particular Characters, in which the separate duties of the different orders of society are inculcated, and in which those dangers are pointed out by which every state is immediately besieged. From his writings may youth learn to avoid Negligence, and old age to beware of Avarice; Prosperity may be warned against Wantonness and Pride, and Power against Cruelty and Oppression; Poverty may be taught Resignation and Disappointment may be supported against Despair.[4]

In the quoted text he sees 'the whole doctrine of civil Polity':

The King is placed above the Rest that he may from his exalted Station survey all the Subordinations of Society, that he may observe and obviate those Vices and Corruptions by which Peace is disturbed, Justice violated, or Security destroyed; he *sitteth in the Throne of Judge-ment* to scatter *away Evil,* and is required to scatter it away *with his Eyes* by constant care, and vigilant Observation.[5]

---

[1] Ibid., p. 512.   [2] Ibid., p. 513.   [3] Ibid., p. 516.
[4] Yale MS., pp. 2–3.   [5] Ibid., p. 3.

Johnson then notes that the duties of the king 'claim likewise the attention of all Magistrates in a degree proportioned to their dignity and their Power'.[1] The end of all government is to suppress or dissipate evil by means of a just and equitable criminal code, supplemented by a resolute campaign to combat idleness, which is 'the original or parent vice'.[2] The beneficial legislator, unlike the tyrant, derives his happiness from the eradication of idleness; and the happiness of the people 'is best secured by Virtue'.[3] In the conclusion of this sermon Johnson clearly states that the governors and legislators must safeguard both the temporal and the eternal happiness of their subjects.

The one constant theme pervading all Johnson's sermons, then, is the search for happiness, both in this world and in the next: that form of happiness which transcends the vanity of human wishes and the transitoriness of life, and which derives its promise and its strength both from the harmonious workings of society and from the message of the Christian faith. The homilist in Johnson is constantly aware of all the various disturbers of human quiet, extending from man's self-imposed tyrannies and iniquities to that ominous final menace, death itself. It may be said that, within the canon of his sermons, lies the solution to that very problem which vexed him and often appeared to obsess him, the problem of reconciling the misery and the wickedness of the temporal state with the Christian hope of redemption and of happiness eternal.

[1] Yale MS., p. 3.   [2] Ibid., pp. 4, 19.   [3] Ibid., p. 24.

IV

The Form and Style of the Sermons

JOHNSON'S CONCEPTION OF THE SERMON AS A SPECIES OF LITERARY ART

IF he was a traditionalist in his choice and treatment of theological problems, Samuel Johnson was also a treader in the 'old paths' in his approach to the writings of sermons. For one thing, he had memorized The Book of Common Prayer with characteristic thoroughness. It will also be remembered that, in childhood, he had shown an unusual interest in the problems of the faith by attempting to read the *De Veritate Religionis* of Hugo Grotius,[1] and that in young manhood he had begun composing prayers, translating the Collects into Latin, and planning handbooks of devotion.[2] Throughout his career he continued to pursue all these interests, and acquired the habit of reading the New Testament in Greek at the rate of 160 verses every Sunday.[3] His personal library contained a high proportion of Biblical commentaries, volumes of sermons, devotional treatises, and scriptural texts. He not only read, but imbibed and practised the earnest injunctions of theologians like William Law and Richard Baxter and Jeremy Taylor. Persuasive manuals like *The Whole Duty of Man* and *The Causes of the Decay of Piety*, with their stress on rigorous moral discipline, together with solemn hortatives such as Taylor's *Rules and Exercises of Holy Living and Dying* and Thomas à Kempis's *The Imitation of Christ* impressed him more and more as he grew older.[4] Above all, he was a diligent

[1] See *Life*, i. 40, and *Johnsonian Miscellanies*, i. 157.
[2] See *Life*, iv. 381 n. 1, and Hawkins, p. 81.
[3] *Life*, ii. 288. See also *Diaries*, p. 102 and n., where the rate is given as 'six verses a minute'.
[4] See *Life*, i. 527, v. 227, iii. 34 n. 3. In *Life*, iii. 226, Johnson is quoted as saying, 'Thomas à Kempis . . . must be a good book, as the world has opened its arms to receive it.' See also *Life*, iv. 21 and n. 3, where we are told that he read à Kempis in Low Dutch to assure himself that his mental faculties were still sound. Hawkins, p. 543, reports that Johnson later discarded à Kempis, as the main design of the *De*

reader of the Bible, and of several of its leading commentators. 'To be sure, Sir,' he told Boswell, 'I would have you read the Bible with a commentary; and I would recommend Lowth and Patrick on the Old Testament, and Hammond on the New.'[1]

With his vast background of religious inquiry and learning, and his obvious skill in hermeneutics, it is not surprising that Johnson should have become interested in the art of the sermon. What is a little surprising, perhaps, is the fact that he did not much relish listening to sermons. He went more frequently to church, Boswell informs us, when there were prayers only, than when there was also a sermon, 'as the people required more an example for the one than the other; it being much easier for them to hear a sermon, than to fix their minds on prayer'.[2] For that matter, he was not as fastidious about church attendance in general as one might expect, and we find him confessing his shame over this deficiency in his private diaries.[3] Of the many explanations that have been offered for his laxity in church attendance, the simplest are probably the most accurate: his deafness made it difficult for him to hear the service, and the standards of pulpit oratory in his day were such that he was more often bored than edified. He observed to his friend Dr. William Maxwell that 'the established clergy in general did not preach plain enough; and that polished periods and glittering sentences flew over the heads of the common people, without any impression upon their hearts'. He added that 'the new concomitants of methodism' might help to improve the situation by exciting 'the affections of the common people, who were sunk in languor and lethargy'.[4] And to George Steevens he once admitted,

I am convinced I ought to be present at divine service more frequently than I am; but the provocations given by ignorant and affected preachers too often disturb the mental calm which otherwise would

Imitatione was to 'promote monastic piety, and inculcate ecclesiastical obedience', but I have found no corroboration of this elsewhere. It appears that Johnson took up this study on two separate occasions, in 1773 and in 1782. See Johnsonian Miscellanies, ii. 153–4, and Diaries, p. 333.

[1] Life, iii. 58. See also Johnsonian Miscellanies, i. 100, 107, and ii. 19.
[2] Life, ii. 173.
[3] Diaries, pp. 144, 153, 267 (entries for 23 Sept. 1771; 9 Apr. 1773; and 6 Apr. 1777).
[4] Life, ii. 123 and n. 3.

succeed to prayer. I am apt to whisper to myself on such occasions—
How can this illiterate fellow dream of fixing attention, after we have
been listening to the sublimest truths, conveyed in the most chaste
and exalted language, throughout a Liturgy which must be regarded
as the genuine offspring of piety impregnated by wisdom?[1]

This prejudice against the ignorant and affected preacher perhaps
explains, in part, why Johnson, in his own sermons, strives to make
his points on the level of common sense, avoids, in general, emotional outbursts of a hortatory or ejaculatory kind, and relates
what he has to say, whenever possible, to the Liturgy contained
in The Book of Common Prayer. Whether he succeeded in avoiding
the 'polished periods and glittering sentences' which 'flew over
the heads of the common people' is more debatable. But in fairness
we should remember that he quoted with approval Richard Baxter's
rule 'in every sermon that he preached, to say something that was
above the capacity of his audience';[2] and that one of the reasons
Boswell gives for Johnson's not taking holy orders was his conviction that 'his temper and habits rendered him unfit for that
assiduous and familiar instruction of the vulgar and ignorant which
he held to be an essential duty in a clergyman'.[3]

The 'plain and familiar manner' which Johnson considered so
successful in Methodist preaching, and which he described as 'the
only way to do good to the common people', and worthy of emula-
tion by 'clergyman of genius and learning', was evidently beyond
his reach; and yet, as I propose to show later,[4] there is in Johnson's
homiletics a quality of plainness that somehow transcends the
erudite phrases and the neatly turned periods, or more properly,
that is assisted rather than hindered by the magnificence of his
manner.

In writing sermons for other people, Johnson made few concessions to their views and personalities; except in the rare instances,
discussed in the first chapter, where he helped someone of different
opinions to express them adequately, he stuck to his own beliefs
and staunchly defended his own orthodoxy. Hawkins has testified
to the truth of this in his biography of Johnson: '. . . he was not so

---

[1] *Johnsonian Miscellanies*, ii. 319. See Edward Williamson, Bibl. 161.
[2] *Life*, iv. 185.   [3] Ibid., i. 320.   [4] See pp. 186–7 and 200 ff. below.

indifferent to the subjects that he was requested to write on, as at any time to abandon either his religious or political principles'.[1] Indeed, as I have demonstrated, when his political views were in conflict with those of John Taylor, Johnson merely avoided discussion of the controversial issues.[2] In any case, he seemed to feel that the preacher himself could adapt the sermon to his own purposes, and supplement it with anything that might assist the communication of his message, including physical actions in the pulpit: 'Yet as all innocent means are to be used for the propagation of truth, I would not deter those who are employed in preaching to common congregations from any practice which they may find persuasive, for, compared with the conversion of sinners, propriety and elegance are less than nothing.'[3]

Thus the sermon itself is primarily an instrument of persuasion, with which other instruments, such as the force of the preacher's personality, may be combined for effectiveness. Like Richard Hooker, who had considered preaching to be 'the blessed ordinance of God', and to whom sermons were 'as keys to the Kingdom of Heaven, as wings to the soul, as spurs to the good affections of man', he was enough of a realist to understand that 'sermons are not the only preaching which doth save souls'.[4]

In the *Dictionary* Johnson defines a sermon as 'a discourse of instruction pronounced by a divine for the edification of the people', and it is from Hooker that he draws his first illustration: 'As for our *sermons*, be they never so sound and perfect, God's word they are not, as the *sermons* of the prophets were. . . .' This example is in accord with another statement of Hooker's: 'For, touching our sermons, that which giveth them their very being is the wit of man, and therefore they oftentimes accordingly taste too much of that over-corrupt fountain from which they come.'[5]

To avoid the intrusion of his inimitable personality in the sermons he composed for others, Johnson may, as Laetitia Hawkins suggested, have tried to 'keep down' his style,[6] but not with much success. He did, however, succeed in letting the plain word of God

[1] Hawkins, p. 85.   [2] See pp. 25–6 above.
[3] *Idler* 90, Yale Edn. ii. 281.   [4] *Works*, Bibl. 104, ii. 76–7.
[5] Ibid., p. 89.
[6] *Memoirs, Anecdotes, Facts, and Opinions*, i. 163. See p. 10 above.

speak for itself by adhering closely to the scriptural text, and by using, as far as possible, the words of The Book of Common Prayer in the reiteration of his point. He was guided, moreover, by the specifications of the Prayer Book for sermons on special occasions, as Sermon XXIII, written for 30 January, in commemoration of the martyrdom of Charles I, clearly demonstrates. For this day, The Book of Common Prayer requires that the sermon should denounce disobedience and wilful rebellion. In compliance with this requirement, Johnson advances strongly conservative views on the subject of order and disorder. Keeping in mind his text, 'Where envying and strife is, there is confusion' (Jas. 3:16), he observes:

Of the strife, which this day brings back to our remembrance, we may observe, that it had all the tokens of *strife* proceeding from *envy*. The rage of the faction, which invaded the rights of the Church and Monarchy, was disproportionate to the provocation received. The violence, with which hostility was prosecuted, was more than the cause, that was publickly avowed, could incite or justify. Personal resentment was apparent in the persecution of particular men, and the bitterness of faction broke out in all the debates upon publick questions. No securities could quiet suspicion, no concessions could satisfy exorbitance. Usurpation was added to usurpation, demand was accumulated on demand; and, when war had decided against loyalty, insult was added to insult, and exaction to exaction. . . .

Such was the *strife*, and such was the *confusion*. Such are the evils which God sometimes permits to fall upon nations, when they stand secure in their own greatness, and forget their dependence on universal sovereignty, depart from the laws of their Maker, corrupt the purity of his worship, or swerve from the truth of his revelation. Such evils surely we have too much reason to fear again, for we have no right to charge our Ancestors with having provoked them by crimes greater than our own.[1]

Thus Johnson fulfils the requirements of The Book of Common Prayer for the occasion, by denouncing rebelliousness, striking the proper penitential note, and bringing the political theme into close harmony with the spiritual. This was no simple task. Having

[1] *Works*, ix. 504–6.

read a number of the 480 sermons listed in the British Museum *Catalogue of Printed Books* as delivered on the day of the commemoration of the martyrdom, I am convinced that Johnson succeeded more than most.[1]

A similar observance of the Anglican form is to be found in other sermons by Johnson, including two which deal with the significance of the sacrament of Holy Communion and the duties it implies (Sermons IX and XXII), three on the subject of charity (IV, XIX, and XXVII), and two on the obligations of the governors and the governed (XXIV and XXVI), all of which might be described as formal or occasional sermons. Many of the others show that Johnson was mindful of the feast days and fast days of the Church of England, which, as he told Boswell, were 'memorials of important facts', and 'of great use in religion'. In the passage in the *Life* where he records this opinion of Johnson's, Boswell mentions that Robert Nelson's *Festivals and Fasts* (the full title is *A Companion for the Festivals and Fasts of the Church of England*), a book that Johnson admired and used—indeed he annotated Boswell's own copy of it—, was 'a most valuable help to devotion', and, incidentally, that it had had 'the greatest sale of any book ever printed in England, except the Bible'.[2] It was possibly from Nelson's book, used in conjunction with The Book of Common Prayer, that Johnson derived some of his ideas for wedding the text and theme of his sermons to particular occasions of observance. For instance, the text and theme of Sermon VIII ('Be not wise in your own conceits', Rom. 12:16) are those recommended for the third Sunday after Epiphany; those of the charity sermons (IV and XIX) are suitable to the feast of St. John the Evangelist, 27 December; the theme of the need for unity in religion (Sermon XI) is suggested for the feast of St. Barnabas, 11 June; that of the need for humility (Sermon VI) for the feast of the Purification of the Blessed Virgin, 2 February;

[1] The practice of delivering sermons to commemorate the martyrdom of Charles I dates back to 25 Jan. 1661, when Parliament ordered 30 Jan. to be kept as a day of fasting and humiliation. In 1662 Convocation formally issued a special order of service for that day, which was subsequently annexed to The Book of Common Prayer by order of the Crown. In 1859 this service was removed from the Prayer Book by royal warrant and Act of Parliament. For Johnson's views on the continuance of observing the fast of 30 Jan. see *Life*, ii. 151–2.

[2] Ibid., p. 458.

that of judgement, rewards, and punishments (Sermon X) for the
Sundays in Advent; that of the denunciation of false witness and
calumny (Sermon XVII) for the feast of St. Michael and All Angels,
29 September; and the theme of covetousness and fraudulence
(Sermon XVIII) for the feast of St. Matthew, 21 September.[1]

Whether Johnson was wholly guided by Nelson's *Companion* or by
The Book of Common Prayer in the choice of text and theme we
cannot, of course, be sure; but the fact that he follows the Anglican
form so closely in other matters, including the use of a formal
liturgical ending in many of the sermons, would point to similar
adherence to the Anglican tradition in respect of dates and seasons.

In the substance of his sermons Johnson invariably fulfils the
requirement of his own *Dictionary* definition of the sermon as 'a
discourse of instruction . . . for the edification of the people'. His
opening statement is usually an outline of the theme, or an introduction to it. Not for him the histrionic exclamation, the grand
beginning, or the subterfuge of indirection that other preachers
employed. There is a Baconian immediacy, if not economy, a
straight thrust at the heart of the subject, in Johnson's exordium:

One of the mighty blessings, bestowed upon us by the Christian
Revelation, is, that we have now a certain knowledge of a future
state, and of the rewards and punishments, that await us after
death . . . (Sermon X).[2]

Such is the weakness of human nature, that every particular state,
or condition, lies open to particular temptations . . . (Sermon XVI).[3]

To subdue passion, and regulate desire, is the great task of man, as
a moral agent . . . (Sermon XVIII).[4]

To afford adequate consolations to the last hour, to chear the
gloomy passage through the valley of the shadow of death, and to
ease that anxiety, to which beings, prescient of their own dissolution,
and conscious of their own danger, must be necessarily exposed, is
the privilege only of revealed religion (Sermon XXV).[5]

Johnson's fondness for the opening noun clause, or the infinitive
phrase used nominatively, is clearly seen in these opening sentences,

[1] For this information I am indebted to Professor J. H. Hagstrum, Bibl. 43,
pp. 51-3.
[2] *Works*, ix. 377.   [3] Ibid., p. 432.   [4] Ibid., p. 451.
[5] Ibid., pp. 516-17.

indicating his desire to parcel or encapsule his theme at the very start. At times the opening period is lengthy, perhaps too lengthy to be absorbed by the audience at one hearing, and it always makes immediate demands on the intellect. Even when it is an eloquent statement of a truism, or a Johnsonian recapitulation of the scriptural text, it is presented as a challenge to the reader or listener, requiring his alertness and attention.

Johnson sometimes varies this procedure by directing the thoughts of his audience to the occasion of the text. Thus, in Sermon XIII, using the text 2 Timothy 3:5, 'Having a form of Godliness, but denying the power thereof', he begins:

When St. Paul, in the precepts given to Timothy for his instruction how to regulate and purify the conversation of the first Christians, directed him to take care that those men should be avoided, as dangerous and pestilent, who, having the form of godliness, denied the power; it is reasonable to believe, that he meant, in his direct and immediate intention, to awaken his caution against gross hypocrites; such as may easily be supposed to have appeared too often in the most early seminaries of Christianity; who made an appearance of righteousness subservient to worldly interest; and whose conversion, real or pretended, gave them an opportunity of preying upon artless simplicity, by claiming that kindness which the first Believers shewed to one another; and obtaining benefactions which they did not want; and eating bread for which they did not labour.[1]

This is one of the longest of his opening sentences, but it is carefully punctuated, and it has the force and purposefulness of a clear explication of the circumstances as well as the substance of the text.

A slight variation in this procedure is found in Sermon XXVI, where the text is from Proverbs (20:8), 'A king that sitteth in the throne of judgement scattereth away all evil with his eyes.' This time Johnson begins in a more general way:

Among the Precepts delivered by Solomon for the Conduct of Life, and the Attainment of Happiness, some relate to moral duties and general obligations, and therefore are equally to be observed by Men of all Conditions, and all employments; but there are likewise many admonitions directed to particular Characters, in which the separate

[1] *Works*, ix. 404.

duties of the different orders of Society are inculcated, and in which those dangers are pointed out by which every State is immediately besieged.[1]

This is not one of Johnson's most polished beginnings, the structure being uncharacteristically loose and unwieldy, and the double relative clause at the end rendering it clumsy and ineffectual. Perhaps the reason for this unwonted roughness was that the sermon was the product of his collaboration with Taylor. The sentence does, however, illustrate another type of opening device: a general statement about the Biblical context, followed by a narrowing down or particularization of it towards the central theme, which, in this instance, deals with the duties of the governors, or leaders of the nation. (The sermon was addressed, presumably, to the members of the House of Commons at St. Margaret's, Westminster, where Taylor was Minister.)

At other times, as in Sermon XI, Johnson begins with a more extended explication of the text before relating it to the theme. Instead of taking one paragraph to bring the text into focus, he devotes four pages, in Sermon XI, to such introductory material. On occasion, too, as in Sermon XIV, he avoids a direct discussion of the context, and concentrates from the start on the moral implications of the Biblical passage. In this instance, the text is from Isaiah (26:3): 'Thou wilt keep him in perfect peace, whose mind is stayed on thee, because he trusteth in thee.' The sermon begins:

In order to the explication of this text, or the enforcement of the precept implied in it, there seems to be no necessity, either of proving, that all men are desirous of happiness, or that their desire, for the most part, fails of being gratified. Every man is conscious, that he neither performs, nor forbears anything upon any other motive than the prospect, either of an immediate gratification, or a distant reward; that whether he complies with temptation, or repels it, he is still influenced by the same general regard to his own felicity; but that when he yields to the solicitation of his appetite, or the impulse of his passions, he is overborne by the prevalence of the object before him; and when he adheres to his duty, in opposition to his present interest, he is influenced by the hopes of future happiness.[2]

---

[1] Sermon XXVI (Yale MS.), pp. 2–3. [2] *Works*, ix. 414.

This opening is clearly more essayistic than homiletic: the Rambler takes precedence over the preacher. But it is more usual for Johnson to begin his sermons with a direct textual attack, and then to develop the moral theme, always keeping in mind the fact that he is uttering, in the words of his own definition, a 'discourse of instruction'.

When Johnson told Wilkes to remember that sermons 'make a considerable branch of English literature',[1] he implied that there was more to a religious discourse than mere instruction. A sermon, for him, was a work of rhetorical art, having rules and characteristics just as specific and important as those of any other artistic genre. In this respect he followed in the tradition of St. Augustine, whose works, together with those of St. Ambrose, St. Athanasius, and Justin Martyr, were on the shelves of his library. St. Augustine, himself following the prescriptions of Cicero, had insisted that a sermon should do three things: teach, delight, and persuade: 'The eloquent divine, then, when he is urging a practical truth, must not only teach so as to give instruction, and please so as to keep up the attention, but he must also sway the mind so as to subdue the will.'[2] While Johnson's sermons are less calculated to please than to instruct and persuade, there is no doubt that he gave a great deal of attention to matters of form and style, with the intention of making each discourse pleasant to read or hear. Entertainment, in the form of wit, is conspicuously lacking, perhaps because Johnson, unlike the more 'popular' type of preacher, such as Isaac Barrow, felt that levity had no place in the pulpit.[3]

The advice he gave to the young preacher, the Revd. Charles Lawrence, already referred to in this study,[4] illuminates Johnson's own practice in the composition of sermons:

. . . in the labour of composition, do not burthen your mind with too much at once; do not exact from yourself at one effort of excogitation, propriety of thought and elegance of expression. Invent first, and then embellish. The production of something, where nothing was before, is an act of greater energy than the expansion or decoration

---

[1] *Life*, iv. 105.

[2] *On Christian Doctrine*, iv, xiii. 29. Translation from *Nicene and Post-Nicene Fathers*, ii. 584.

[3] See *Life*, iv. 105–6 n.   [4] See pp. 8–9, 17 above.

of the thing produced. Set down diligently your thoughts as they rise, in the first words that occur; and, when you have matter, you will easily give it form; nor, perhaps, will this method be always necessary; for, by habit, your thoughts and diction will flow together.[1]

Then he recommends the use of the traditional sermon 'divisions' as an aid to the memory of the listener as well as a means of guiding the judgement of the writer: 'they supply sources of invention, and keep every part in its proper place'.[1]

The divisions to which Johnson refers in this letter to young Lawrence went back to the old 'three-decker'[2] sermons of the Middle Ages and, beyond those, to the ancient patristic tradition of pulpit rhetoric, which, in turn, was closely associated with the classical oration and its five sections: the exordium, the division or proposition, the confirmation, the confutation, and the conclusion. This structuring of the speech was, of course, adapted and modified in various ways by the authorities on homiletics and by individual preachers themselves. The divisions used by John Donne, for instance, were modifications of those of Keckermann: *praecognitio textus*, which replaced the earlier exordium, *partitio et propositio*, *explicatio verborum*, the amplification, and the application. Donne's practice was to follow these divisions in the main, but to interlace them with personal reflections and dilatations, often with the result that his sermon became a sustained lyric in prose. Other preachers made frequent use of the medieval *exemplum*, of the kind made familiar to us in Chaucer's *Pardoner's Prologue* and *Tale*.[3]

[1] *Life*, iii. 437.
[2] The 'three-decker' sermon was approved by the French homiletic authorities such as Bourdaloue, Massillon, Fléchier, and Bossuet, but the rules for a threefold division go back very early in the history of sermon literature. Quintilian expressly disapproved of the restriction to three parts, but suggested a maximum of five. See John Quincy Adams, *Lectures on Rhetoric and Oratory*, Bibl. 54, ii. 20–5. A critical objection to such divisions is expressed by Vicesimus Knox, *Winter Evenings*, ii. 282: 'The anticipation of matter by a previous declaration of your method, as is frequently done in sermons, renders the whole languid and flat. Divisions and subdivisions of the subject, which appear in sermons, have a powerful effect in realizing Hogarth's sleeping congregation.'
[3] On the history, use, and modifications of the sermon *exempla*, see G. R. Owst, *Literature and Pulpit in Medieval England*, Bibl. 133, pp. 149–209. W. Fraser Mitchell, *English Pulpit Oratory from Andrewes to Tillotson*, Bibl. 130, Chs. I–IV, particularly pp. 94–9, provides a useful summary of Bartholomew Keckermann, *Rhetoricae Ecclesiasticae, Siue Artis Formandi et Habendi Conciones Sacras, Libri Dvo: Methodice Adornati per Praecepta et Explicationes . . .* Editio tertia (Hanoviae, 1606), on which I have drawn.

On the whole, Johnson elected to follow the same divisions, but, unlike Donne, he used a severely impersonal tone, very rarely obtruding himself into the discourse (no doubt because his sermons were to be delivered by others), and only occasionally employing an *exemplum*. In the sermons, moreover, we find no fictitious characters of the kind encountered in Law's *Serious Call* and in his own moral essays, but now and again there is a reference to an unnamed personage, like the 'great Eastern monarch' in Sermon XIV, or to a historical figure, such as Charles I in Sermon XXIII.[1] His rare use of the *exemplum* from a non-Biblical context is characterized by brevity:

The story of the great Eastern Monarch, who, when he surveyed his innumerable army from an eminence, wept at the reflection, that in less than a hundred years not one of all that multitude would remain, has often been mentioned; because the particular circumstances, in which that remark occurred, naturally claim the thought, and strike the imagination; but every man that places his happiness in external objects, may every day, with equal propriety, make the same observations. Though he does not lead armies, or govern kingdoms, he may reflect, whenever he finds his heart swelling with any present advantage, that he must, in a very short time, lose what he so much esteems, that in a year, a month, a day, or an hour, he may be struck out from the book of life, and placed in a state, where wealth or honour shall have no residence, and where all those distinctions shall be for ever obliterated, which now engross his thoughts, and exalt his pride (Sermon XIV).[2]

As has been shown, Johnson occasionally introduces his sermons with a *praecognitio textus*, in which he sets his text against its scriptural and historical background, but more frequently he adopts the older method of the exordium, emphasizing the moral import of the text, or offering a general statement as a prelude to his theme. Following this, he defines his theme more precisely, and introduces the partition of the argument, dividing it into two, three, or four main lines. Each of these lines or divisions of the argument is then amplified or expatiated upon, not so much illustratively as discursively and abstractly. The reasoning of each argument is logical,

---

[1] *Works*, ix. 418, 504 ff.   [2] Ibid., pp. 418–19.

balanced, mindful of alternative possibilities, and careful in its recognition of cause and motive. In moving from the general to the particular and from the theoretical to the practical, Johnson often embodies in his thinking the words and implications of the text itself, which he weaves skilfully into the fabric of the whole discourse.

It is interesting to note that Johnson's *partitio* in each sermon (with the exception of Sermon XXV,[1] the funeral eulogy, which has no conventional divisions) takes one of three traditional forms: the division of the text itself into parts, the sectioning of the theme, or the partitioning of the textual explication. In the first of these the text is divided into words or phrases; in the second the subject arising from the text is split into headings; and in the third the interpretation of the text is similarly divided. Johnson's practice in these matters was similar to that of Tillotson, who, however, went further by sub-dividing his *partitio* on occasion.[2]

When each strand of his argument has been carefully examined, Johnson proceeds to the application of his text or theme or both. This application sometimes takes the form of an exhortation or appeal or *epiphonema*, and at other times that of a recapitulation of the text as it applies directly to the particular audience or congregation to whom the sermon is addressed. Occasionally, as in Sermon IV, which was delivered at Bath, and addressed especially to those who had come to seek healing from the waters there, the appeal and the recapitulation of the text are combined. The appeal in this instance was for the congregation's support of a local charity school:

To those to whom languishment and sickness have shewn the instability of all human happiness, I hope it will not be requisite to enforce the necessity of securing to themselves a state of unshaken security, and unchangeable enjoyment. . . . To the sick therefore I may be allowed to pronounce the last summons to this mighty work, which perhaps the divine Providence will allow them to hear. Remember

---

[1] Unless the two 'heads' under which the purposes of a funeral celebration are discussed (*Works*, ix. 521) can be regarded as divisions.

[2] e.g. in *A Sermon on Stedfastness in Religion*, he sub-divides both halves of his *partitio*, the first into 2, the second into 4; in *A Sermon Concerning Family-Religion*, his *partitio* consists of four divisions, each one sub-divided; 1 (4), 2 (2), 3 (2), and 4 (2): *Six Sermons by His Grace John Lord Archbishop of Canterbury* (Bibl. 155), pp. 1–88.

thou! that now faintest under the weight of long-continued maladies, that to thee, more emphatically, the night cometh in which no
man can work; and therefore say not to him that asketh thee, 'Go
away now, and to-morrow I will give;' To-morrow? To-morrow is to
all uncertain, to *thee* almost hopeless; to-*day* if thou wilt hear the voice
of God calling thee to repentance, and by repentance to Charity;
harden not thy heart, but what thou knowest that in thy last moment
thou shalt wish done, make haste to do, lest thy last moment be now
upon thee.

And let us all, at all times, and in all places, remember, that they
who have given food to the hungry, raiment to the naked, and instruction to the ignorant, shall be numbered by the Son of God, amongst
the blessed of the Father.[1]

Thus, in his closing words, Johnson has neatly combined his appeal
with a reiteration of part of the text of his sermon, Isaiah 58: 7, 'Is
it not to deal thy bread to the hungry, and that thou bring the
poor that are cast out, to thy house?'

As a rule, Johnson's endings are quite brief and formal, repeating
the text or using the liturgical formula, or combining both, but an
interesting exception is to be found in the address he wrote for Dr.
William Dodd, the convicted forger, to which reference has already
been made.[2] In this address the ending takes the form of a long and
moving prayer, to be spoken on behalf of Dodd and his fellow
prisoners at Newgate. In the printed copy[3] of the text of this
extraordinary sermon, *The Convict's Address to His Unhappy Brethren*,
now deposited in the Yale Rare Book Library, Boswell, who owned
the copy, wrote these words on the title-page: 'This Copy Dr.
Samuel Johnson who composed the Address, revised for me, and
marked Dr. Dodd's additions with a D. on the margin.' According
to Johnson's own testimony, then, the opening of the prayer which
concludes the *Address*, together with one other paragraph of it, was
composed by Dodd himself. Here is the first paragraph, composed
by Dodd:

O almighty Lord God, the righteous JUDGE of all the earth, who
in thy providential justice dost frequently inflict severe vengeance

---

[1] *Works*, ix. 329–30.   [2] See pp. 7, 159–62 above.
[3] Permission to examine this copy is gratefully acknowledged.

upon sinners in this life, that thou mayest by their sad examples effectually deter others from committing the like heinous offences; and that they themselves, truly repenting of their faults, may escape the condemnation of hell:—look down in mercy upon us, *thy sorrowful servants*, whom thou hast suffered to become the unhappy objects of offended justice in this world![1]

It might be noted at this point that, even without Johnson's marginal 'D' against this paragraph, we could have recognized it as not being of his composition, for, as we have already shown, Johnson did not subscribe to the view that people are punished frequently for their sins in this world.[2] The two following paragraphs of the concluding prayer are Johnson's own:

Give us a thorough sense of all those evil *thoughts*, *words*, and *works*, which have so provoked thy patience, that thou hast been pleased to permit this public and shameful judgment to fall upon us; and grant us such a portion of grace and godly sincerity, that we may heartily confess, and unfeignedly repent of every breach of those most *holy laws and ordinances, which if a man do, he shall even live in them.*

Let no root of bitterness and malice, no habitual and deadly sin, either of *omission* or *commission*, remain undisturbed in our hearts! But enable us to make our repentance universal, without the least flattering or deceitful reserve, that so we may clear our consciences before we close our eyes.[3]

Then comes another paragraph of Dodd's interpolation:

And now that thou hast brought us within the view of our long home, and made us sensible, that the time of our dissolution draweth near; endue us, we humbly pray thee, O gracious Father, with such Christian fortitude, that neither the terrours of thy present dispensations, nor the remembrance of our former sins, may have power to sink our spirits into a despondency of thy everlasting mercies in the adorable Son of thy love.[4]

Once again, for the reasons stated earlier, Johnson would not have subscribed to the phrase, 'the terrours of thy present dispensations',

---

[1] *The Convict's Address*, p. 22.   [2] See pp. 71 ff. above.
[3] *The Convict's Address*, pp. 22–3.   [4] Ibid., p. 23.

as it suggests divine vengeance in this life. The rest of the prayer is of Johnson's own composition:

Wean our thoughts and affections, good Lord, from all the vain and delusive enjoyments of this transitory world; that we may not only with patient resignation submit to the appointed stroke of death, but that our faith and hope may be so elevated, that we may conceive a longing desire to be dissolved from these our earthly tabernacles, and to be with Christ, which is far better than all the happiness we can wish for besides!

And in due sense of our own extraordinary want of forgiveness at thy hands, and of our utter unworthiness of the very least of all thy favours—of the meanest crumbs which fall from thy table—Oh! blessed Lord Jesus! make us so truly and universally charitable, that in an undissembled compliance with thy own awful command, and most endearing example, we may both freely forgive and cordially pray for our most inveterate *enemies, persecutors,* and *slanderers*!—Forgive them, O Lord, we beseech thee—turn their hearts, and fill them with thy love!

Thus, may we humbly trust, our sorrowful prayers and tears will be acceptable in thy sight. Thus shall we be qualified, through Christ, to exchange this dismal bodily confinement (and these uneasy fetters) for the glorious liberty of the sons of God.—And thus shall our legal doom upon earth be changed into a comfortable declaration of mercy in the highest heavens:—and all thro' thy most precious and all-sufficient merits, O blessed Saviour of mankind!—who with the Father, and the Holy Ghost, livest and reignest ever, *One God*, world without end. Amen.[1]

This was, of course, no ordinary sermon. It called forth from Johnson an unusually fervent display of emotion, rarely seen elsewhere except in the charity sermons and in his private prayers, and it befitted the desperate plight into which Dodd had fallen. The gratitude of the condemned man, as reported by Boswell, is understandably eloquent:

I am so penetrated, my ever dear Sir, with a sense of your extreme benevolence towards me, that I cannot find words equal to the sentiments of my heart. . . .

---

[1] *The Convict's Address*, pp. 23–4.

You are too conversant in the world to need the slightest hint from me, of what infinite utility the Speech on the aweful day has been to me. I experience, every hour, some good effect from it. I am sure that effects still more salutary and important must follow from *your kind and intended favour*. I will labour—God being my helper,—to do justice to it from the pulpit. I am sure, had I your sentiments constantly to deliver from thence, in all their mighty force and power, not a soul could be left unconvinced and unpersuaded. . . .

May GOD ALMIGHTY bless and reward, with his choicest comforts, your philanthropick actions, and enable me at all times to express what I feel of the high and uncommon obligations which I owe to the *first man* in our times.[1]

The *Address* for which Dodd was so grateful is undoubtedly the most remarkable of all the products of Johnson's collaboration with clergymen in the composition of sermons: a much more exacting exercise than his works for Aston or Taylor, which had been more or less routine assignments, and one that called for a rare combination of empathy and imagination as well as plain communication of the kind that would impress itself upon the hearts and minds of condemned prisoners. It is significant that, even here, Johnson avoided excessive rhetorical amplification, and followed his restrained but moving peroration with a fervent prayer. Once again, his supreme sense of occasion, combined with his rare ability to adapt the tone of his discourse to the needs of the preacher who was to deliver it, is skilfully brought to bear on the task in hand.

In some respects, the talents Johnson had displayed as an essayist are quite similar to those he employed as a homilist. The typical *Rambler* essay, although only half the length of the average Johnsonian sermon, follows the rhetorical pattern proposed by Aristotle: introduction, proposition, proof, and conclusion. Many of the same rhetorical devices, such as amplification and climax, are employed in both forms to similar effect. But the differences are also to be noted. The essay is inevitably more discursive than the sermon; it contains, as a rule, no formal divisions; and, while preceded by epigraphs and interlarded with quotations, it does not adhere rigidly to a text. At the same time, it is interesting to observe

[1] *Life*, iii. 144.

that the same kinds of adaptation by which the Rambler invented and composed the letters of 'correspondents' like Hymaenus and Bucolus and Victoria are applied to the task of writing sermons to be preached by men like Aston and Taylor and Dodd. In both instances, however hard Johnson may have tried, to use Laetitia Hawkins's phrase, to 'keep down' his style,[1] the inimitable *cachet* of the master is stamped on every piece he composed.

HIS HOMILETIC STYLE

While we have no means of assessing the effectiveness of Johnson's sermons as pulpit discourses, we can learn something of their reception, at the time of their publication, from two notices which appeared in *The Critical Review* for December 1788 and November 1789. The first of these, discussing the first volume published by Hayes, notes that the sermons 'possess the manly strength, the nervous perspicuity, the pointed energy' of Johnson's other works, and describes the language as 'clear and forcible, without studied refinement or laboured obscurity'. Although he finds some of the subjects commonplace, and the author inclined to lean 'a little too securely' on the authority of the 'earlier fathers' of the Church, the reviewer commends the 'great precision' of his explanations and interpretations, as well as the excellence of his precepts. 'We have seldom seen sermons', he concludes, 'where a rational piety was more closely united with sound judgment; and where the most salutary lessons are in general better enforced by energetic and perspicuous language.'[2]

The second review, dealing with the 1789 volume, is equally enthusiastic. 'We can truly say that these discourses possess all the energy, all the perspicuity, all the pointed accuracy of the former volume', writes the critic, and he goes on to describe the second volume as 'a valuable acquisition to the literature of the pulpit', and to recommend it, 'not only to those young divines who are unable or unwilling to compose their own sermons, but to masters of families, as admirably calculated for the evening instructions.'[3]

[1] *Memoirs, Anecdotes, Facts, and Opinions*, i. 163. See p. 10 above.
[2] *The Critical Review*, LXVI (Dec. 1788, London: printed for A. Hamilton), pp. 443–6.
[3] Ibid. LXVIII (Nov. 1789), pp. 402–3. The reviewer is probably right in implying

In short, the contemporary commentator, whose favourable verdict was widely endorsed, saw in Johnson's homiletic style the same classical qualities which characterize his other prose work: strength, energy, perspicuity, clarity, and precision. The tightly aphoristic manner in which the homilist formulated his observations and presented his interpretations commended itself particularly to the reviewer. What he seemed to miss, however, was the unusual rhetorical skill, supported and enhanced by a special poetical quality, which Johnson brought to the task of composing sermons.

In discharging this task, Johnson took his own precepts, as applied to the art of the essay, as his guide:

> The task of an author is, either to teach what is not known, or to recommend known truths by his manner of adorning them; either to let new light in upon the mind, and open new scenes to the prospect, or to vary the dress and situation of common objects, so as to give them fresh grace and more powerful attractions, to spread such flowers over the regions through which the intellect has already made its progress, as may tempt it to return, and take a second view of things hastily passed over or negligently regarded.[1]

This is the opening of *Rambler* 3, where Johnson explains that his essays will follow the second plan, 'to recommend truths by his manner of adorning them'. In a word, he will employ the arts of rhetoric.

Professor W. K. Wimsatt, in his detailed study of Johnson's prose style, observes: 'There can be no doubt that Johnson considered his own prose as leaning toward the poetic.' In this respect he finds Johnson 'nearer to the romantic essayists than to the neoclassic': 'He made a kind of poetry of abstraction; out of emptiness he conjured weight, out of the collapsible he made structures. By limiting himself faithfully to the abstract he achieved more with it than did any other neoclassicist.'[2] While Johnson, according to his own prescription, gave primary place to 'invention' and secondary

---

that the sermons in the Taylor collection were intended for evening service, as they are relatively short.

[1] *Works*, ii. 11; Yale Edn. iii. 14–15.
[2] *The Prose Style of Samuel Johnson* (Bibl. 53), pp. 96, 103.

to 'embellishment',[1] while he sedulously avoided extravagances of expression in his sermons, and, it will be remembered, even went on record as saying that 'contemplative piety, or the intercourse between God and the human soul, cannot be poetical',[2] he did indeed make 'a kind of poetry of abstraction', and frequently employed figures of speech and other embellishments in his sermons. The resultant style of his homiletic prose is a distinctively Johnsonian blend of reflective poetry and persuasive oratory, characterized as it is by what the eighteenth century liked to call 'harmonious numbers', 'turns', 'figures', and other rhetorical ornaments.

The use of such a style for sermons was a matter of debate long before Johnson's time. The desire for a mathematically simple style, which had been expressed and promoted in Dryden's day by the first members of the Royal Society, still lingered at the beginning of the eighteenth century. The author of *Christian Eloquence in Theory and Practice*, however, argued, at least in part, against it in its application to sermons:

Are Men to be touched and converted by fine Expressions? Shall I consider how to shine when I am to publish Truths of so sublime and terrible a Nature as those of Christianity? Would not this be extream Weakness, not to say Folly in me? Of what use, says St. *Austin*, is a golden Key, if we can open nothing with it? And what matter is it, if it be of Wood, provided it will serve the Purpose? Let the Expressions be ever so grave and unpolished, if they affect me, they are certainly to be preferred before the most delicate and lively ones, which would only please me.

The Turns too and Figures of your Discourse should be varied. I am not of their Opinion, who would allow no Figures in Sermons,

---

[1] *Works*, ii. 11 (*Rambler* 3). In sermon rhetoric *inventio* (invention) embraced *praecognitio textus* (consideration of the text), *partitio* (division), and *explicatio verborum* (explanation of the passage); *embellishment* could be effected by sheer simplicity and clarity (*simplici perspicuitate*), by wealth of language (*copia*), by effective arrangement (*efficacia*), or by figures (*figuris*) (W. Fraser Mitchell, op. cit., p. 95). Johnson was well aware of the fine dividing line between excess and deficiency in the use of figurative expressions. He criticized Cowley, for instance, for losing 'the grandeur of generality' by 'pursuing his thoughts to their last ramifications', and he adds, 'the force of metaphors is lost when the mind by the mention of particulars is turned more upon the original than the secondary sense, more upon that from which the illustration is drawn than that to which it is applied': *Lives*, i. 45 (Life of Cowley).

[2] *Works*, vii. 213 (Life of Waller); *Lives*, i. 291.

under Pretence, that they look too much like Artifice, and become only a Sophist and Declaimer, who would have our Discourses be plain and simple with an air of Conversation, at most of familiar Instruction. They cannot think Figures at all suitable to the Character of *Christ*'s Ambassador: The Truths of our Religion, say they, are great enough of themselves, and want not the help of Art, and the Ornaments of Rhetorick to support them. I confess, an infinite difference should be made between a Christian Orator, and a Sophist and Declaimer; and grant, that the Ornaments wherewith these set themselves out would serve only to disfigure him. But the consequence to be drawn from this Principle is not, that the Christian Orator should reject the Turns and Figures that are proper for his Use, but those only that are peculiar to the Sophist and Declaimer.[1]

Elsewhere, the same author suggests that Christian oratory should sometimes be simple, at other times figurative: 'A well managed Metaphor is of wonderful Assistance to diversify Expressions, the diversity of Objects, which Nature presents to us, supplying us with an almost infinite diversity of Expressions.'[2]

In his practice, Johnson adopted a similar view, although in theory—at least as applied to non-homiletic literature—he appeared to be strongly opposed to it, as has been shown.[3] The rhetorician, and to some extent the poet, in him evidently overcame the prejudices of the critical theorist when it came to the composition of sermons.

Johnson's homiletic style has, of course, many of the rhetorical earmarks of the neo-classic manner, particularly in its resort to prosopopeia, personification, and hypallage. He talks, for instance, of 'the insolent triumphs of intellectual superiority',[4] and tells his audience that the apostle Peter warned new converts to Christianity that the heathen would watch their conduct with 'suspicious vigilance'.[5] In discussing 'the pernicious effects' which arise from 'harsh strictness and sour virtue; such as refuses to mingle in harmless gaiety, or give countenance to innocent amusements, or which transacts the petty business of the day with a gloomy ferociousness that clouds existence',[6] he slips into the familiar

---

[1] D'Oyley, op. cit., pp. 154–5.   [2] Ibid., p. 152.
[3] See p. 128 above.   [4] *Works*, ix. 362.
[5] Ibid., p. 386.   [6] Ibid., p. 394.

rhetorical mould, combining the transferred epithet with several forms of personified abstraction.

When we turn to the richly aphoristic sentences of the sermons, we find that very combination of the figurative and the simple which the author of *Christian Eloquence* had recommended. At times the simple expression provides a gloss on the figurative, as in this passage, discussing monastic retirement:

... it cannot be allowed, that flight is victory; or that he fills his place in the creation laudably, who does no ill, *only* because he does *nothing*.[1]

At other times, the simple conclusion forms a pendant to the figurative:

The slave of pleasure soon sinks into a kind of voluptuous dotage; intoxicated with present delights, and careless of everything else; his days and nights glide away in luxury or in vice, and he has no cure, but to keep thought away; for thought is always troublesome to him, who lives without his own approbation.[2]

Frequently, too, there is a compression of thought, reminiscent of the terser passages in the work of Francis Bacon:

To hope for our recompense in this life, is not beneficence, but usury.[3]

In each of these examples the weight of the aphorism is reserved for the conclusion of the sentence, a practice in keeping with Johnson's principle of 'cadence' in prose style, which required the placing of the emphasis at the end.[4] In the sermons the application of this principle serves to reinforce the proverbial quality of the statement:

Poverty, for the greatest part, produces ignorance; and ignorance facilitates the attack of temptation.[5]

In this example the personifications are strengthened both by the repetition of 'ignorance' and by the thrust of the final phrase. A

[1] *Works*, ix. 313 (Sermon III).   [2] Ibid., p. 317 (Sermon III).
[3] Ibid., p. 323 (Sermon IV).
[4] See *Life*, iii. 257 and n.; and Wimsatt, op. cit., p. 156.
[5] *Works*, ix. 327 (Sermon IV).

variation of this method is found in a passage from Sermon V, in which Johnson is discoursing on rationalization:

... few men have been made infidels by argument and reflection; their actions are not generally the result of their reasonings, but their reasonings of their actions.[1]

Here the order of the repeated words is reversed, with ellipsis, in the second phrase. This particular form of parallel structure, a special kind of chiasmus called 'antimetabole',[2] is found in several places in the sermons, sometimes with minor substitutions in the phrasing:

... Knowledge is to be attained by slow and gradual acquisitions, by a careful review of our ideas, and a regular superstructure of one proposition on another; and is, therefore, the reward only of diligence and patience. But patience is the effect of modesty; pride grasps at the whole; and what it cannot hold, it affects to despise; it is rather solicitous to display, than increase its acquisitions: and rather endeavours by fame to supply the want of knowledge, than by knowledge to arrive at fame.[3]

Once again the emphasis comes at the end of the sentence, and is given power by the repetition and reversal.

Another variation of this parallelism may be illustrated by this extract from a passage in which Johnson is warning teachers against the abuse of their authority:

In this state of temporary honour, a proud man is too willing to exert his prerogative; and too ready to forget that he is dictating to those, who may one day dictate to him.[4]

In this instance a simple shift of pronominal phrase, from 'to those' to 'to him', achieves the desired effect.

The more common form of this chiasmus, however, is that of the following example:

He that will eat bread, must plough and sow; though it is not certain that he who ploughs and sows shall eat bread.[5]

---

[1] Ibid., p. 332 (Sermon V).
[2] Although the terms 'antimetabole' and 'chiasmus' do not appear in Johnson's *Dictionary*, they were in current rhetorical use.
[3] *Works*, ix. 365.   [4] Ibid., p. 366.   [5] Ibid., p. 399.

Johnson liked to give such structures the flavour of paradox, just as he did in other contexts:

Of things that terminate in human life the world is the proper judge: to despise its sentence, if it were possible, is not just; and if it were just is not possible (*Life of Pope*).

. . . he who praises everybody, praises nobody (*Misc.* 2. 327).

It ought to be the first endeavour of a writer to distinguish nature from custom; or that which is established because it is right, from that which is right only because it is established . . . (*Rambler* 156).

> The drama's laws the drama's patrons give,
> For we that live to please, must please to live. . . .
>
> (Drury Lane Prologue.)

This habit of Johnson's expression, which falls somewhere between parallelism and antithesis, is equally effective in epigrammatic verse and in homiletic prose. At times, in the sermons, the antithesis is made even more emphatic by a kind of musical pointing, as in psalmody:

. . . he who spoke, and the world was made, can speak again, and it will perish.[1]

This is reminiscent of a similar thought expressed in *Rasselas*:

'But the being,' said Nekayah, 'whom I fear to name, the being which made the soul, can destroy it.'[2]

While both passages are chopped up by the punctuation, the first is more methodically, and more musically, balanced; the second, though retaining its parallelism more consistently through the use of the active voice, is somehow more prosaic.

When the antithesis and chiasmus are combined in the sermons with a paradoxical 'turning', a characteristically Johnsonian counterpoint is achieved:

---

[1] *Works*, ix. 385. Cf. Ps. 148: 5, which Johnson paraphrases in the Life of Cowley: 'Such events as were produced by the visible interposition of Divine Power are above the power of human genius to dignify. The miracle of Creation, however it may teem with images, is best described with little diffusion of language: "He spake the word, and they were made" ' (*Lives*, i. 49).

[2] *Works*, i. 308 (*Rasselas*, Ch. XLVIII).

Not only our speculations influence our practice, but our practice reciprocally influences our speculations. We not only do what we approve, but there is danger lest in time we come to approve what we do, though for no other reason but that we do it. A man is always desirous of being at peace with himself; and when he cannot reconcile his passions to his conscience, he will attempt to reconcile his conscience to his passions; he will find reason for doing what he resolved to do, and, rather than not walk after his own lusts, will scoff at religion.[1]

Occasionally the phrasing takes on a regularity close in manner to that of the Psalms and the Proverbs of the Old Testament, and not unlike the insistent rhythm of the Beatitudes:

He that rises to greatness finds himself in danger; he that obtains riches perceives that he cannot gain esteem. He that is caressed, sees interest lurking under kindness; and he that hears his own praises, suspects that he is flattered. Discontent and doubt are always pursuing us. Our endeavours end without performance, and performance ends without satisfaction.[2]

When Hazlitt complained that all Johnson's periods were 'cast in the same mould' and were 'of the same size and shape', with the result that they had 'little fitness to the variety of things he professes to treat of',[3] he was underestimating his subject's capacity for producing antiphonal effects and musical cadences which are only partially related to the conventional beat of the heroic couplet. 'The structure of his sentence', argues Hazlitt, 'is a species of rhyming in prose.'[3] Elsewhere, he elaborates on this point: 'There is a tune in it, a mechanical recurrence of the same rise and fall in the clauses of his sentences, independent of any reference to the meaning of the text, or progress or inflection of the sense . . . his periods complete their revolutions at certain stated intervals, let the matter be longer or shorter, rough or smooth, round or square, different or the same.'[4] This criticism is not entirely applicable to Johnson's sermon prose. It is true that Johnson often arranges his ideas in almost a couplet

[1] *Works*, ix. 472 (Sermon XX).   [2] Ibid., p. 399.
[3] 'On the Periodical Essayists', Lecture V in the series *Lectures on the English Comic Writers*, in *The Complete Works of William Hazlitt*, ed. P. P. Howe (Bibl. 107), vi. 101–2.
[4] Ibid. (*The Plain Speaker*, 1826), xii. 6.

form, as in this passage, in which he is discussing the ideal community:

If we consider it with regard to publick happiness, it would be opulent without luxury, and powerful without faction: its counsels would be steady, because they are just; and its efforts vigorous, because they would be united.[1]

In the first half of this sentence the main clause is divided into two parallel complements, each consisting of an adjective–preposition–noun sequence ('opulent without luxury', 'powerful without faction'). The second part has two further main clauses, followed by adverbial clauses of reason in the form of subject–conditional verb–adjective. But the parallelism has a special appropriateness to the subject: it is not merely mechanical recurrence. The following paragraph from the same sermon, moreover, illustrates the antiphonal balance and *anaphora* Johnson used to produce a special homiletic emphasis:

Every man would be industrious to improve his property, because he would be in no danger of seeing his improvements torn from him.

Every man would assist his neighbour, because he would be certain of receiving assistance, if he should himself be attacked by necessity.

Every man would endeavour after merit, because merit would always be rewarded.

Every tie of friendship and relation would add to happiness, because it would not be subject to be broken by envy, rivalship, or suspicion.

Children would honour their parents, because all parents would be virtuous;

all parents would love their children, because all children would be obedient.[2]

Here the rhythm of the sentence is not merely a couplet-like rhythm; nor is it only the product of parallelism of syntax. Conscious of the value of Biblical sentence rhythms, and particularly knowledgeable in the Psalms, Johnson evidently modelled his homiletic prose on scriptural lines. In addition, he used a whole

---

[1] *Works*, ix. 338 (Sermon V).
[2] Ibid. The paragraph has been broken up to illustrate the parallelism.

range of rhetorical devices, such as multiplication, repetition, parallel phrasing, and climax. One passage will serve to illustrate all these qualities:

To determine the degrees of virtue and wickedness in particular men, is the prerogative only of that Being that searches the secrets of the heart, that knows what temptations each man has resisted; how far the means of grace have been afforded him, and how he has improved or neglected them; that sees the force of every passion, knows the power of every prejudice, attends to every conflict of the mind, and marks all the struggles of imperfect virtue. He only, who gave us our faculties and abilities, knows when we err by insurmountable ignorance, or when we deviate from the right by negligence or presumption. He only, that knows every circumstance of life, and every motion of the mind, can tell how far the crimes, or virtues, of each man are to be punished or rewarded.[1]

More obvious echoes[2] of Biblical phrasing are to be found in passages like these, on pride:

Pride has been able to harden the heart against compassion, and stop the ears against the cries of misery. . . .

It makes masters cruel and imperious, and magistrates insolent and partial. It produces contempt and injuries, and dissolves the bond of society. . . .

A proud man is opposed in his rise, hated in his elevation, and insulted in his fall.[3]

Sometimes, too, there is some interweaving of various Biblical texts, as in the peroration of Sermon IV, where Proverbs 3 : 28 becomes the point of departure for an earnest injunction to repentance and charity, expressed in a paraphrase of at least three separate scriptural quotations:

Remember thou! that now faintest under the weight of long-continued maladies, that to thee, more emphatically, the night

---

[1] *Works*, ix. 438–9 (Sermon XVI).
[2] Sometimes these 'echoes' are acknowledged by Johnson as points of departure from the text: e.g. in the opening of Sermon VI, where his text is Proverbs 11: 2, he produces a series of Solomon-like proverbs of his own (*Works*, ix. 343).
[3] *Works*, ix. 345–8 (Sermon VI).

cometh in which no man can work; and, therefore, say not to him that asketh thee, 'Go away now, and to-morrow I will give.' To-morrow! To-morrow is to *all* uncertain, to *thee* almost hopeless; to-*day*, if thou wilt hear the voice of God calling thee to repentance, and by repentance to charity, harden not thy heart. . . .[1]

Both the sound and the sense of the Bible are thus incorporated in Johnson's concluding sentences.

THE POETIC IMAGERY

Johnson's homiletic style is not solely a matter of careful sentence structuring, rhetorical devising, and scriptural echoing. It depends very largely for its effects on certain kinds of poetic imagery, of the power and uses of which he was acutely aware. His descriptions of various styles in the *Lives of the Poets*, his perceptive if sometimes punctilious notes on Shakespeare's figures of speech, and his definitions of *imagery*, *metaphor*, *trope*, *catachresis*, *simile*, and *wit* in the *Dictionary* all testify to his detailed knowledge of the subject. In particular, he defines *imagery* as consisting of 'representations in writing, such descriptions as force the image of the thing described upon the mind'. As W. K. Wimsatt has suggested, however, Johnson's own imagery,

is imagery only in the most diluted sense. One of the . . . most deliberate students of imagery, Professor Spurgeon, writes: 'When I say "images" I mean every kind of picture, drawn in every kind of way, in the form of simile or metaphor—in their widest sense.' If one may judge from Professor Spurgeon's extended treatment of the subject, she means that imagery is not only non-literal but pictorial—that it is simile or metaphor which has a strong imaginative appeal. . . . But if imagery is to be taken in this way, the question how much imagery is to be found in a writing will have a close connection with . . . how much sensory terminology is to be found, how many of the author's terms suggest sense impressions, or images. . . . Johnson's terms tend to be non-sensory, his meaning to be general and abstract. If Johnson's writing may be said to contain imagery, we must understand the term in another sense, that of simply non-literal expression. If it be remembered that not all non-literal expression, that is, not all

[1] *Works*, ix. 330.

metaphor, need be highly sensory, it can be admitted that in some sense Johnson's writing contains imagery. . . .[1]

Professor Wimsatt here assumes that there is a clear-cut distinction between 'sensory terminology' and other kinds of non-literal expression. But, as J. H. Hagstrum has pointed out,

Our present conception of imagery includes but does not always distinguish two functions of language, that of introducing sensuous concreteness and that of making comparisons. Dr. Johnson recognized both but carefully distinguished them. His definition of imagery does not include comparison. . . . The imagination was in part conceived of as the image-making faculty; and an idea was defined as a 'mental image'. Imagery, although of course it included the sensuous, was therefore not exclusively confined to it. When Johnson praised Gray's *Elegy* for its 'happy selection of images' or Milton's *L'Allegro* and *Il Penseroso* because 'the images are properly selected and nicely distinguished' or when he wrote late in life that one of the comforts of having old friends is that they have 'many images in common,' he probably referred in all these cases to mental pictures of reality, both phenomenal and intellectual. . . .[2]

In Johnson's sermons there are images that could be described as almost exclusively 'intellectual', others that blend abstraction with concretion, and others still that are predominantly sensuous or concrete. To illustrate the way in which Johnson interweaves the 'phenomenal' and the 'intellectual' in his 'mental pictures of reality' we might consider his statement in Sermon XV that 'pain lies in ambush behind pleasure, and misfortune behind success'.[3] While there is nothing sensuous here, the word 'ambush' is at least suggestive of a 'phenomenal' mental image, while the words 'pain', 'pleasure', and 'success' are personified abstractions. There is also, perhaps, a temporal implication in the use of the word 'behind'. Johnson's memorable phrase in *The Vanity of Human Wishes*, 'the secret ambush of a specious prayer',[4] provides a similar example of this mixture of phenomenal and intellectual imagery. In neither

---

[1] Wimsatt, op. cit., p. 65. Professor Donald Greene, in ' "Pictures to the Mind": Johnson and Imagery' (Bibl. 100), questions Professor Wimsatt's championship of the theory of Johnson's 'abstractness'.

[2] J. H. Hagstrum, *Samuel Johnson's Literary Criticism*, p. 114.

[3] *Works*, ix. 429.

[4] *The Vanity of Human Wishes*, l. 357; Yale Edn. vi. 108, l. 354.

instance is the reader or listener expected to imagine a military ambush, but there is at least the hint of a visual image within the phrase or sentence.

A variant of this process of blending the phenomenal with the intellectual is the personification of tyranny in Sermon I:

> But cruelty and pride, oppression and partiality, may tyrannize in private families without control; meekness may be trampled on, and piety insulted, without any appeal, but to conscience and to heaven.[1]

This is a familiar Augustan succession of abstractions, rendered concrete by the verbs 'trampled' and 'insulted', but only to a limited extent as phenomenal images. The same effect of concretion by remote implication is found in Johnson's assertion that 'one of the chief acts of love is readily to forgive errours, and overlook defects',[2] in which he appears to be echoing the Pauline catalogue of love's attributes[3] and adopting a similar mode of expressing them. The proverbial is thus elevated by the phenomenal. The Pauline manner in which a man without love is described as 'sounding brass, or a tinkling cymbal' (1 Cor. 13: 1) has such Johnsonian counterparts as the passage in which he describes the man of wealth and power who lacks the protection of God, 'without which, wealth is only a floating vapour, and policy an empty sound'.[4]

The abstract and the concrete are often amalgamated in adjective–noun phrases like 'glittering follies and tempting delusions',[5] as well as in the more extended metaphor of the kind we notice in Sermon XIV, where Johnson is talking of young pleasure-seekers:

> Instead of founding happiness on the solid basis of reason and reflection, they raise an airy fabrick of momentary satisfaction, which is perpetually decaying, and perpetually to be repaired.[6]

This method of illustrating an abstract idea by a concrete metaphor is so habitual with Johnson that the metaphor tends to become submerged:

> . . . the fabrick of terrestrial happiness has no foundation that can long support it.[7]

---

[1] *Works*, ix. 291.   [2] Ibid., p. 299.   [3] See 1 Cor. 13.
[4] *Works*, ix. 320.   [5] Ibid., p. 331 (Sermon V).   [6] Ibid., p. 415.
[7] Ibid., p. 426.

Here the 'fabrick' is much less of a mental image than it is in the previous example, which recalls 'the baseless fabric of this vision' raised by Prospero in *The Tempest*.[1]

The submerged metaphor, in which the concrete image gives way almost entirely to the abstraction, is found again in sentences like this one:

That *ardour* of *kindness*, that *unbounded confidence*, that *unsuspecting security* which friendship requires, cannot be extended beyond a single object.[2]

In addition to the abstract metaphors underlined here, we see Johnson's tendency to restore words to their etymological meaning, a practice noted specifically by the Revd. Robert Burrowes with reference to *ardour*:

Ardour, which in his preface to his Dictionary, he observes, is never used to denote material heat, yet to an etymologist would naturally suggest it; and Johnson accordingly, speaking of the '*ardour* of posthumous fame', says that 'some have considered it as little better than *splendid* madness; as a *flame kindled* by pride and *fanned* by folly'.[3]

Another striking instance of this revitalizing of a metaphor by wedding abstraction to concretion through the agency of etymology is found in Sermon VII, where, after noting that every age in history has its own peculiar approach to questions of morality, Johnson comments:

These changes of conduct or opinion may be considered as the revolutions of human nature, often necessary, but always dangerous. Necessary, when some favourite vice has generally infected the world, or some errour, long established, begins to tyrannize, to demand implicit faith, and refuse examination. But dangerous, lest the mind, *incensed* by oppression, *heated* by contest, and *elated* by victory, should be too far transported to attend to truth, and, out of zeal to secure her conquest, set up one errour to depress another.[4]

Here the successive images suggested by *incensed*, *heated*, and *elated* are given special force by the physical analogies they convey and

[1] *The Tempest*, IV. i. 151.   [2] *Works*, ix. 295.
[3] 'Essay on the Stile of Dr. Samuel Johnson', Bibl. 37, Vol. I, 49.
[4] *Works*, ix. 350–1.

by their etymological associations. The word *elated*, for instance, means not only 'excited' but 'drawn or brought out', and, in its botanical application, 'burst out by an elastic filament serving to disperse spores'. Thus the series of verbs is both logical in its progression and phenomenal in its application.

The precision with which Johnson defines words in the sermons is partly the product of his etymological knowledge and of his skill in exegesis. In some cases, such as his discussion of *compassion*[1] in Sermon XI, he supplies both the derivative meaning and the textual application. In others, such as his analysis of *pride*[2] in Sermon VI, he follows a general definition of the term with an account of its 'speculative' or philosophical connotation and its application to 'real' life. In most of the sermons he provides a lexicographic explanation of his terms, such as *repentance* (Sermon II), *fear* and *hardness of heart* (III), *charity* (IV), *communion* (IX), *self-deceit* (X), *vanity* (XII), *false witness* (XVII), and *fraud* (XVIII).[3] The last two are discussed as legal terms, and *trust* (XIV)[4] is given a very comprehensive definition from several points of view. This rare enunciative talent, which enabled Johnson to give an added dimension to his imagery, is particularly in evidence when he introduces scientific terms and analogies.

The fact that he was interested in the sciences is so well known as to need little comment, but the readiness with which he expressed his ideas in scientific equivalents is perhaps less frequently acknowledged. Professor Wimsatt notes what he considers to be 'pre-eminently the Johnsonian trait of vocabulary—the use of general or abstract words which have a scientific or philosophic flavour',[5] and Heinrich Schmidt points out his fondness for the 'technical terms of philosophy, medicine and law',[6] but it was Johnson himself who formulated the principle: 'As by the cultivation of various sciences, a language is amplified, it will be more furnished with words deflected from their original sense; the geometrician will talk of a courtier's zenith, or the eccentrick virtue of a wild hero, and the physician of sanguine expectations and phlegmatick

---

[1] *Works*, ix. 388–9.   [2] Ibid., p. 344.
[3] Ibid., pp. 311 ff., 322, 371, 380, 397 ff., 441 ff., 454 ff.   [4] Ibid., p. 420.
[5] Wimsatt, op. cit., p. 106.
[6] *Der Prosastil Samuel Johnson's* (Bibl. 48), pp. 4–8.

delays.'[1] The theory here implied, of the absorption of scientific terms into metaphorical language, has several applications in Johnson's prose. In the sermons it sometimes takes the form of a direct analogy:

... he that neglects the improvement of his own mind, will never be enabled to instruct others. Light must strike on the body, by which light can be reflected.[2]

Again, the analogy with the laws of physics seems to appeal to Johnson as being particularly applicable to the human condition:

... as the force of corporeal motion is weakened by every obstruction, though it may not be entirely overcome by it, so the operations of the mind are by every false notion impeded and embarrassed, and though they are not wholly diverted or suppressed, proceed at least with less regularity, and with less celerity.[3]

In the same context, he talks of 'the settled and predestined motions of a machine impelled by necessity',[4] but, using another scientific analogy, makes it clear that not all human conduct is the work of a superhuman agency:

The materials for building are naturally combustible; but when a city is fired by incendiaries, God is not the author of their destruction.[5]

Elsewhere, the connection between the physical and the moral world is made even more explicit:

As it appears, by examining the natural system of the universe, that the greatest and smallest bodies are invested with the same properties, and moved by the same laws; so a survey of the moral world will inform us, that greater or less societies are to be made happy by the same means, and that, however relations may be varied, or circumstances changed, virtue, and virtue alone, is the parent of felicity.[6]

For the purpose of such analogies, too, the 'engine' simile is especially apt:

As every engine of artificial motion, as it consists of more parts, is in more danger of deficience and disorder; so every effect, as it requires

[1] Works, v. 47 (Preface to the Dictionary).   [2] Ibid., ix. 363–4 (Sermon VIII).
[3] Ibid., p. 332 (Sermon V).   [4] Ibid., p. 334 (Sermon V).
[5] Ibid., p. 335 (Sermon V).   [6] Ibid., p. 298 (Sermon I).

the agency of greater numbers, is more likely to fail. Yet what pleasure is granted to man, beyond the gross gratification of sense, common to him with other animals, that does not demand the help of
others, and the help of greater numbers, as the pleasure is sublimated
and enlarged?[1]

A more domesticated scientific metaphor is that which identifies
the contemplation of human afflictions with the taking of
unpleasant medicine:

To consider the shortness, or misery, of life . . . is one of those intellectual medicines, of which the nauseous essence often obstructs the
benefit, and which the fastidiousness of nature prompts us to refuse.[2]

The language of chemistry and physics often appears in a little less
obvious form, as when Johnson suggests of marriage that

it sometimes *condenses* the gloom, which it was intended to dispel, and
increases the *weight*, which was expected to be made lighter by it. . . .[3]

The natural world is also a favourite source of imagery, as the
following example, depending as it does on a volcanic–meteorolo-
gical analogy, serves to show:

The end of learning is, to teach the publick, to superintend the
conduct, watch over the morals, and regulate the opinions of parishes,
dioceses, and provinces; to check vices in their first eruption, and
suppress heresies in the whispers of their rise.[4]

Johnson's habit of incorporating scientific terms into his language
and converting them into poetic phrases is effectively manifested
here. The sibilance of the last part of the sentence cleverly sustains
the image of the seething volcano, reminding us that Johnson well
knew the onomatopoeic values of words, as he had demonstrated
in lines like these:

> Here beauty falls, betray'd, despis'd, distress'd,
> And hissing infamy proclaims the rest.

and

> Must helpless man, in ignorance sedate,
> Roll darkling down the torrent of his fate?

---

[1] *Works*, ix. 401 (Sermon XII).
[2] Ibid., p. 423 (Sermon XV). See *Life*, iii. 386–7 and n.
[3] *Works*, ix. 292 (Sermon I).   [4] Ibid., p. 366 (Sermon VIII).

and

> Approach, ye minstrels, try the soothing strain,
> Diffuse the tuneful lenitives of pain.[1]

In the last example, incidentally, we have another illustration of his employment of a scientific metaphor.

Like the language of science, the language of finance was a useful source of imagery for Johnson, who was, of course, fully aware of the many financial interests of John Taylor, for whom the sermons were for the greatest part composed, and those of his congregation in the City. Talking of friends in Sermon I, for instance, he points out that, as a man

> divides his affection and esteem between them, he can in *return claim* no more than a *dividend* of theirs; . . .[2]

Again, in Sermon VIII he comments that a man of learning is often tempted to compare himself favourably with others,

> and in all disputable cases, turns the *balance* in his own favour, by *superadding*, from his own conceit, that wisdom which by nature he does not *possess*, or by industry he has not *acquired*.[3]

An image, or series of images, suggestive of military manœuvres occurs in the same sermon, where he talks of

> every condition of humanity being exposed on one side, and guarded on the other; so that every man is burdened, though none are overwhelmed; every man is obliged to vigilance, but none are harassed beyond their strength. The great business, therefore, of every man is to look diligently round him, that he may note the approaches of an enemy; and to bar the avenues of temptation, which the particular circumstances of his life are most likely to lay open; and to keep his

---

[1] *The Vanity of Human Wishes*, ll. 341–2, 345–6, and 267–8; Yale Edn. vi. 104–8, ll. 341–2, 345–6, 267–8. In the *Dictionary* Johnson defines *eruption* as 'the act of breaking or bursting forth from any confinement', and illustrates it from Bacon's *Natural History*, No. 361: 'In part of Media there are *eruptions* of flames out of plains.' In the Sermon quoted there may be an echo of the phrase from Milton's *Paradise Lost* with which he illustrates another sense of the word, 'sudden excursion of a hostile kind':

> Thither, if but to pry, shall be perhaps
> Our first *eruption*, thither or elsewhere;
> For this infernal pit shall never hold
> Celestial spirits in bondage.

[2] *Works*, ix. 295. [3] Ibid., p. 362.

heart in perpetual alarm against those sins which constantly besiege him. . . .

There are some conditions of humanity, which are made particularly dangerous by an uncommon degree of seeming security; conditions, in which we appear so completely fortified, that we have little to dread, and, therefore, give ourselves up too readily to negligence and supineness; and are destroyed without precaution, because we flattered ourselves, that destruction could not approach us. . . . And the sin to which we are particularly tempted, may be of that insidious and seductive kind, as that, without alarming us by the horrours of its appearance, and shocking us with the enormity of any single acts, may, by slow advances, possess the soul, and in destroying us differ only from the atrociousness of more apparent wickedness, as a lingering poison differs from the sword. . . .[1]

This unusually prolonged series of metaphors and similes, forged around a military analogy, is reminiscent of some of the homiletic procedures of John Donne, who was fond of expatiating from a central image as the kernel of his theme.[2]

In addition to those categories of imagery we have already discussed—the intellectual–phenomenal, the abstract–concrete, the scientific, the financial, and the military—there are three groups which, because of their frequent appearance, call for special comment: images of motion, images of abruption or impediment, and images of extinction or obliteration. None of these types can be said to be exclusive, but they represent dominant patterns in the sermons, and contribute to the poetic thrust of Johnson's homiletic prose.

In the first of these groups we see very clearly Johnson's particular fondness for verbs denoting motion and nouns depicting the channels of motion, such as roads, paths, streams, rivers, and gateways. 'The different methods of life', he says in Sermon XVI, 'have each of them their *inlets* to sin, and their *avenues* to perdition.'[3] And in Sermon XXIII the tortuous ways of deception and trickery are expressed in these terms:

The man whose duty gives way to his convenience, who, when once he has fixed his eye upon a distant end, hastens to it by violence

---

[1] *Works*, ix, pp. 359–60.   [2] See W. Fraser Mitchell, op. cit., pp. 156–7, 186–7.
[3] *Works*, ix. 432.

over forbidden ground, or creeps on towards it through the crooked paths of fraud or stratagem, as he has evidently some other guide than the word of God, must be supposed to have likewise some other purpose than the glory of God, or the benefit of man.[1]

In this example the verbs of motion effectively match the nouns of thoroughfare. Johnson's penchant for such combinations is again evident in the following passage from Sermon XXV, which neatly sums up, in a succession of infinitives and participles, the excellence of the Christian gospel:

To bring life and immortality to light; to give such proofs of our future existence, as may influence the most narrow mind, and fill the most capacious intellect; to open prospects beyond the grave, in which the thought may expatiate without obstruction; and to supply a refuge and support to the mind amidst all the miseries of decaying nature, is the peculiar excellence of the gospel of Christ. Without this heavenly Instructor, he who feels himself sinking under the weight of years, or melting away by the slow waste of a lingering disease, has no other remedy than obdurate patience, a gloomy resignation to that which cannot be avoided; . . .[2]

Bring, give, influence, fill, open, expatiate, supply, decaying, sinking, melting, lingering. . . . The homilist cleverly changes key from the verbs of action, which for him connote the vital strength of the gospel, to the participles of decline, which suggest, in their turn, the hopeless state of the non-believer. In the same sermon he points out that, in pre-Christian times, there were many who went their heedless ways,

many who dissolved themselves in luxurious enjoyment, and, when they could lull their minds by any present pleasure, had no regard to distant events, but withheld their imagination from sallying into futurity, or catching any terrour that might interrupt their quiet. . . .[3]

Once again the images are sharpened by expressive verbs and participles, suggestive of 'melting' and rapid action in alternate phrases.

Yet another typical series of metaphors of motion, largely dependent on active verbs, occurs in this passage from Sermon XXIV:

But that authority may never swell into tyranny, or languish into supineness, and that subjection may never degenerate into slavery,

[1] Ibid., p. 501.   [2] Ibid., p. 520.   [3] Ibid., p. 517.

nor freedom kindle into rebellion, it may be proper, both for those who are entrusted with power, and those from whom obedience is required, to consider . . . how much it is the duty of those in authority to promote the happiness of the people.[1]

Swell, *languish*, *degenerate*, and *kindle*, all favourite words of Johnson's, are used in imaginative juxtaposition to their nouns, *tyranny*, *supineness*, *slavery*, and *rebellion*, giving the abstractions force and concreteness and shape.

Johnson had the poet's awareness, too, of the aural qualities of certain verbs of motion:

Accustomed pleasures rush upon the imagination; the passions clamour for their usual gratifications; and sin, though resolutely shaken off, will struggle to regain its former hold.[2]

He is capable, moreover, of giving his images of motion a 'romantic' cast:

The highest flights of the soul soar not beyond the clouds and vapours of the earth; . . .[3]

This is a passage of which the poet of *Adonais* would not have been ashamed.[4]

From images of motion it is an easy leap to images of abruption and impediment, of which there are many instances in the sermons. These take several quite distinct forms. One is the image which suggests an obstacle on a road or path.

In a smooth course of prosperity, an unobstructed progression from wish to wish, while the success of one design facilitates another, and the opening prospect of life shows pleasures at a distance; to conclude that the passage will always be clear, and that the delights which solicit from far, will, when they are attained, fill the soul with enjoyments, must necessarily produce violent desires, and eager pursuits, contempt of those that are behind, and malignity to those that are before.[5]

---

[1] *Works*, ix. 507.   [2] Ibid., p. 428 (Sermon XV).
[3] Ibid., p. 412.
[4] The sentiment is not, of course, the same as that typically expressed by Shelley, who liked to take the more optimistic view of the soul soaring beyond the clouds.
[5] *Works*, ix. 402 (Sermon XII).

Here Johnson sees life as a road, a prospect, a view, and the obstacles on that road as desires, jealousies, scorn, and hatred. Another form of the 'impediment' image is associated with shackles and chains:

Age is shackled with infirmity and diseases. Immediate pain and present vexation will then do what amusement and gaiety did before, will enchain the attention, and occupy the thoughts, and leave little vacancy for the past or future.[1]

He obtains a similar effect with images of hills, mountains, uphill struggles, and barriers of various kinds. Not surprisingly, death, that great disturber of human quiet, is presented frequently in the sermons as an obstacle, and the consequence of death as a yawning chasm or a gaping void in the mind of the bereaved:

The whole mind becomes a gloomy vacuity, without any image or form of pleasure, a chaos of confused wishes, directed to no particular end, or to that which, while we wish, we cannot hope to obtain; . . .[2]

The sharpness of death is also suggested by the simple abruption of 'no more' in a passage of personal grief, evoked by the death of Johnson's wife:

. . . he who has seen kindness snatched from his arms, and fidelity torn from his bosom; he whose ear is no more to be delighted with tender instruction, and whose virtue shall be no more awakened by the seasonable whispers of mild reproof, . . .[2]

Even here, the images expressive of the writer's own deeply-felt agony are carefully shaped, and the sense of loss is etched by concrete verbs animating a series of abstractions, and given a sad, Tennysonian refrain by the repetition of 'no more'.[3] Thus the sermon takes on the shape of a threnody, the more moving as it comes closer to poetic utterance.

A combination of the 'shackles' image and the mental pictures which the contemplation of death produces in Johnson's mind is found in the following passage:

When the mind had broken loose from the shackles of sense, and made excursions to remote consequences, the first consideration that

---

[1] Ibid., p. 384 (Sermon X).   [2] Ibid., p. 521 (Sermon XXV).
[3] Cf. *The Princess*, Part IV.

would stop her course must be incessant waste of life, the approach of age, and the certainty of death; the approach of that time, in which strength must fail, and pleasure fly away, and the certainty of that dissolution which shall put an end to all the prospects of this world.[1]

Here the images of motion are placed in opposition to images of abruption, and death is imagined as the last barrier, the end of the prospect, the cessation of activity, the final dissolution. When reading passages like this, we can understand why Johnson would be so deeply impressed by the lines from Shakespeare's *Measure for Measure*:

> Ay, but to die and go we know not where;
> To lie in cold obstruction and to rot;
> This sensible warm motion to become
> A kneaded clod; and the delighted spirit
> To bathe in fiery floods, . . .
>
> (III. i. 118–22.)

Images of obliteration and extinction also occur frequently in the sermons. In Sermon XX, for example, where Johnson describes as 'the summit of impiety'[2] that state of mind which causes men not only to neglect, but to insult religion, and to add to their viciousness a contempt for virtue, he goes on to observe:

Wickedness in this state seems to have extended its power from the passions to the understanding. Not only the desire of doing well is extinguished, but the discernment of good and evil obliterated and destroyed. Such is the infatuation produced by a long course of obstinate guilt.[2]

The phrase 'obstinate guilt' serves to underline the destructive force impersonally suggested in the 'extinction' image, and somehow to activate the succession of passive verbs in the preceding sentence.

An interesting variant of the 'extinction' image is the surgical or horticultural metaphor in Sermon VII, where Johnson is talking of the violence with which changes in religion have been brought about:

---

[1] *Works*, ix. 517–18 (Sermon XXV).
[2] Ibid., p. 472 (Sermon XX).

Rage has been called in to the assistance of zeal, and destruction joined with reformation. Resolved not to stop short, men have generally gone too far, and, in lopping superfluities, have wounded essentials.[1]

This progression from a series of abstractions to the picture of the knife or the shears is yet another instance of a characteristic manipulation of the style in which Johnson cast so much of his homiletic prose.

Allied to the imagery of 'extinction' are images which suggest evanescence, the transitoriness of life, the dashing of hopes, and the suddenness of death. Perhaps the favourite image of evanescence is that of the 'phantom', which takes several forms. It is, of course, familiar to readers of *Rasselas*, which is addressed to those 'who listen, with credulity, to the whispers of fancy, and pursue, with eagerness, the phantoms of hope',[2] and of *The Vanity of Human Wishes*, which is set in that environment

> Where wav'ring man, betray'd by vent'rous pride
> To tread the dreary paths, without a guide,
> As treach'rous phantoms in the mist delude,
> Shuns fancied ills, or chases airy good; . . .[3]

In Sermon V Johnson describes a state of true happiness, based firmly upon 'the practice of the duties of religion', as the only one which is not illusory:

Let no man charge this prospect of things, with being a train of airy phantoms; a visionary scene, with which a gay imagination may be amused in solitude and ease, but which the first survey of the world will show him to be nothing more than a pleasing delusion.[4]

This has something in common with the 'shadow and bubble' image which he evokes in Sermon XIV:

It will easily appear, that men fail to gain what they so much desire, because . . . they waste their lives in successive delusions, in idle schemes of imaginary enjoyment; in the chase of shadows which

---

[1] *Works*, ix. 351 (Sermon VII). I am indebted to Professor William Kinsley for his suggestion that this might be interpreted as a horticultural metaphor.
[2] Ibid., i. 199.
[3] *The Vanity of Human Wishes*, ll. 7–10; Yale Edn. vi. 92.
[4] *Works*, ix. 339.

fleet before them, and in attempts to grasp a bubble, which, however it may attract the eye by the brightness of its colour, is neither solid nor lasting, but owes its beauty only to its distance, and is no sooner touched than it disappears.[1]

Images of illusion occur again and again in the sermons. One of the most striking, and one of the most poetic, combines two metaphors in a single context:

Religion is not only neglected by the projector and adventurer, by men who suspend their happiness on the slender thread of artifice, or stand tottering upon the point of chance.[2]

Here the image of the projector, the man of grand designs, is identified with that of the acrobat: the 'slender thread of artifice' is the scheme on which he stakes everything, and which may easily fail. The 'adventurer' or gambler, to give the word its eighteenth-century meaning, is depicted as the tightrope walker, poised uncertainly on one foot. Johnson is using this double image to underline the hazards of neglecting the practice of religion and leaving all to chance or 'art'. It is interesting to note that, in *Adventurer* 99, which has as its epigraph *Magnis tamen excidit ausis*, projectors are applauded for their contributions to human progress, even though 'they all fail by attempting things beyond their power'.[3] While some of them are censured for excessive ambition and ruthlessness, no mention is made of their lack of religion; the difference between the essay and the homily is small, but significant.

Johnson's images of illusion are closely related to his images of the transitoriness of life, many of which are expressed in terms of cliffs, rivers, seas, rocks, storms, and calms. The edge of eternity is depicted as 'the brink of life', on which the charitable man 'shall stand without fear', for 'his recompense shall flow upon him from the fountain of mercy'.[4] Johnson often refers, in his conversations as well as his writings, to the 'ocean of life'—in *Rambler* 102,[5] for instance, where this analogy is fully exploited; in the third-last paragraph of Chapter 12 of *Rasselas*;[6] and in the early part of his *Life of Richard Savage*, where he describes his subject as having been

[1] *Works*, ix. 415.   [2] Ibid., p. 381 (Sermon X).
[3] Yale Edn. ii 429, 434.   [4] *Works*, ix. 324–5 (Sermon IV).
[5] Ibid., ii. 481 ff.; Yale Edn. iv. 179–84.   [6] *Works*, i. 229.

'launched upon the ocean of life, only that he might be swallowed by its quicksands, or dashed upon its rocks'.[1] One also recalls his famous description of 'the full tide of human existence' at Charing Cross (*Life*, ii. 337). In the sermons the image assumes several forms. In Sermon XIII it is placed within a metaphor of sailing. Arguing that men of learning, because of their retirement from the gay and active world, are blind to the peculiar dangers to which they are exposed, he observes:

... they are willingly persuaded to believe, that because they are at a great distance from the rocks on which conscience is most frequently wrecked, that, therefore, they sail with safety, and may give themselves to the wind, without a compass. . . .[2]

In Sermon XX a similar image is treated with greater elaboration, after a characteristic passage in which abstract and concrete are presented in juxtaposition:

Wickedness is in itself timorous, and naturally skulks in coverts and in darkness, but grows furious by despair, and, when it can fly no further, turns upon the pursuer.[3]

Then follows the familiar, but somewhat expanded, 'wrecks and rock' analogy:

A man ventures upon wickedness, as upon waters with which he is unacquainted. He looks upon them with horrour, and shudders at the thought of quitting the shore, and committing his life to the inconstancy of the weather; but, by degrees, the scene grows familiar, his aversion abates, and is succeeded by curiosity. He launches out with fear and caution, always anxious and apprehensive lest his vessel should be dashed against a rock, sucked in by a quicksand, or hurried by the currents beyond sight of shore. But his fears are daily lessening, and the deep becomes less formidable. In time he loses all sense of danger, ventures out with full security, and roves without inclination to return, till he is driven into the boundless ocean, tossed about by the tempests, and at last swallowed by the waves.[4]

Here we are back, for a moment, in the world of allegory and parable, the image swelling into a homiletic *exemplum*, and the author carried away by the suggestive richness of his extended simile.

---

[1] Ibid., viii. 137. *Lives*, ii. 324.   [2] *Works*, ix. 361.
[3] Ibid., p. 470.   [4] Ibid., pp. 470–1.

Images of storm and calm are also found in association with thoughts of death, which, as Johnson reminds us in Sermon XIV, are not to be avoided even 'in the most rapid whirl of pleasure, or the most incessant tumults of enjoyment'.[1] Feelings of guilt, too, are represented as storms, from which 'pious intentions' afford a kind of refuge:

When remorse and solitude press hard upon the mind, they afford a temporary refuge, which, like other shelters from a storm, is forsaken, when the calm returns. The design of amendment is never dismissed, but it rests in the bosom without effect.[2]

To such turbulence of conscience the author of the sermons was far from immune, and to such pious intentions his private prayers and meditations frequently bear witness.

The more closely one examines the imagery of Johnson's sermons, the more one is struck by its essential grace and simplicity, and by the way in which it reflects the character and conviction of its composer. At times, indeed, the imagery is so unobtrusive as to slip by unnoticed, and the most eager image-hunter must restrain himself with the reminder that, in all human discourse, literal and figurative expressions are often blended in such a way that the boundaries between them become imperceptible. Perhaps in the end, as Shelley said, 'the deep truth is imageless'.[3] And certainly there are moments when Johnson, coming close to the heart of a favourite theme, chooses to express a deep truth in a virtually 'imageless' meiosis:

To live in a world where all is vanity, has been decreed by our Creator to be the lot of man—a lot which we cannot alter by murmuring, but may soften by submission.[4]

But his constant care and concern for words, and his conscious artistry in the shaping and re-shaping of a phrase, in the careful measuring of a sentence, and in the imaging forth of abstract ideas, lead me to believe that his figurative expressions are rarely accidental or merely commonplace.

---

[1] *Works*, ix. 418.   [2] Ibid., p. 427 (Sermon XV).
[3] Demogorgon in *Prometheus Unbound*, II. iv. 116.
[4] *Works*, ix. 402.

Even his simplest passages are often assisted by a musical pointing, as in this sentence from Sermon XIV, in which he suggests that
the only security from thoughts of death is to be found in

the protection of a Being mighty to save; a Being whose assistance
may be extended equally to all parts of his duration, who can equally
defend him in the time of danger, and of security; in the tumults of
the day, and the privacy of the night; in the time of tribulation, and
in a time more frequently fatal, the time of wealth; and in the hour
of death, and in the day of judgment.[1]

The simplicity and the balance are sometimes combined with a
memorable analogy:

We may pass by men, without being able to distinguish whether
they are to be numbered among those whose felicities, or whose
sorrows, preponderate; as we may walk over the ground, without
knowing whether its entrails contain mines of gold, or beds of sand.[2]

The poet keeps breaking in, perhaps in spite of the preacher. There
is a constant searching for poetic equivalents, for those 'images
which find a mirrour in every mind', and for those 'sentiments to
which every bosom returns an echo'.[3] Sometimes these poetic
equivalents take the form of a chain of images, rather like those in
the celebrated 'sleep' passage in *Macbeth*. In Sermon XXV, for
instance, we are told,

. . . the fear of death has always been considered as the great enemy of
human quiet, the polluter of the feast of happiness, and embitterer of
the cup of joy.[4]

Again, the series of images may be threaded on a single string, as
in Sermon VII, where, to express the idea that 'the innocence of
errour accompanied with sincerity' has become a favourite rationalization of the age, Johnson pictures a garden, in which

This doctrine has been cultivated with the utmost diligence, enforced with all the arts of argument, and embellished with all the
ornaments of eloquence, but perhaps not bounded with equal care. . . .[5]

[1] Ibid., p. 419.   [2] Ibid., p. 359 (Sermon VIII).
[3] *Works*, viii. 487 (Life of Gray); *Lives*, iii. 441.   [4] *Works*, ix. 518.
[5] Ibid., p. 354 (Sermon VII).

Finally, the series of images may issue from a central notion, as in this passage from Sermon XV, where Johnson observes that

... the power of doing good is not confined to the wealthy. He that has nothing else to give, may often give advice. Wisdom has likewise benefits in its power. A wise man may reclaim the vitious, and instruct the ignorant, may quiet the throbs of sorrow, or disentangle the perplexities of conscience. He may compose the resentful, encourage the timorous, and animate the hopeless.[1]

This is no random collection of ideas, but a carefully, poetically balanced selection of figurative phrases, congruously and logically arranged: reclamation is followed by instruction, pacification by disentanglement, reconciliation by encouragement and animation. The parallelism assists and educes the succession of ideas, just as surely as the heroic couplet measures the sequence of thought in Johnson's verse:

> Yet, when the sense of sacred presence fires,
> And strong devotion to the skies aspires,
> Pour forth thy fervours for a healthful mind,
> Obedient passions, and a will resign'd;
> For love, which scarce collective man can fill;
> For patience, sov'reign oe'r transmuted ill;
> For faith, that, panting for a happier seat,
> Counts death kind nature's signal of retreat;
> These goods for man the laws of heav'n ordain;
> These goods he grants, who grants the pow'r to gain;
> With these celestial wisdom calms the mind,
> And makes the happiness she does not find.[2]

CONCLUSION

Enough has been said in this concluding chapter to show that Johnson's approach to the writing of sermons was that of the studied prose stylist, the rhetorician, and the poet. In addition, his remarkable talents as lexicographer, etymologist, philosopher, legal expert,

---

[1] *Works*, ix. 431-2 (Sermon XV).
[2] *The Vanity of Human Wishes*, ll. 357-68; Yale Edn. vi. 108, ll. 357-68.

scientist, textual scholar, exegete, and theologian were all combined in their composition. But what emerges most clearly, in my view, is the special quality in Johnson which enabled him to combine homily with poetry. Both the vision and the method which are so much in evidence in his didactic and moralistic verse are seen again in the sermons. More precisely, Johnson in these discourses exhibits the character of the poet as it was defined by Imlac in *Rasselas*:

His character requires, that he estimate the happiness and misery of every condition; observe the power of all the passions in all their combinations, and trace the changes of the human mind, as they are modified by various institutions, and accidental influences of climate or custom, from the sprightliness of infancy to the despondence of decrepitude. He must divest himself of the prejudices of his age or country; he must consider right and wrong in their abstracted and invariable state; he must disregard present laws and opinions, and rise to general and transcendental truths, which will always be the same. . . . He must write, as the interpreter of nature, and the legislator of mankind, and consider himself, as presiding over the thoughts and manners of future generations; as a being superiour to time and place.[1]

This is not to deny Johnson's own dictum that 'the good and evil of Eternity are too ponderous for the wings of wit; the mind sinks under them in passive helplessness, content with calm belief and humble adoration'.[2] But I do not believe that the spheres of religion and poetry were for him two separate worlds, as one of his commentators has contended:

The two [religion and poetry] belong to two different spheres, involving means of expression so diverse as to make them incompatible. The themes which the mind dwells upon in devotion are awful and incomprehensible; poetry must deal with the easily comprehensible. The mood of religion is overwhelming and direct; poetry requires leisure and control. In devotion the appropriate expression is a simple cry for mercy; in poetry there are the embellishments of wit and fancy. . . . If T. E. Hulme is right in saying that romanticism is 'spilt religion' and that concepts 'right and proper in their own

---

[1] *Works*, i. 222–3.   [2] *Works*, vii. 135 (Life of Milton); *Lives*, i. 182.

sphere' are poured out like 'a pot of treacle over the dinner table,' then Johnson is one of the least 'romantic' of all English writers.[1]

If Johnson divorced poetry from religion in his literary theory, he failed to do so in his own practice. All his greatest themes—the vanity of human wishes, the fear of death, the mystery of the future state, the search for happiness—are too closely allied to poetic literature to be isolated. It was Johnson, after all, who found a passage in Congreve's *Mourning Bride*, a passage describing death, as 'the most poetical paragraph' in 'the whole mass of English poetry'.[2]

The sermons are not, of course, prose poems. Nor are they rhapsodic visions cast in a homiletic mould. They are, as this study has attempted to demonstrate, the unique productions of a great mind, steeped in the sermon literature of the past and in the Bible and in the Book of Common Prayer, nurtured in the Anglican tradition, and at the same time aware of the other tides and cross-currents of belief and interpretation that had swept the English-speaking world. They take their place as part of 'that considerable branch of English literature'[3] which Johnson considered important, because of their clarity, perspicuity, and reasoned eloquence, as well as the consistent neatness and regularity of their design. They have something in common with poetry as Johnson understood that art, and as the Psalms and the Proverbs and the Book of Ecclesiastes appealed to him as poetry. They deal with similar themes; they survey the pleasures, the wisdom, the folly, the iniquity of this life, the illusory nature of earthly happiness, the human preoccupation with the things of this world, the mystery of God's purposes, and the certainty of worldly disappointment.

Finally, they contain an important part of their author's own poetic vision. Just as, at the end of *The Vanity of Human Wishes*, there is a hint of the golden world, centred in 'the celestial wisdom' that 'calms the mind',[4] and, at the end of *Rasselas*, 'the choice of eternity' becomes more significant to the princess than 'the choice of life',[5] so in the final sermon, written for his own wife's funeral,

---

[1] J. H. Hagstrum, *Samuel Johnson's Literary Criticism*, p. 68.
[2] *Works*, viii. 31 (Life of Congreve); *Lives*, ii. 229.   [3] *Life*, iv. 105.
[4] *The Vanity of Human Wishes*, l. 367; Yale Edn. vi. 109, l. 367.
[5] *Works*, i. 308.

Johnson concludes that 'whenever disease, or violence, shall dissolve our bodies, our souls may be saved alive, and received into everlasting habitations; where, with angels and archangels, and all the glorious host of heaven, they shall sing glory to God on high, and the Lamb, for ever and ever'.[1] Thus religion becomes for Johnson 'spilt poetry'. The poetry is in the piety.

[1] *Works*, ix. 525 (Sermon XXV).

APPENDIX

A Letter to Samuel Johnson, LL.D. on the Subject of a Future State

By

John Taylor, LL.D.

A

LETTER

TO

SAMUEL JOHNSON, L.L.D.

MY DEAR SIR,

ACCORDING to my promise, I here send you my thoughts upon the subject of a future state, and the best arguments, I could think of, to prove the immortality of the soul, and the resurrection of the body. If the fare I have provided for you, be not so delicate, or so highly seasoned, as you may have expected, you must remember, that it was all to pass your digestion, and your finish. (A new word for you.)

A very superficial inquiry into the nature of the human mind will convince us, that the fear of death is the great disturber of human quiet; and therefore, of all speculations, none can be so interesting to the wise and to the good, as such as will discover to us the most efficacious remedies against the restless horrors of these most terrifying expectations, and afford us the best and most certain lights to cheer the gloomy passage through the valley of the shadow of death.

To do this, is the prerogative and privilege only of religion, of that religion which shews us, by irresistible evidence, the certainty of a state of future existence; a state, in which we shall see all the objections to the divine government of the world solved; all the seeming inequalities of providence adjusted; and all the distributions of our Creator justified; a state, in which it will appear, that in the course of existence, the Judge of all the earth has done right; and in which, every man shall receive the due reward of his works, whether they be good, or whether they be evil.

That there will be in some other place a review of our present life; that what seems a total dissolution of our nature, and absolute privation of all sensitive and intellectual powers, is, in reality, only a change of the manner of life, only a removal to some other state, and a separation of our immortal from our perishable part, has been indeed generally believed, and evinced by many moral and physical arguments.

It has been always discovered by the most negligent observer, that this world afforded to human understandings no proof of a distribution of happiness or misery, according to the deserts of virtue or of wickedness; or according to the sacred rules of reason and of justice. It was found, that men were often prosperous in their crimes, and distressed by their virtues; at least, that good and bad men were promiscuously happy and miserable without distinction. And therefore, since truth and falsehood, benevolence and cruelty, seemed unalterably opposite; since the one seemed universally worthy of approbation, and the other unchangeably detestable; they could not but imagine, in every age, that a time would come, in which, practices so different in their natures, would differ likewise in their consequences; and in which, those who had endeavoured to spread happiness over human life, would be distinguished by the universal Author of existence from them, who had only laboured to deface his works, and to blast, with misery and discontent, the being which his bounty has bestowed.

As they saw the world wisely made, they very reasonably supposed it to be wisely governed; and as they could not reconcile the appearance of the present state with the idea they had formed of the wisdom of the Creator, they concluded, and concluded with great justice, that they saw only part of his works; that the present state was imperfect, and that there was another existence necessary to complete the scheme of divine wisdom.

There were some Philosophers, men capable of the most abstruse ratiocination, who both embraced the same opinion, and also, with diligence and sagacity, examined further into the nature of the soul; in which there appeared nothing common with corruptible and changeable matter, nothing which could involve it in the dissolution of the body, or subject it to the same laws with an organical and compounded frame, of which, each part is subjected to external accidents, and of which, one particle wears out another by attrition, till the whole is consumed by corruption. In contemplating the faculties of the mind, they found it able to perform more than the necessities of the present life require; able to comprehend a thousand powers to which the body cannot attain, and form a thousand wishes, which, thus entangled, it never can enjoy.

They perceived that it was always soaring beyond the senses, and the appetites; therefore they could not imagine that the Creator, who in other instances has so exactly proportioned the means to the end, should lavish upon the mind of man such superfluous excellencies; should create a being to desire so much, and to obtain so little; whose performances are so inadequate to his conceptions; and of whom, one part should know the imperfection of the other; and know it only to lament it; know it without hope of remedy, and feel it only to despair.

These Philosophers, by the mere light of reason, even without any assistance from, or knowledge of, revelation; by inquiring into the nature of the soul of man, discovered that it is a substance distinct from matter; and upon the most steady contemplation and investigation of matter, they established this truth; that as matter is incapable by any powers of its own, either of action or sensation, that therefore the soul is independent of the body, and therefore immaterial, and consequently immortal. Here you see that natural religion alone proves beyond a doubt, the immortality of the soul, consequently the absurdity and folly of annihilation.

When I told you that I had heard from Mr. Jodrell, of your conversation with Dr. Brocklesby about annihilation; you said, 'that nothing could be more weak than any such notion; that life was indeed a great thing; and that you meant nothing more by your preference of a state of torment to a state of annihilation, than to express at what an immense value you rated vital existence.' Upon this part of the subject it is very necessary that you should be precisely exact, and very forcible.

But the reasons above, as they could only be collected by the speculative and the wise, could not exert sufficient influence upon the generality of mankind.

It was therefore necessary that the doctrine of the immortality of the soul, and the resurrection of the body, that it might influence all, should be established upon such evidence, as all could understand; which might operate upon the passions as well as the judgment; which might be learned in infancy, and which in old age could not be forgotten.

Such evidence we have by an actual exemplification. He therefore, who taught the great doctrine of the resurrection, has given an invincible attestation to its truth by rising himself.

Our all-merciful Creator has made men free and moral agents; as such he has sent them into this world, into a state of probation; suffers them to be masters of themselves, and restrains them only by coercions applied to their reason; by the hope of rewards, or the fear of punishments. But to prevent the sin of suicide, a sin that most opposes the designs and schemes of his providence, and the most heinous of all sins in his sight, our God omnipotent has applied every exertion of his almighty power; and by his prescient care at our creation in framing, in mixing, and in uniting, in our nature, in our reason, and in our senses, this first principle, this miraculous law of self-preservation, He, the mighty Lord, hath taught us how offensive in his sight is the crime of self-murder; a sin certainly unpardonable, because it seems impossible, if death be the instantaneous consequence of the act, that it can be repented of; and by his miraculous care to prevent it we cannot but deduce this conviction, how outrageously they must offend him, who shall dare to desert the station in which their God has a right to place them.

I was once desired by a Friend to give him my opinion of the crime of suicide. My answer was the argument above; and the effect of it was most amazing. He immediately turned pale; his lips were convulsed; and it was some time before he could recover himself. You have frequently, and very lately, reminded me of this occurrence.

The doctrine of the immortality of the soul is, doubtless, clear to our reason; and the doctrine of the resurrection of the body sufficiently evident for our faith; but the constitution of man is such, that abstruse and intellectual truths cannot by any other means be so forcibly impressed upon our minds, as by sensible evidence;

and it may be a speculation worthy the chase and pursuit of men of the strongest reasoning, and most clear intuitive powers, to examine for what wise cause or causes, our omniscient Creator, who has already established these doctrines by evidence so clear to our reason, and so sufficient for our faith, should refuse to gratify our curiosity with such lights to our senses.

The laws, by which the propagation of our species is enforced, and our existence continued, are the laws of sense in a very eminent degree. And if our omniscient God had given those lights to our senses to see farther by them beyond the grave, than he has permitted us, he could not but know how these lights must militate against those first laws of nature; and that by the power of such lights to our senses the present constitution of the world must be destroyed, and infinite mischief and inextricable confusion be the consequences.

By these lights, our faith, that faith which in our present state of probation will be the test of our belief in God and our obedience to his laws, for which we shall be judged, condemned, or acquitted; that faith that hath saved thee, and by which we shall be justified: Luke 7: 50 that faith which hath subdued kingdoms, wrought righteousness, obtained promises, stopped the mouths of lions: Heb. 11: 33, that faith which our God has taught us; and by every impulse of persuasion, and every inducement of privilege, and promise of blessings, hath impressed upon us, would be totally annihilated. St. Paul's definition of faith is, that faith is the substance of things hoped for, the evidence of things not seen: But by these lights things hoped for would be seen, and hope changed into certainty.

The shallow powers with which we are endued cannot foresee, nor circumscribe, the dreadful consequences of thus overturning the omniscient schemes of providence, and the grand and stupendous miracle of nature.

The temptations to the sin of suicide must be infinitely multiplied, and the law of self-preservation to prevent it would become of little effect. The impatience of man under the pressure of his common and daily afflictions must be infinitely magnified, and existence (existence in this world) must be intolerable to him, who sees how the penitent thief, in one moment, is conveyed from the misery of the cross, to the felicities of Paradise; from a state of the most agonizing torture, to a state of bliss, such as eye hath not seen, nor ear heard, neither hath it entered into the heart of man to conceive.

I have somewhere read, that whilst an almost Christian Philosopher was descanting to his audience, on the immortality of the soul, and describing, with all the warmth of a fine imagination, the pure and inexhaustible source of intellectual pleasures, to which it would be admitted, on being separated from the body, some virtuous Youths were so transported with the idea, that they could hardly be restrained from laying violent hands upon themselves, in order to anticipate those supreme enjoyments, from which the immortal spirit was detained, by its present connection with gross, unthinking matter—not considering that the social duties of life were first to be discharged, and its various trials sustained, ere the soul could be entitled to a blissful immortality.

The following tetrastick of Callimachus is to the same purport.

Εἶπας, "Ηλιε χαῖρε, Κλεόμβροτος 'Ωμβρακιώτης
"Ηλατ᾽ἀφ᾽ ὑψηλοῦ τείχεος εἰς Ἀΐδην,
Ἄξιον οὐδὲν ἰδὼν θανάτου κακόν, ἀλλὰ Πλάτωνος
"Εν τὸ περὶ ψυχῆς γράμμ᾽ ἀναλεξάμενος.

Cleombrotus exclaim'd, 'Farewell, O light!'
From the high tow'r then plung'd to Stygian night,
No ills he felt that urg'd the desp'rate thought,
But wish'd to realize what Plato taught.

From hence you must observe, how nearly the force of reason in the Heathen Philosophers equipoizes the powers of the law of self-preservation, and see, how infinite the wisdom and mercy of our Creator is, in withholding from us any fuller prescience of the blessed state in the world to come; to enter upon which, nothing could prevent mankind from storming the avenues and gates of death, but the grand obligation to a patient continuance in well doing, enjoined them by the Gospel.

We have another very stupendous instance of our Creator's infinite prescience and provident solicitude for the happiness of mankind, by the covenant which our God established between himself and man, from the foundation of the world. Since from the moment that man was created liable to sin, from that same moment a remedy was prepared, and the propitiation offered by the Son was accepted. The Lamb was sacrificed from the foundation of the world, and took place from the first formation of man. Here you see that the tender mercy of God the Father, and God the Son, hath delivered the posterity of him who broke the covenant, from the consequences of his fault, and given us the means of grace and the hope of glory.— Upon the whole, I am for my part convinced, that the evidence which God has given to my reason, and by the Scriptures to my faith, is sufficient and perfect; that God hath done all, and left nothing undone, that is necessary for our guidance in the ways which he hath set before us. We are in this world, as I before observed, in a state of probation; and by our belief in God, and our obedience to his laws, we are to be tried, punished, or rewarded. We are very certain (Acts 17: 31) that the Lord will judge the world, and (Prov. 31: 9) that he will judge righteously; that he does not require us to know what he has hid from us; and that he will punish us for the neglect or misapplication of talents, and not for the want of them.

We know that the schemes of unerring providence cannot be improved or amended, either by adding new, or taking away the old lights; and with great truth and sincerity I say, to God only wise be glory through Jesus Christ for ever. Amen.

All the knowledge that we have of the resurrection of the body we derive from the Scriptures; which, as it may give you much comfort, and me little trouble, I will extract for your consideration.

In considering the doctrine of the resurrection, we can only declare what is delivered in the holy Scriptures. It is not necessary, nor proper, to examine all the wild opinions which enthusiasm or folly have published to the world; or examine all the questions which presumptuous curiosity, or subtilty, ill employed, have ventured to propose; questions, to which, since God has not been pleased to resolve them, no answer can be given by human wisdom. The Scriptures are written with pity to the infirmities of man, but with no indulgence to his pride; and they who will not humbly stop at those limits which their Creator has set to their knowledge, are deservedly left to wander in the labyrinths of endless intricacy, when they have forsaken the light of revelation, to wander after the illusive meteors of fanciful conjectures.

It is indeed not necessary that man should wholly restrain himself from searching into the government of God, even farther than God has expressly revealed it.

An inquiry into the general scheme of providence is surely a very noble and interesting speculation. But let such inquiries be begun with humility, and conducted with piety. Let him that searches into the ways of God, remember the boundless disparity between his intellectual powers, and the subject that employs them! And first, resolving to rest his soul upon the word of God, let him exert his reason with due subordination to his faith; let him search with reverence, and assert with modesty, and he may indulge his curiosity without a crime, and perhaps with some advantage both to others and himself.

But the discoveries of one man's reason will be sometimes doubtful to the reason of another; and the utmost that any man can hope, is but to arrive at ingenious conjectures, which may gain applause; but the word of God alone can demand our faith. And in the word of God, though the vain inquirer may sometimes fail of satisfaction, there will be found all that is necessary to comfort misery, to repress pride, to reform corruption, and to encourage virtue. Though those are condemned as fools who arrogantly ask how are the dead raised, and with what bodies will they rise; we are however told that this corruptible shall put on incorruption, and this mortal shall put on immortality; and shewn that this change is possible, because it has already been effected, for Christ is now risen from the dead.

These Scriptures farther inform us, that those who at this great day shall be left alive, shall not die but be changed. From whence we may conclude, without much straining for a conjecture, that this change will be from an earthly to an heavenly body, with which we are assured the dead shall arise.

In the Scriptures we have also sufficient information to fill the heart with awe, to raise devotion to ecstasy, and turn our thoughts from the present life to the great day of total consummation: That day in which death, the last enemy, shall be overcome; on which the trumpet shall sound, and the universe, at the command of God, assume a new form, as it first arose, when the voice of creation summoned it to being. When those who have long slept in the grave shall rise again, and the sea shall give up her dead; when all, from the east and the west, and the north and the south, shall be assembled together, and all the generations of men, from the first to the last day, shall stand ranged before the tribunal of all powerful justice. Then will that Jesus who died to redeem us appear in the clouds, surrounded by the armies of heaven, and shining with the visible splendors of divinity. Then will every one see the genuine and unmingled effects of vice and virtue. Those who have passed their lives in charity and piety; who have loved God with all their might, and their neighbour as themselves; who have clothed the naked, and whose houses have been open to the destitute; who have prayed without ceasing, have watched against temptation, and laboured to make themselves perfect, even as their Father which is in heaven is perfect; shall appear before their judge with humble faith, and support the day of the Lord with hopes of mercy. Then shall those who have despised the threatenings of God, who have walked after their lusts, and known no other motive of action than the enjoyment of present vices; those who have laid up treasures by oppression, and looked on misery without pity; who have persuaded themselves to say there is no God, or have drawn near him with their lips, when their hearts were far from him; shall now feel those terrors which luxury or pomp had formerly laid asleep. They shall then find themselves without refuge; the time past not to be recalled, and the time to come insusceptible of change. They shall wish to fly from the sight of omniscience, and to withdraw themselves from the presence of infinity, and shall call upon the mountains to fall on them, and upon the rocks to cover them. But all wishes are now too late, the trial is now past, and the sheep are severed from the goats, the wicked are for ever divided from the good. Those that have done well enter with their Saviour into the kingdom of his Father, and they that have done wickedly are sentenced to the everlasting fire prepared for the Devil and his Angels.

I hope you will approve the part which I have done; and I have no doubt but that I shall be perfectly satisfied with your superstructure upon this foundation.

I am, my dearest Sir,
Yours, &c.
JOHN TAYLOR

BIBLIOGRAPHY

I. WORKS

1. *The Works of Samuel Johnson, LL.D.*, ed. F. P. Walesby, 9 vols. Oxford: published by Talboys & Wheeler; and London, W. Pickering. 1825.

2. *The Yale Edition of the Works of Samuel Johnson*, general editor Allen T. Hazen. New Haven and London: Yale University Press. 1958-.
   Vol. i: *Diaries, Prayers, and Annals*, ed. E. L. McAdam, Jr., with Donald and Mary Hyde (1958).
   Vol. ii: '*The Idler*' and '*The Adventurer*', eds. W. J. Bate, John M. Bullitt, and L. F. Powell (1963).
   Vols. iii–v: '*The Rambler*', eds. W. J. Bate and Albrecht B. Strauss (1969).
   Vol. vi: *Poems*, ed. E. L. McAdam, Jr., with George Milne (1964).
   Vols. vii and viii: *Johnson on Shakespeare*, ed. A. Sherbo (1968).

3. *Sermons on Different Subjects, Left for Publication by John Taylor, LL.D.* Late Prebendary of Westminster, Rector of Bosworth, Leicestershire, and Minister of St. Margaret's, Westminster. Published by the Revd. Samuel Hayes, A.M. Usher of Westminster School. London: Printed for T. Cadell, in the Strand. 1788.

4. *Sermons on Different Subjects, Left for Publication by John Taylor, LL.D.* Late Prebendary of Westminster, Rector of Bosworth, Leicestershire, and Minister of St. Margaret's, Westminster. Volume the Second. Published by the Revd. Samuel Hayes, A.M. Late Senior Usher of Westminster School. To which is added, A Sermon written by Samuel Johnson, LL.D. for the funeral of his wife. London: Printed for T. Cadell, in the Strand. 1789.

5. *The British Prose Writers.* 25 vols. London: published by John Sharpe, Piccadilly. 1819–21. (Vol. xv contains the Taylor Collection of the *Sermons*.)

6. ASTON, HENRY HERVEY. *A Sermon Preached at the Cathedral Church of St. Paul, Before the Sons of the Clergy, On Thursday the Second of May, 1745, Being the Day of their Annual Feast.* By the Honourable and Reverend Henry Hervey Aston, A.M. Rector of Shotteley in the County of Suffolk. London: Printed for J. Brindley, Bookseller to His Royal Highness the Prince of Wales, at the Feathers in New-Bond-Street; and sold by M. Cooper, in Paternoster-Row. 1745. (Reprint, ed. James L. Clifford (Los Angeles: Augustan Reprint Society, Publication No. 50, 1955).)

7. MS. Sermon—by Dr. Johnson, found in the library at Bradley by R. Gifford, and given to him by Hugo Maynell, Esq. Undated. New Haven: in the Beinecke Rare Book Library, Yale University.

8. DODD, WILLIAM. *The Convict's Address to His Unhappy Brethren.* Delivered in the Chapel of Newgate, on Friday, June 6, 1777. London: printed for G. Kearsly, at No. 46, in Fleet-Street. 1777.

9. *A Sermon Written by the Late Samuel Johnson, LL.D. for the Funeral of his Wife.* Published by the Revd. Samuel Hayes, A.M. Usher of Westminster School. London: printed for T. Cadell, in the Strand. 1788.

10. *The Letters of Samuel Johnson, with Mrs. Thrale's genuine letters to him,* coll. and ed. by R. W. Chapman (3 vols., Oxford: Clarendon Press, 1952).

11. *The Lives of the Poets by Samuel Johnson, LL.D.,* ed. G. B. Hill (3 vols., Oxford: Clarendon Press, 1905).

12. *Papers Written by Dr. Johnson and Dr. Dodd in 1777,* ed. R. W. Chapman (Oxford: Clarendon Press, 1926).

13. TAYLOR, JOHN. *A Letter to Samuel Johnson, LL.D. on the Subject of a Future State.* By John Taylor, LL.D. Prebendary of Westminster, Rector of Bosworth, Leicestershire, and Minister of St. Margaret's, Westminster. London: Printed for T. Cadell, in the Strand. 1787.

2. BIOGRAPHICAL STUDIES AND MEMOIRS

14. ANDERSON, ROBERT, M.D. *The Life of Samuel Johnson, LL.D.,* with Critical Observations on his works (London: J. & A. Arch, 1795).

15. [ARMITAGE, ROBERT]. *Dr. Johnson: his Religious Life and his Death* (London: Richard Bentley, 1850).

16. BALDERSTON, K. C. *Thraliana* (2 vols., Oxford: Clarendon Press, 1951).

17. CLIFFORD, JAMES L. *Young Sam Johnson* (New York: McGraw Hill, 1955).

18. CRADOCK, JOSEPH. *Literary and Miscellaneous Memoirs* (4 vols., London: J. B. Nichols, 1828).

19. HAWKINS, SIR JOHN. *The Life of Samuel Johnson, LL.D.* (London: printed for J. Buckland, J. Rivington, etc., 1787).

20. HAWKINS, LAETITIA MATILDA. *Memoirs, Anecdotes, Facts, and Opinions.* Collected and preserved by Laetitia Matilda Hawkins. 2 vols. London: printed for Longman, Hurst, Rees, etc. 1824.

21. HILL, G. B. (ed.). *Boswell's Life of Johnson,* revised and enlarged by L. F. Powell (6 vols., Oxford: Clarendon Press, 1934–50).

22. —— *Dr. Johnson: his Friends and his Critics* (London: Smith, Elder, 1878).

23. —— *Johnsonian Miscellanies* (2 vols., Oxford: Clarendon Press, 1897).

24. KRUTCH, J. W. *Samuel Johnson* (New York: Henry Holt, 1944).

25. MURPHY, ARTHUR. 'Essay on the Life and Genius of Dr. Johnson', in *Works,* vol. i.

26. NICHOLS, JOHN. *Literary Anecdotes of the Eighteenth Century* (9 vols., London: Nichols, Son, & Bentley, 1812–15).

27. PIOZZI, HESTER LYNCH. *Anecdotes of the Late Samuel Johnson, LL.D.* (London: T. Cadell, 1786).

28. —— 'Anecdotes of the Late Samuel Johnson', in *Johnsonian Miscellanies*, ed. G. B. Hill (2 vols., Oxford: Clarendon Press, 1897), i. 147–350.

29. READE, ALEYN LYELL. *Johnsonian Gleanings* (10 parts, London: privately printed, 1909–46).

30. TAYLOR, THOMAS. *A Life of John Taylor, LL.D.* (London: St. Catherine Press and J. Nisbet, 1910).

31. TYERS, THOMAS. *A Biographical Sketch of Dr. Samuel Johnson*. Reprint of revised version issued as a separate pamphlet in 1785, with marginal additions by Tyers. Introduction by Gerald D. Meyer (Los Angeles: Augustan Reprint Society, Publication No. 34, 1952).

32. TYSON, M. and GUPPY, H. *The French Journals of Mrs. Thrale and Dr. Johnson* (Manchester: John Rylands Library, 1932).

33. WAINGROW, MARSHALL. 'Five Correspondences of James Boswell Relating to the Composition of the *Life of Johnson*.' Unpublished Ph.D. dissertation (New Haven: Yale University, 1951).

3. CRITICAL COMMENTARIES AND BIBLIOGRAPHICAL STUDIES

34. BATE, WALTER JACKSON. *The Achievement of Samuel Johnson* (New York: Oxford University Press, 1955).

35. BEECHING, H. C. *Johnson and Ecclesiastes: a sermon preached in Lichfield Cathedral* (London: Hugh Rees, 1909), reprinted from *Guardian*, 22 Sept. 1909, p. 1478.

36. BRONSON, B. H. *Johnson Agonistes and Other Essays* (Cambridge: University Press, 1946).

37. BURROWES, ROBERT. 'Essay on the Stile of Dr. Samuel Johnson', *Transactions of the Royal Irish Academy* (Dublin: 1787).

38. CHAPIN, CHESTER F. *The Religious Thought of Samuel Johnson* (Ann Arbor: University of Michigan Press, 1968).

39. CLIFFORD, JAMES L. *Johnsonian Studies, 1887–1950* (Minneapolis: University of Minnesota Press, 1951).

40. —— and DONALD J. GREENE. 'A Bibliography of Johnsonian Studies, 1950–1960', in *Johnsonian Studies*, ed. Magdi Wahba (Cairo: 1962; distributed outside the U.A.R. by Oxford University Press). A supplement to *Johnsonian Studies, 1887–1950*, with additions and corrections thereto.

41. GREENE, DONALD J. *The Politics of Samuel Johnson* (New Haven: Yale University Press, 1960).

42. HAGSTRUM, JEAN H. *Samuel Johnson's Literary Criticism* (Minneapolis: University of Minnesota Press, 1952).

43. —— 'The Sermons of Samuel Johnson'. Unpublished Ph.D. dissertation (New Haven: Yale University, 1941).

44. —— 'The Sermons of Samuel Johnson', *Modern Philology*, xl, no. 3 (Feb. 1943), 255–6.

45. HILLES, F. W. (ed.). *New Light on Dr. Johnson* (New Haven: Yale University Press, 1959).

46. MOSER, EDWIN. 'A Critical Examination of the Canon of the Prose Writings of Samuel Johnson.' Unpublished Ph.D. dissertation (New York: New York University, 1959). Abstract in *Dissertation Abstracts*, xx (1960), 3283–4.

47. QUINLAN, MAURICE J. *Samuel Johnson: a Layman's Religion* (Madison: University of Wisconsin Press, 1964).

48. SCHMIDT, HEINRICH. *Der Prosastil Samuel Johnson's* (Marburg: Inaugural-Dissertation zur Erlangung der Doktorwürde der Hohen Philosophischen Fakultät der Universität Marburg, 1905).

49. VOITLE, ROBERT. *Samuel Johnson the Moralist* (Cambridge, Mass.: Harvard University Press, 1961).

50. WAHBA, MAGDI. *Johnsonian Studies*, including *A Bibliography of Johnsonian Studies, 1950–1960*, compiled by James L. Clifford and Donald J. Greene (Cairo: 1962; distributed outside the U.A.R. by the Oxford University Press).

51. WATKINS, W. B. C. *Perilous Balance: The Tragic Genius of Swift, Johnson, and Sterne* (Princeton, N.J.: University Press, 1939).

52. WIMSATT, WILLIAM K., JR. *Philosophic Words: A Study of Style and Meaning in the 'Rambler' and 'Dictionary' of Samuel Johnson* (New Haven: Yale University Press, 1948).

53. —— *The Prose Style of Samuel Johnson* (New Haven and London: Yale University Press, 1941).

4. MISCELLANEOUS

54. ADAMS, JOHN QUINCY. *Lectures on Rhetoric and Oratory* (2 vols., Cambridge, Mass.: Hilliard & Metcalf, 1810).

55. ATKINSON, A. D. 'Dr. Johnson and Some Physico-Theological Themes', *Notes and Queries*, 5 Jan. 1952, pp. 16–18; 12 Apr. 1952, pp. 162–5; 7 June 1952, pp. 249–53.

56. —— 'Donne Quotations in Johnson's Dictionary', *Notes and Queries*, 1 Sept. 1951, pp. 387–8.

57. BALDERSTON, KATHERINE C. 'Dr. Johnson and William Law', *PMLA*, lxxv, no. 4, pt. I (Sept. 1960), 382–94.

58. —— 'Dr. Johnson's Use of William Law in the Dictionary', *Philological Quarterly*, xxxix (July 1960), 379–88.

59. BALDESHWILER, SISTER JOSELYN. 'Johnson's Doctrine of Figurative Language.' Unpublished Ph.D. dissertation (Fordham University, 1954).

60. BAXTER, RICHARD. *Reliquiae Baxterianae: or, Mr. Richard Baxter's Narrative of the most memorable passages of his Life and Times.* Faithfully published from his own Original Manuscript, by Matthew Sylvester. London: printed for T. Parkhurst, J. Robinson, J. Lawrence, and J. Dunton. 1696.

61. —— *The Autobiography of Richard Baxter*, being the *Reliquiae Baxterianae* abridged from the folio (1696), ed. J. Lloyd Thomas (London: Everyman Liby., Dent, 1931).

62. —— *A Call to the Unconverted* (New York: American Tract Society, 1825).

63. —— *The Practical Works of Richard Baxter* (4 vols., London: George Virtue, 26 Ivy Lane, Paternoster Row, 1828).

64. —— *The Reasons of the Christian Religion.* The second part, of Christianity, etc. London: R. White, for F. Titon. 1667.

65. —— *Richard Baxter's Account of His Present Thoughts Concerning the Controversies about the Perseverance of the Saints.* London: For T. Underhill and F. Tyton. 1657.

66. BENNETT, HIRAM R. 'Samuel Johnson, Churchman', *Anglican Theological Review*, xl (Oct. 1958), 301–9.

67. BIRON, SIR CHARTRES. 'Dr. Johnson and Dr. Dodd', in *Johnson Club Papers by Various Hands* (London: Fisher Unwin, 1920), pp. 13–28.

68. *The Book of Common Prayer* (Oxford: Clarendon Press, 1787).

69. BRACEY, ROBERT. 'Dr. Johnson's Catholic Friends' and 'Dr. Johnson as a Preacher', *Eighteenth-Century Studies and Other Papers* (Oxford: Basil Blackwell, 1925), pp. 1–9 and 10–19.

70. BRODERICK, JAMES H. 'Dr. Johnson's Impossible Doubts', *South Atlantic Quarterly*, lvi (Apr. 1957), 217–23.

71. BROWN, DAVID D. 'Johnson and Pulpit Eloquence', *New Rambler* (London: published by the Johnson Society, June 1969), pp. 19–37.

72. BROWN, STUART GERRY. 'Dr. Johnson and the Christian Tradition.' Unpublished Ph.D. dissertation (Princeton, N.J.: Princeton University. 1937; Ann Arbor, Michigan: University Microfilms, 1952).

73. —— 'Dr. Johnson and the Religious Problem', *English Studies*, xx (Feb., Apr. 1938), 1–17, 67.

74. CAIRNS, WILLIAM T. 'The Religion of Dr. Johnson', in *The Religion of Dr. Johnson and Other Essays* (London: Oxford University Press, 1946, pp. 1–23; reprinted from *Evangelical Quarterly*, xvi (Jan. 1944), 53–70).

75. CHAPIN, CHESTER F. 'Johnson, Rousseau, and Religion', *Texas Studies in Literature and Language*, ii (Spring 1960), 95–102.

76. —— *Personification in Eighteenth-Century Poetry* (New York: Columbia University Press, 1955).

77. —— 'Samuel Johnson's "Wonderful" Experience', in *Johnsonian Studies*, ed. Wahba (q.v.), pp. 51–60.

78. CHAPMAN, R. W. 'A Sermon by Dr. Johnson?' London *Times*, 29 Sept. 1933, p. 13.

79. —— 'Dr. Johnson and Dr. Taylor', *Review of English Studies*, ii, no. 2 (1926), 338–9.

80. CLARKE, SAMUEL. *A Discourse Concerning the Unchangeable Obligations of Natural Religion, and the Truth and Certainty of the Christian Revelation.* Being eight sermons preach'd at the Cathedral Church of St. Paul in the year 1705, at the Lecture founded by the Honourable Robert Boyle, Esq. London: James Knapton. 1706.

81. —— *A Discourse Concerning the Unchangeable Obligations of Natural Religion, and the Truth and Certainty of the Christian Revelation*, 5th edn. (London: James Knapton, 1719).

82. —— *Sermons on Several Subjects and Occasions.* 2 vols. Dublin: printed by S. Powell, for Stearne Brock at the Corner of Sycomore-Alley in Dame-Street, Bookseller. 1734.

83. —— *The Scripture-Doctrine of the Trinity* (London: James Knapton, 1712).

84. —— *Works* (4 vols., London: J. & P. Knapton, 1738).

85. COCHRANE, J. A. *Dr. Johnson's Printer: the Life of William Strahan* (London: Routledge & Kegan Paul, 1964).

86. COLSON, PERCY. *A Story of Christie's* (London: Sampson Low, 1950).

87. DERHAM, WILLIAM. *Physico-Theology: or, a Demonstration of the being and attributes of God, from his works of creation.* Being the substance of XVI sermons preached in St. Mary le Bow Church, London, at the Honourable Mr. Boyle's Lectures, in the years 1711 and 1712 with large notes and many curious observations never before published. London: W. Innys. 1713.

88. [DODSLEY, ROBERT]. *The Art of Preaching.* In Imitation of Horace's Art of Poetry. London: printed for R. Dodsley, at Tully's Head, in Pall Mall. 1741.

89. DOWNEY, JAMES. *The Eighteenth-Century Pulpit: a Study of the Sermons of Butler, Berkeley, Secker, Sterne, Whitefield and Wesley* (Oxford: Clarendon Press, 1969).

90. D'OYLEY, SAMUEL. *Christian Eloquence in Theory and Practice.* 2nd edn. London: printed for W. and J. Innys, at the West End of St. Paul's. 1722. (A translation of Blaise Gisbert, *L'Éloquence chrétienne dans l'idée et dans la pratique.*)

91. FINNERTY, SISTER M. JEAN CLARE. 'Johnson the Moralist: Friend and Critic of the Clergy and Hierarchy.' Unpublished Ph.D. dissertation (Fordham University, 1959).

92. FLEW, R. NEWTON. *The Idea of Perfection in Christian Theology* (Oxford: Clarendon Press, 1934; reissue 1968).

93. FOSTER, W. E. 'Samuel Johnson and the Dodd Affair', *Transactions of the Johnson Society, Lichfield, 1951–2*, pp. 36–49.

94. FREESE, JOHN HENRY, translator. *Aristotle: The 'Art' of Rhetoric* (Loeb Classical Liby., Cambridge, Mass.: Harvard University Press, 1939; London: Heinemann).

95. GRAHAM, W. H. 'Dr. Johnson and Law's *Serious Call*', *Contemporary Review*, cxci (Feb. 1957), 104–6.

96. GRAY, JAMES. 'Dr. Johnson and the King of Ashbourne', *University of Toronto Quarterly*, xxiii, no. 3 (Apr. 1954), 242–52.

97. —— 'Johnson as Boswell's Moral Tutor', *The Burke Newsletter*, iv, nos. 3 & 4 (1963), 202–10.

98. GREENE, DONALD J. 'Dr. Johnson's "Late Conversion": a Reconsideration', in *Johnsonian Studies*, ed. Wahba (q.v.), pp. 61–92.

99. —— 'Johnson and Newman', *Johnsonian News Letter*, xviii, no. 3 (Oct. 1958), 4–6. See also Sister M. Jean Clare, ibid. xx, no. 1 (Mar. 1960), 12.

100. —— ' "Pictures to the Mind": Johnson and Imagery', in *Johnson, Boswell, and their Circle*: Essays Presented to Lawrence Fitzroy Powell in Honour of his Eighty-Fourth Birthday (Oxford: Clarendon Press, 1965), pp. 137–58.

101. HAGSTRUM, JEAN H. 'On Dr. Johnson's Fear of Death', *Journal of English Literary History*, xiv (Dec. 1947), 308–19.

102. HAZEN, ALLEN T. *Samuel Johnson's Prefaces and Dedications* (New Haven: Yale University Press, 1937).

103. HILLES, FREDERICK W. *Portraits by Sir Joshua Reynolds*, ed., with Introduction and notes, by Frederick W. Hilles (New York: McGraw-Hill; London: Heinemann, 1952. Vol. 3 of the Yale Edition of the *Private Papers of James Boswell*).

104. HOOKER, RICHARD. *Works*, a new edn. (3 vols., Oxford: Clarendon Press, 1807).

105. —— *The Works*, ed. John Keble (3 vols., Oxford: Clarendon Press, 1836).

106. HOPKINSON, ARTHUR W. *About William Law* (London: S.P.C.K., 1948).

107. HOWE, P. P. (ed.). *The Complete Works of William Hazlitt* (21 vols., London and Toronto: Dent, 1930–4).

108. HUMPHREYS, A. R. 'Dr. Johnson, Troubled Believer', in *Johnsonian Studies*, ed. Wahba (q.v.), pp. 37–49.

109. HUTTON, ARTHUR WOLLASTON. 'Dr. Johnson's Library', in *Johnson Club Papers by Various Hands*, ed. George Whale and John Sargeaunt (London: Fisher Unwin, 1899).

110. JOHNSTONE, J. (ed.). *The Works of Samuel Parr* (8 vols., London: privately printed, 1828).

111. JOOST, NICHOLAS. 'Poetry and Belief: Fideism from Dryden to Eliot', *Dublin Review*, no. 455 (1st Quarter, 1952), 35–53.

112. KIRCHHOFER, K. HERMANN. 'Dr. Johnson's Religion.' Unpublished Ph.D. dissertation (Syracuse, N.Y.: Syracuse University, 1947).

113. KNOX, VICESIMUS. *Winter Evenings, or Lucubrations on Life and Letters* (3 vols., London: printed for Charles Dilly, 1788).

114. KOLB, GWIN J. 'Johnson Echoes Dryden (*The State of Innocence*)', *Modern Language Notes*, lxxiv (Mar. 1959), 212–13.

115. LANDA, LOUIS A. 'Introduction to the Sermons', in *Irish Tracts and Sermons*, ed. Herbert Davis (Oxford: Clarendon Press, 1963).

116. LAW, WILLIAM. *A Serious Call to a Devout and Holy Life* (London: 1729). Boswell's copy, consulted in the Beinecke Rare Book Library.

117. —— *A Serious Call to a Devout and Holy Life* (London: Everyman's Liby., Dent, 1906). See Ch. II, p. 54, fn. 4.

118. —— *A Practical Treatise upon Christian Perfection*, 3rd edn. (London: W. Innys & R. Manby, 1734).

119. —— *Works* (9 vols., London: privately printed, 1893).

120. LEAVIS, F. R. 'Johnson as Poet', in *The Common Pursuit* (London: Chatto & Windus, 1952), pp. 116–20.

121. LOCKE, JOHN. *An Essay Concerning Human Understanding*, collated and annotated, with prolegomena, biographical, critical, and historical, by Alexander Campbell Fraser (2 vols., Oxford: Clarendon Press, 1894).

122. MACKAY, H. F. B. 'The Religion of Dr. Johnson', in *Saints and Leaders* (London: Philip Allan, 1928), pp. 163–79.

123. MARSHALL, JOHN S. *Hooker and the Anglican Tradition* (London: A. & C. Black, 1963).

124. MATTHEWS, A. G. *The Works of Richard Baxter—an Annotated List* (Oxted: A. G. Matthews, 1932).

125. MAY, GEORGE LACEY. 'Religious Letters of Dr. Johnson', *Church Quarterly Review*, cliv (Apr.–June 1953), 168–75.

126. McADAM, E. L., JR. *Dr. Johnson and the English Law* (Syracuse, N.Y.: University Press, 1951).

127. McCUTCHEON, ROGER P. 'Johnson and Dodsley's *Preceptor*, 1748', *Tulane Studies in English*, iii (1952), 125–32.

128. METZDORF, ROBERT F. 'Isaac Reed and the Unfortunate Dr. Dodd', *Harvard Library Bulletin*, vi (Autumn 1952), 393–6.

129. MICHOT, PAULETTE. 'Doctor Johnson on Copyright', *Revue des langues vivantes* (Brussels), xxiii (1957), 137–47.

130. MITCHELL, W. FRASER. *English Pulpit Oratory from Andrewes to Tillotson* (London: S.P.C.K., 1932).

131. MOSSNER, E. C. *The Forgotten Hume* (New York: Columbia University Press, 1943).

132. NORTH, RICHARD. 'The Religion of Dr. Johnson', *Hibbert Journal*, lvi (Oct. 1957), 42–6.

133. OWST, G. R. *Literature and Pulpit in Medieval England*, 2nd edn. (Oxford: Basil Blackwell, 1961).

134. PAULL, H. M. 'Some Unidentified Writings of Dr. Johnson', *Fortnightly Review*, N.S. cxxiv (Oct. 1928), 570–3.

135. POWELL, L. F. 'Dr. Johnson and a Friend', London *Times*, 25 Nov. 1938, pp. 15–16.

136. PRESTON, THOMAS R. 'The Biblical Context of Johnson's *Rasselas*', *PMLA*, lxxxiv, no. 2 (Mar. 1969), pp. 274–81.

137. PRIMROSE, C. L. 'A Study of Dr. Johnson's Religion', *Theology*, xii (Apr. 1926), 207–16.

138. QUINLAN, MAURICE J. 'On Dr. Johnson's Fear of Death', *Philological Quarterly*, xxvii (Apr. 1948), 146–7.

139. READE, ALEYN LYELL. 'A New Admirer for Dr. Johnson', *London Mercury*, xxi (Jan. 1930), 247.

140. ROBERTS, S. C. 'Dr. Johnson as a Churchman', *Church Quarterly Review*, clvi (Oct.–Dec. 1955), 372–80. Reprinted in *Dr. Johnson and Others* (Cambridge: University Press, 1958).

141. SANDERSON, BISHOP ROBERT. *Fourteen Sermons Heretofore Preached* (London: printed by R. N. for Henry Seile, 1657).

142. SCHAFF, PHILIP (ed.). *A Select Library of the Nicene and Post-Nicene Fathers of the Christian Church* (14 vols., Buffalo: Christian Literature Company, 1887).

143. SILVESTER, JAMES. *Samuel Johnson: a Man of Faith* (Stirling, Scotland: Drummond's Tract Depot, 1926).

144. SOUTH, ROBERT. *Sermons Preached upon Several Occasions* (2 vols., Oxford: Clarendon Press, 1842).

145. SOUTH, ROBERT. *Works* (6 vols., Oxford: Clarendon Press, 1823).

146. SOUTHEY, CHARLES CUTHBERT. *The Life and Correspondence of Robert Southey* (6 vols., London: G. Routledge, 1849).

147. STEPHEN, LESLIE. *English Literature and Society in the Eighteenth Century* (London: Duckworth, 1904).

148. —— *History of English Thought in the Eighteenth Century* (2 vols., London: Smith, Elder, 1881). A recent 2-vol. edn. is published by Hart-Davis.

149. SUTHERLAND, RAYMOND C. 'Dr. Johnson and the Collect', *Modern Language Quarterly*, xvii (June 1956), 111–17.

150. SYKES, NORMAN. *From Sheldon to Secker* (Cambridge: University Press, 1959).

151. TAYLOR, JEREMY. *Works* (15 vols., London: C. & J. Rivington, 1828).

152. TEMPLE, WILLIAM JOHNSON. *An Essay on the Clergy: Their Studies, Recreations, Decline of Influence*, etc. etc. By the Reverend W. J. Temple, LL.B. Rector of Mamhead, in Devonshire. London: printed for Edward and Charles Dilly. 1774.

153. TILLEY, JOSEPH. *The Old Halls, Manors, and Families of Derbyshire* (4 vols., London: Simpkin, Marshall, Hamilton, Kent, 1893).

154. TILLOTSON, JOHN. *The Works of the Most Reverend Dr. John Tillotson, late Lord Archbishop of Canterbury*. Containing Two Hundred Sermons and Discourses on Several Occasions: Published from the Originals By Ralph Barker, D.D. Chaplain to his Grace. 4th edn. 3 vols. London: printed for John Darby, Arthur Bettesworth, Jacob Tonson, etc. 1728.

155. —— *Six Sermons by His Grace John Lord Archbishop of Canterbury* (London: printed for B. Aylmer and W. Rogers, 1694).

156. TUCKER, SUSIE I. and HENRY GIFFORD. 'Johnson's Poetic Imagination', *Review of English Studies*, N.S. viii (Aug. 1957), 241–8.

157. TURBERVILLE, A. S. (ed.). *Johnson's England* (2 vols., Oxford: Clarendon Press, 1933).

158. WHITE, T. H. *The Age of Scandal* (London: Cape, 1950).

159. WILLEY, BASIL. *The Eighteenth-Century Background* (London: Chatto & Windus, 1949).

160. WILLIAMS, PHILIP. 'Samuel Johnson's Central Tension: Faith and the Fear of Death', *Tòhoku Gàkuin Daigaku Ronshū* (*Journal of Literary Studies*, North Japan College, Sendai), nos. 33–4 (Sept. 1958), pp. 1–35.

161. WILLIAMSON, EDWARD (Bishop of Swansea and Brecon). 'Dr. Johnson and the Prayer Book', *Theology*, liii (Oct. 1950), 363–72.

162. WILLOUGHBY, EDWIN E. 'The Unfortunate Dr. Dodd: the Tragedy of an Incurable Optimist', *Essays by Divers Hands* (Royal Society of Literature), xxix (1958), 124–43.

163. WIMSATT, W. K., JR. 'Johnson's *Dictionary*', in *New Light on Dr. Johnson*, ed. F. W. Hilles (New Haven: Yale University Press, 1959).

Index

(Main entries in italic figures)

Abercrombie, James, 13–14
Adams, John Quincy, 193 n.
Adams, William, Master of Pembroke College, 76, 90
Addison, Joseph, 18
Allestree, Richard, reputed author of *The Whole Duty of Man* and *The Causes of the Decay of Piety*, 183
Ambrose, Saint, 49, 192
Anderson, Robert, 11
Andrewes, Lancelot, 49, 114, 125 n., 193 n.
Anselm, Saint, 49
Aquinas, Saint Thomas, 49
Aristotle, 131, 199
Armitage, Robert, 1 n.
Astle, Daniel, 14–15
Aston, Henry Hervey, 3, 7, 60 n., 91 n., 199–200
Athanasius, Saint, 49, 192
Atonement, The, 58, 86 *et passim*
Atterbury, Francis, 2, 47, 49
Augustine, Saint, 16, 49, 51, 192, 202
Australia, National Library of, 9 n.

Bacon, Francis, 16, 189, 204, 217 n.
Balderston, Katherine C., 5, 51–2, 53, 57–9, 62
Barrow, Isaac, 17, 38, 192
Bate, Walter Jackson, 3, 51, 64, 135
Bateman, Edmund, 19
Batty, W. R., 90 n.
Baxter, Richard, 3, 5, 35, 49, 50, *92–114* (SJ's reading of him and other Nonconformist writers, 92; SJ's admiration for his *Reasons of the Christian Religion* and *Call to the Unconverted*, 93; fullest on the future state, 93; his 'scruple' and fears, 94–5; SJ shares his view on usefulness of fear, anxiety, and sorrow, 95–6; SJ's arguments in Sermon II resemble those of Baxter's *Call*, 96–9; differences of emphasis between them, 99–104; parallels between them, 104 ff.; on the pre-Christian state, 104; on self-deceit, procrastination and the Devil, 104; on delaying conversion, 105; on annihilation and the future state, 105–8; on death, 108; SJ tempers Baxter's message, 109–10; his *Directions for . . . Spiritual Peace and Comfort*, 110–11; and SJ on the fear of death, 112–14), 129, 131, 183, 185
Beinecke Rare Book Library, Yale University, 8, 14 n., 42, 44, 54 n., 196
Bible, The (general), 4, 47, 52, 66, 67, 87, 92, 97, 114, 119, 123, 141, 147, 163, 179, 183–4, 188, 191, 208, 210, 230, 240, 241–2; Exodus, 155; Isaiah, 37, 191, 196; Jeremiah, 100, 145; Job, 178; Psalms, 38, 40, 97, 159, 206 n., 207, 208, 230; Proverbs, 109, 181, 190, 207, 209 and n., 230, 241; Ecclesiastes, 151 n., 230; Matthew, 99; Mark, 96 n.; Luke, 141, 239; John, 130, 139; Acts, 241; Romans, 152, 188; Galatians, 74, 170; 1 Corinthians, 100, 141–2, 212; Philippians, 100; 2 Timothy, 190; Hebrews, 239; James, 55, 187; 1 Peter, 92; 2 Peter, 108, 171; 1 John, 139
Blair, Hugh, 49
Boerhaave, Herman, 38
Boethius, Anicius Manlius Severinus, *De consolatione philosophiae*, 49
Book of Common Prayer, The, 47, 52, 58, 83, 142, 171, 183, 185, 187, 188–9, 230 *et passim*
Boothby, Brooke, Jr., 31
Boothby, Sir Brooke, 31
Boothby, Miss Hill, 5, 130 n.
Bossuet, Jacques Bénigne, 193 n.
Boswell, James, 10–11, 12, 13–15, 19, 21, 23, 24, 29, 35, 41, 43, 47–8, 50–1, 60, 61, 66, 76, 80–3, 88, 89, 92, 93, 107, 112–13, 123–5, 133–4, 143–4, 153, 160, 184, 185, 188, 196, 198–9; *Life of Johnson, passim*